THE NEW POLITICS OF CONFIDENCE

THE NEW
POLITICS OF
CONFIDENCE

PIERRE S. PETTIGREW

TRANSLATED BY PHYLLIS ARONOFF AND HOWARD SCOTT

Original title: Pour une politique de la confiance
Copyright © 1998 Les Éditions du Boréal, Montreal
English translation copyright © 1999 by Phyllis Aronoff and Howard Scott

Published in 1999 by Stoddart Publishing Co. Limited
34 Lesmill Road, Toronto, Canada M3B 2T6

Distributed by:
General Distribution Services Ltd.
325 Humber College Boulevard, Toronto, Canada M9W 7C3
Tel. (416) 213-1919   Fax (416) 213-1917
Email customer.service@ccmailgw.genpub.com

03 02 01 00 99 1 2 3 4 5

Canadian Cataloguing in Publication Data

Pettigrew, Pierre S., 1951–
The new politics of confidence

Translation of: Pour une politique de la confiance
Includes bibliographical references and index.
ISBN 0-7737-3180-6

1. Canada — Politics and government — 1993– .*
2. International relations. 3. International economic relations.
4. Federal government — Canada. 5. Canada — Foreign relations.
6. Quebec (Province) – Politics and government — 1994– .*
7. Quebec (Province) — History — Autonomy and independence movements.
I. Aronoff, Phyllis, 1945– . II. Scott, Howard, 1952– . III. Title.

FC635.P4713 1999   971.064'8   C99-930089-X
F1034.2.P4713 1999

Jacket Design: Bill Douglas @ The Bang
Text Design and Page Composition: Joseph Gisini/Andrew Smith Graphics Inc.

Printed and bound in Canada

*Stoddart Publishing gratefully acknowledges the Canada Council for the Arts
and the Ontario Arts Council for their support of its publishing program.*

*This book was made possible in part through the
Canada Council's Translation Grants Program.*

In memory of my grandparents,
Bernard Grenier (1904–1968),
Eugénie Giguère (1907–1990),
Ethel Aubin (1901–1986), and
René Pettigrew (1904–1990),
who, each in his or her own way, has given me
deep roots in my society and, at the same time,
an openness to the rest of the world,
an appetite for ideas from here and elsewhere,
and, the greatest legacy,
a love of freedom.

Try as one may to limit political objectives,
to make them as simple as possible,
as crude as one would wish,
all politics always implies an idea of man and mind,
a representation of the world.

— Paul Valéry, *Variété*

Contents

Acknowledgments

I COULD NOT HAVE WRITTEN THIS BOOK WITHOUT THE INVALUABLE support of several friends and associates. First of all, I would like to thank Yves-Marie Morissette for his contribution and support throughout this project and for the close and stimulating intellectual dialogue that has been part of our friendship over the past twenty-five years. Michel Bédard's research and speeches made a tremendous contribution to this book, and I have the greatest appreciation for his professionalism, his attention to detail, and his consistent good humour. He was ably assisted by Jean-François Gascon, who has been associated with many of my projects since October 1995 and to whom I am very grateful. Jacques Hudon was the first one to believe in this project, and he did a great deal to facilitate it. He is always there for what is important. He and Francine Brousseau were my first readers. Their encouragement sustained me much more than they realize. Andrée Côté and Sean Riley were my final readers before I handed the manuscript in to the publisher; I could not have done so without the enlightened comments of these dear friends of many years. In addition, I was fortunate to have Yvonne Rialland-Morissette's help at the proof stage. I greatly appreciate her encouragement, which is a constant source of inspiration. Finally, I have appreciated the enthusiasm and professionalism of Boréal, the publisher of the French version of this book. I am delighted that I have developed a good relationship of trust with Stoddart for the English version. I am most grateful to Phyllis Aronoff and Howard Scott. This book reads as though it were penned in English, to me a reflection of the excellence of their translation.

Preface

For every glance behind us, we have to look twice to the future.
— Arabic proverb

DAY-TO-DAY EVENTS HAVE A POWERFUL HOLD OVER US. OUR LIVES ARE dominated by the constraints and controversies of the moment. However, if we want to contribute to the development of the society we live in and maintain control over our individual destinies, we absolutely must look higher and further.

As a minister in the government of Canada, I have a special responsibility to work for the advancement of Canadian society in the area—a key one, in my view—of human development. But this responsibility also gives rise to the opportunity, indeed the obligation, to play an active role in the fundamental debate concerning the future of our society. This book seemed a good way for me to contribute to that debate, as public personalities and other members of the Cabinet do in their various ways, because for me writing is one of the most effective ways to achieve some distance and escape the powerful grip of day-to-day events and immediate concerns.

It is my deep conviction that we have good reasons to be optimistic. I have set myself the goal of presenting the future of Canada and of Quebec society from a global perspective rather than from a narrowly national point of view. I hope to reach a wide range of readers among the participants in political debate in the broadest sense: activists of various allegiances, leaders of civil society and the business world, intellectuals, and observers of public affairs. But I would also like to reach another readership: they are the leaders of tomorrow, those who see society with a fresh eye and who will take on important responsibilities in the first quarter of the coming century. I thought a great deal about them as I wrote these pages. I feel an urgent need for this dialogue with young people.

Everything has changed so quickly in the space of a single generation. I have the feeling that many of my compatriots, especially those of the upcoming generation, want to be free of the debates and polemics of yesterday. This is also true for other new political players: women, immigrants, and members of minority groups. Considering the tide of change that is sweeping over the world today, many of our internal debates seem amazingly narrow. Canadian society and the Canadian federation have been changing at an accelerating rate. The global context is changing even more quickly. If we want to satisfy not only the present but the future needs of our society, we must look upon this future as one element in a world that is being "remade."

Remaining optimistic in the face of globalization does not prevent us from being realistic. Our world is still afflicted with too many calamities: the appalling suffering of many human beings who are like us but have had the misfortune to be born elsewhere, the marginalization or utter exclusion of so many others, the everyday tragedies resulting from racism, violence in all its forms, and the countless attacks on basic rights. Human life, that priceless thing, and human dignity, our instinctive aspiration, are worth very little in many places in the modern world. Yet Canada, in my opinion, has a bright future, in spite of our own difficulties; I see Quebec society and Canada as beacons for the world as we approach the third millennium. We can show here and now that we are able to live together, equal and different. My attachment to our common endeavour and to the values of tolerance and respect, embracing pluralism, is at once visceral, emotional, and rational. In our efforts to improve things in Canada, we must not lose sight of our obligations to humanity as a whole. While I may have touched here and there on the broad theme of justice in the modern world, there is too much to say on this to deal with it adequately in one short book.

Over the years, I have had the good fortune to be able to move back and forth between the world of action and that of ideas. This book began to take shape long before my appointment to the Cabinet. In fact, like a craftsman who refines his skill by plying his trade, I tackled the subjects dealt with in these pages through practice. I have been working on the book for many years. Substantial portions of it come from speeches I have given to various audiences or from articles published in major newspapers, particularly on the issue of globalization. The manuscript was already quite advanced when I entered politics. And then, somewhat to my surprise, the urge to finish it became very pressing. To balance the concerns of a life absorbed daily in politics, I felt an even greater need to clarify these ideas acquired over the years, to take stock, and at the same time to share my thoughts on the fundamental themes that guide my actions. Now those moments stolen for writing late in the evening and early in the morning have finally borne fruit.

I must make it absolutely clear that this book is in no way binding on the government in which I have the honour of serving, or on the ministry I have the pleasure of leading. I am solely responsible for its contents. I beg my readers' indulgence and ask them to see this work as my contribution to the coming generation, which is fortunate to be coming of age at a time when there is so much to be rethought and remade in the world. Behind any action, whatever it is, there must be thought. It is up to each of us to discover how we can add our stone to the collective edifice. What is important is that we accept that responsibility—each one of us for ourself—and do the best we can.

Pierre S. Pettigrew
Montreal, February 1999

Introduction

IF THERE IS A CONNECTING THREAD RUNNING THROUGH THE THREE parts and twenty chapters of this book, it is the need to rethink political activity, which has been so discredited yet which is so essential. At a time when the economy is pushing everything else aside, I have written this book to show that politics still has an essential role in the proper development of societies.

At the outset, I must say that I do not believe that the economy, left to itself, would serve humanity well. Just as the economic sphere is the best place for individual development and self-fulfilment, so the political sphere is the best place for the fostering of our collective well-being. Human beings need both. The economy itself needs the arbitration of politics to fulfil its potential. And it is this relationship between the economic and the political that today needs to be redefined.

Part One of this book, Globalization and the Art of Governing, explores the evolution of the political function, especially its relationship to the economy, from the emergence of the state and modernity nearly four hundred years ago to the radical and revolutionary challenge that globalization represents today. Political power as exercised by the state in its territory made possible the development of the economy and the growth of freedom as never before in human history. In fact, it is this form of political power that made possible the creation of national markets in that space, larger than cities and smaller than empires, where capitalism was born. And capitalism is now the sole model of economic development with which humanity is entering the twenty-first century. However, it is precisely that balance between economic and political spheres that globalization, the revolutionary force of our time, challenges.

If we are not able to reinvent the political, to redefine its relationship with the economic, if we surrender completely to the laws of the market, society will be penalized, because democracy will disappear and the economy itself will suffer greatly. The "too exclusively political" state, unable to understand the signals of the market, has made enormous blunders; the "too exclusively economic" market, unable to perceive the signals of the state, would commit equally serious errors.

This new relationship between the economy and politics will take into account the fact that individuals are remaking their lives in order to fulfil themselves in freedom, and that in so doing they will remake a world that today is undergoing disorders and dislocations.

This remaking of the world, which is absolutely necessary, will be subject to passions that are more ethical than political. New players, who had little power in modernity, will take on a much more important role in this new world. These new players are among the people who have had the most experience in remaking their lives, those best able to reconcile private and public life: they are first of all women, but also young people and immigrants.

In Part Two, The Canadian Exception, I describe Canada as a country that is more "political" than economic, marked from its beginnings by an extremely original choice—that of pluralism and a third path in economic and social matters. The Canadian state seems to me to be a credible response to those who are tempted to see everything as economic. Having already resisted the fashions and all the truisms of the nineteenth century, when the traditional nation-state was the rule, Canada, a composite political space, has refused to become a nation-state, and has made choices that enable it to adapt in a unique way to the phenomenon of globalization.

Canada is a country in constant evolution. It is different with each generation. It will continue to change according to the needs of its people and the values deeply rooted in its character, its identity, and its citizenship, which is more political than ethnic or national.

In Part Three, Quebec: Towards a Postmodern Society, I propose that Quebeckers, who have been politically astute throughout their history, embark on a new Quiet Revolution, this time a postmodern one. Quebec would become the first postmodern society.

This new Quiet Revolution would be postmodern in two ways. Unlike the earlier revolution, which marked Quebec's entry into modernity, this transition would not involve a further reinforcing of the powers of the state but would channel energy into the horizontal and transnational networks that are emerging outside the state. Furthermore, this second Quiet

Revolution would give a large role to women, who were forgotten in the first one, as they have been in modernity in general; this is only reasonable. It would also give a large role to young people, immigrants, and members of minority groups—all those who have had more experience in remaking their lives.

But, in order for this to occur, we must move beyond the old dichotomies of Quebec's traditional politics, the *rouge* and the *bleu*. Quebeckers, who are stronger and better educated today than in the past, can allow themselves to put mistrust behind them and adopt the attitude of trust and confidence that so many observers see as an essential condition for development.

Part One

Globalization and the Art of Governing

Chapter I

History, Politics, and Freedom

WITH THE FALL OF THE BERLIN WALL IN 1989, THE LONG IDEO-
logical and historical struggle between socialism and liberalism
came to an end.

The role of human autonomy in history has always been one of the
basic points of contention between these two philosophies. Liberals have
emphasized a voluntarist reading of history, one that gives the actors,
whether they are individuals or groups, the power and freedom to take
charge of their destiny. Socialists have opposed this view with the doctrine
of historical materialism and a deterministic interpretation of events;
according to this theory, human affairs do not escape the inexorable laws of
history, which are dictated by factors such as class membership.

Actors or factors—what determines the evolution of our societies and of
history? Socialists, on the basis of historical materialism, have asserted that
the victory of their ideology is inevitable. Liberals, on the other hand, have
considered the basis of evolution and progress to be human freedom, conceived as the ability of individuals to influence their destiny. In other words,
liberals have always acknowledged the possibility that their ideal might not
be attained. Uncertainty and doubt are for them at the very heart of freedom.

Freedom: That is what best explains the undeniable victory of liberals
over socialists. Why? Because freedom and the human capacity to act have
been won through long struggle, and they represent humanity's most pre-
cious legacy. Freedom and the capacity to act are also what fundamentally
distinguishes traditional societies from modern societies: for the former, destiny is the result of arbitrary divine will, whereas for the latter, free will plays
a decisive role. This explains the progress of modern societies. And if the
liberals deserved their victory over the socialists, it is, in the final analysis,
because of this respect for the human being. It is through freedom that human
beings are able gradually to escape the uncertainties of their condition.

My aim here is to establish that human beings are fundamentally free to make choices, individually and collectively, and that it is up to them to reduce the impact of the inevitable as much as possible. Because that, in my view, is the human challenge par excellence: to conquer and control freedom.

Differences of opinion with respect to human autonomy have been a constant in the history of humanity. These differences once opposed traditional societies to modern societies, or socialist societies to liberal societies; today they are being transposed into a debate concerning the phenomenon of globalization.

Politics, the Economy, and Globalization

We constantly talk about globalization, often without making any judgments. I want to start by saying that globalization seems to me to be capable of serving individuals and their societies *if and only if* it respects the freedom of action of human beings and allows them room to manoeuvre.

Let us agree immediately that the question of freedom is now being raised in a new context, although it is still characterized by the quest for the appropriate place, on the one hand, of the economy and even of the entire economic sphere, and, on the other hand, of politics. The dignity and nobility of the political function seem self-evident to me. Political activity is essential to enable the economy to achieve its purpose of order. Does not the word *economy* mean "management of the house" in ancient Greek? But the political sphere also fulfils an essential function in that it forces the economy to remain faithful to its human purpose. The economy is the arena in which human beings can fulfil themselves, innovate, and create. Adam Smith, who observed how deeply human beings are characterized by the need to trade, considered the market essential to freedom and human development.[1] That said, only politics, through careful intervention, can keep the market in line and prevent the intolerable inequalities that would result from unbridled materialism.

I believe, moreover, that the "everything is politics" approach, such as we saw under totalitarian Communist régimes, has led to catastrophic failures. Where the state has been unable to perceive the signals of the market because it had destroyed or irreparably distorted it, it has made enormous errors (for example, with respect to the environment) and revealed its inability to achieve the economic development of society. Similarly, I am convinced that the market also commits colossal errors when it ignores signals from the state. The development of the capitalist system demonstrates this: left to itself, the market is quite often unreliable and lacking in direction. It must be acknowledged that when capitalism collapsed in 1929 it was political actors of a rather conservative nature who enabled it to regain control, through the introduction of the measures we now know as the New Deal and the welfare state. And the Asian financial crisis reminds us again of the dangers of the present imbalance between the rules or institutions of public administration and the laws of the market.

It is imperative that we go beyond all the slogans we are hearing with respect to globalization in order to better understand this phenomenon that is clearly emerging as a revolutionary force of our time. It is still too early to say whether globalization will be a positive or a negative force in history. The initial signs may be seen as confirmation of either judgment. On the one hand, globalization has brought about remarkable improvements in productivity, and it is accompanied by a significant logic of global integration. In fact, countries that were left out in the past have been able in recent years to become part of the world economy and to improve appreciably the quality of life of their citizens. On the other hand, globalization also entails a logic of exclusion both internationally and within individual societies. This logic of exclusion is worrying. It could lead almost inevitably to social disruption, demonstrating that globalization does not produce the results needed for the progress of humanity.

This is where politics and the political come in. In the past, the market needed the state to fulfil its potential. Similarly, today, globalization will be able to fulfil its potential only if the state or, at the very least, a redefined political function, is able to force it to be more orderly and more respectful of all individuals. The political sphere can humanize globalization.

The art of governing is more difficult than ever, because we are encountering unprecedented situations and having to deal with extremely powerful economic and technical forces involving incredible numbers of unknowns. The complexity of the problems has increased exponentially with the spread of democracy and knowledge. Fortunately, the information available to help us make wise decisions has reached an unimagined level of reliability, mainly thanks to information technology and advances in the study of administration.

The Economy and Politics: A Relationship That Needs to Be Reconsidered

The role of the political actor needs to be reconsidered in the light of what societies have become, with their bureaucracies and technocracies and their remarkable but cold expertise. This presents a stimulating challenge. The political function itself needs to be reinvented at every level—local, national, and international. But, above all, the art of governing should lead us gradually to a more global conception of the political, and this should enable us to define a certain number of broad endeavours that might rally humanity to an unprecedented solidarity.

If globalization has given rise to the view that unfettered capitalism is the only course of action—what the French are aptly calling "la pensée unique," the only view that is accepted—then it seems to me that the liberals did not deserve their victory over the socialists in 1989, and that, in the more or less short term, liberalism could become rigid and then paralyzed, like communism before it. This is the fate of any system that sees itself as scientific truth; that is what led to the fall of communism.

The following chapters deal with the art of governing in this time of turbulence caused by the beginning of globalization. In them I will attempt to place this situation in context. In order to do so, it will be necessary to define the phenomena being examined and clarify concepts such as *order* and *disorder* and *power* and *strength*. I will also look at some of the philosophical and political aspects of liberalism and consider how it may truly deserve its victory of 1989. I will then discuss the capacity capitalism must develop to acknowledge the human purpose of the economy. And since we are talking about capitalism, we will have to distinguish between capitalism as a model for the production of wealth and capitalism as a form of social organization. It is also important to distinguish between Anglo-Saxon "liberal" capitalism, Japanese "community" capitalism, European capitalism with a "social market economy," and even a fourth form of capitalism that is emerging, a "Chinese-style" capitalism. I will also look at other themes in philosophical and political thought, such as *confidence,* or *trust,* and *mistrust,* particularly with respect to their influence on economic development, and examine the well-known theories of Alain Peyrefitte and Francis Fukuyama.[2]

Among other things, I would like to show that, if we embark on the road to globalization as understood and desired by hard-line capitalists, we will probably be witness to a kind of "revenge of Marx." Marx eliminated all metaphysics in reducing human beings to the single role of economic actors and giving "scientific" historical materialism a central place in the evolution of history. Thus, when those who sing the praises of globalization regard the individual only as a consumer and producer, they are coming very close to Marxism; their perspective is far too reductive. When we attribute a scientific nature to the laws of the market, we make the same egregious error. Human beings—not some scientific dogma—are the engine of history. So, again, when globalization presents health and education as mere "commodities," we are coming dangerously close to the errors of Marxism. Faced with the irresistible trend of the past fifteen years, we must without delay conceive a new humanism that will be a match for globalization.

To appreciate the importance of the historical shift we are experiencing with globalization, we have to look back at the distance we have covered in terms of the state, the market, and economic development. It is particularly important to take a brief look at the evolution of the state since 1648, because the state developed as the engine of modernity, acquiring a vertical authority within the limits of its territory and thus replacing the horizontal authority held in their time by the feudal aristocracies and the medieval clergy. We need to examine the role of the state in the development of modernity and, especially, to explain the nature of the state's vertical authority over its territory, which is now being challenged by horizontal pressures coming, for example, from the transnational flows of globalization.

We must understand that states, under these conditions, have diminished room to manoeuvre. This trend challenges the established order, and we will have to find human answers to this challenge. The creation of states, as the case of England illustrates, led to the formation of the first large national markets. The state granted legal rights to business, and properties and contracts were able to expand in a market covering a growing territory. This made possible the development of industry, which depends heavily on the degree of trust or confidence that exists in a society. For the moment, it is important to further our understanding of globalization and triumphant liberalism.

Upheavals and Global Disorder: The Internal Contradictions of Triumphant Capitalism[1]

A "NEW WORLD ORDER" HAS NOT YET EMERGED, IN SPITE OF THE profound ideological harmony that has reigned since the fall of the Berlin Wall in 1989. In the euphoria of the end of the Cold War, we hoped that the old order, born of the balance of terror and the nuclear arms race, might be replaced with a better way of organizing international relations, one based on cooperation and solidarity and the ability to foresee and manage crises. Instead we were confronted with upheavals, a general reorganization of geostrategic and social forces, a repositioning of economic actors, and a breakdown of common cultural references. Many people feel we have gone from the international order of yesterday to global disorder today.[*]

In fact, the current international system, as the term implies, is based essentially on cooperation and coordination among states. To work well, therefore, it needs the power that the state exercises domestically, over its own society. During the period of internationalization, this system brought order. But in this era of globalization, challenge to the state, and the emergence of new actors and new transnational stakes, this system of cooperation among states is no longer capable of organizing relations among societies and managing crises. It is therefore unable to prevent disorder.

From International Order to Global Disorder

The international order of yesterday was based on the power of the state and its vertical authority over its society. The state controlled military and economic strength on its territory. Globalization breaks this connection of vertical authority between the power of the state and the strength of the market. But the international system has not yet begun to reflect this new reality. Hence the disorder.

---

[*] As Paul Valéry said, there are two threats to the world: order and disorder.

The new order will have to be built around a founding principle of the post-Communist world, a world in which—and I will come back to this point—the primary force, a revolutionary one, is the radical phenomenon of globalization. This book is an attempt precisely to determine the elements that will constitute this founding principle. In this new context, in fact, ideological harmony is not enough to ensure and promote order. Because the international order of yesterday was based on the power of the state and its vertical authority over society, the Cold War actually helped the state affirm itself, since it forced the state to assert its power. Conversely, because it frees the strength of civil society from state trusteeship, globalization entails a disengagement by the state. The current crisis of the international system is therefore a crisis of the nation-state, because the international system is still based on the state as the sole actor in international relations, as if state power and sovereignty were still intact.

The new ideological harmony has a name: liberalism. Liberalism has triumphed over socialism because of its performance in terms of both economic development and freedoms. However, the two fundamental tenets of triumphant liberalism—liberalization and democratization—contribute to the current disorder. Economic liberalization and political democratization both limit the authority of government and, therefore, the state's power to act, thus weakening the international order.

Democratization subordinates the apparatus of the state to civil society; the state now becomes responsible to civil society. Democratization demands political freedoms from the state: freedom of speech, association, assembly, freedom for individuals to be what they want. Liberalization reduces the role of the state in the economy and demands from it economic freedoms: freedom to own property, work, invest, produce, and consume without the impediment of regulation—or, at least, with a minimum of regulation—by the state.

In his lectures at the Collège de France, Alain Peyrefitte recognized these freedoms as being at the heart of the Dutch miracle of trade, the British miracle of industrialization, and the American miracle of invention and innovation.[2] Peyrefitte speaks of "miracles," since natural causes, visible data, and material factors are not sufficient to account for the economic takeoff of certain societies and the stagnation of others. Deprivation has been the lot of humanity since its origins. It is nothing short of miraculous that certain societies over the past two hundred years have managed to overcome high mortality rates, endemic diseases, food shortages, and illiteracy. In religion, miracles are related to faith: they nourish faith and are nourished by it. In the economic and social realms, the metaphorical miracle must be associated with *confidence*. As Peyrefitte points out, faith and confidence are counterparts, one religious and the other secular; in English, as in French, the words share the same root.[3]

Democratization and liberalization continue today in the form of globalization, which undermines the conventional international order and entails—for the moment—major global disorder. While democratization increases society's control and expectations with respect to the state, liberalization reduces the state's control and means of action with respect to society. Democratization increases people's expectations of the state, while liberalization tends to limit the state's ability to meet these expectations. This is the combination of phenomena that triumphant liberalism faces. There was a time when the challenge of socialism forced liberalism to compromise, which helped it overcome this internal contradiction of its two fundamental tenets. Now that the ideological competition is over, will capitalism be able to adapt to the needs of individuals and their communities and societies? That is now the crucial question.

Whether in its Anglo-Saxon "liberal" form, its German "social" form, or its Japanese "community" form, capitalism has prevailed because of its performance in the areas of both economic growth and individual and collective freedoms. However, the accelerating globalization that is so organically linked to capitalism entails considerable costs and unexpected consequences.

Globalization is now recognized as the predominant force of our time, and one that is revolutionary. The word *revolutionary* is no exaggeration, because globalization has led to major global disorder and radical breaks with the past in many areas. The state and the market, politics and the economy, no longer operate in the same spaces or the same time frames. The consequences for societies are enormous, as they are for individuals. Concretely, in the absence of pressure from a competing ideological system, the challenge of liberalism, with its internal contradictions, is further complicated by the fact that free trade, which has historically benefited all those who have practised it, is no longer capable of improving the situation for all; although there are variations in degree, many are excluded from its benefits.

The End of the Dogma of Free Trade

Without redistribution, what hope can we offer to the excluded in most of the countries of the South, and even to many citizens in the industrialized countries? What hope can we give them in this era of globalization in which the benefits of free trade are no longer assured?

As history has shown, the market was right in offering the solution of free trade to societies seeking development, and for a long time, this worked.

In the international order, where we thought primarily in terms of trade, all the countries that have followed the rules of GATT[4] and accepted its discipline, as well as the strict laws of the market, have benefited greatly. The productivity of these countries has increased, and their development and growth have accelerated. The other countries, those that rejected these rules and this discipline, primarily the Communist countries and the countries of the South, have lost considerable ground. David Ricardo clearly showed that free trade benefits all those who practise it. In Ricardo's time, however, the factors of production were essentially immobile. This is no longer the case, and that is a crucial difference.

In the new economy, all the decisive factors—trade, production, technology, distribution, and finance—are integrated. On a world scale, these factors are extremely mobile. Consequently, the effects of free trade are no longer *necessarily* positive for everyone. Why is this? In a context of extreme mobility, indeed of international volatility of capital, as soon as producers feel sufficiently safe to invest almost anywhere, they will go where the profits are greatest. The mobility of these economic factors thus leads inevitably to the standardization of their economic returns. Competition therefore increases. In fact, the nature of competition changes radically.

The gap between rich and poor is increasing as a result of the global scarcity of capital and the huge reserve of workers, who are in many cases better educated than ever before. This explains the increase in unemployment and social inequalities, over-indebtedness, and the downward pressure on all kinds of local community institutions, public health services, occupational safety standards, income security, pollution controls, and so on. Business now occupies much of the area the state previously did, since it constitutes a true global system of trade and commerce. This is increasingly the case as the pace of globalization accelerates, with trade increasing three times faster than production.[5]

In turn, competition goes beyond firms and involves states themselves in networks of industrial and commercial competition. The effectiveness of the state, particularly in terms of the extensiveness and, especially, the quality of its infrastructures, is now decisive in the competitiveness of an economic space. Grey matter—intelligence, knowledge, and will—is becoming the raw material of the economy. This dematerialization of the economy and the ability to communicate instantaneously across the planet make it possible for firms to optimize their activities on a worldwide basis. New relationships are thus emerging between states and firms. The traditional pre-eminent role of the state is eroding in favour of companies.

Vertical Power and Horizontal Strength:*
Internationalization and Globalization

The intense feeling of having moved from a condition of international order to one of global disorder is not unfounded. It is far from obvious how the vertical power of the state can be reconciled with the horizontal strength of the market. We will discover the founding principle of the post-Communist world only by asking essential philosophical questions and finding completely new concepts to comprehend the new threats to humanity. It is in this perspective that I will discuss the need for a new aesthetic experience.

It is not enough to acknowledge that the era of internationalization has definitively given way to that of globalization. It is also important to understand the ways in which these phenomena are not merely distinct but contradictory. Internationalization implies two things: first of all, the broadening of the geographic area in which more and more economic and commercial activities are carried out, and, second, the existence of national borders which this broadening movement seeks to subsume within everlarger wholes. Internationalization thus increases the interdependence of societies conceived as nation-states. Moreover, the word *internationalization* itself denotes increased trade "among nations" and thus suggests a certain imperviousness of economic spaces and national—that is, political—borders.

Internationalization thus gives a decisive role to the state in international relations, as the sole actor in law and one with no serious rival. Involving states in mutual cooperation, internationalization gives them major responsibility for both their societies and their territoriality. Even when internationalization entails states giving up certain of their powers and responsibilities to some supranational level, it recreates at that level the vertical authority of the state, only on a broader territory comprising two or more countries.

Globalization is qualitatively different. It reduces the role of the state in international relations and profoundly alters its powers over the society living in its territory. Globalization implies a high degree of functional integration of economic, industrial, and financial activities dispersed across various spaces. This inevitably leads to an attenuation of the vertical authority of the state over the economic, financial, and industrial forces in its territory. Thus placed in a precarious situation, the state can no longer assume the responsibilities its citizens have become accustomed to it assuming. It becomes even less able to do so as the diminution of its vertical authority in many cases makes its attempts at cooperation with other states ineffectual.

---

* In French the author distinguishes between *pouvoir* and *puissance*, translated here as *power* and *strength*.

A recent phenomenon, this aspect of globalization results from the liberalization of trade, deregulation, and progress in various information technologies, in particular telematics, a combination of telecommunications and informatics. Firms can now choose to carry out a certain *industrial* function in a particular *geographic* space according to economic logic, and without regard for any *political* consideration. This new global distribution of work follows a technological hierarchy. Unlike the multinational corporation that had to heavy-handedly reproduce the model of the head office from country to country, the global firm has much more flexibility and often, through strategic networks or alliances, integrates its various functions of production, research, financing, marketing, and data processing, discharging each of these functions in the space best suited to it. In short, globalization ignores political borders and merges economic spaces.

In this particular sense, globalization appeared in the mid-1980s. In terms of the economy, its birth can be symbolically placed on the day when the three major stock exchanges, in London, New York, and Tokyo, were linked electronically, enabling capitalists throughout the world to invest day and night in large multinational corporations. Politically, it is the fall of the Berlin Wall in November 1989 that constitutes the symbolic consecration of globalization as the prime mover of recent history and world affairs. Inevitably, countries where the state had controlled everything, where politics completely dominated the economy, were the first to experience the great revolutionary upheavals of this new era. Though these great changes do not affect all societies at the same pace or to the same degree, they still represent a global trend, one that is inescapable.

The Breakdown of Spaces and Times

In the era of globalization, economic spaces tend to integrate, whereas political spaces tend to become fragmented. This is taking place in many different ways. First, over the last decade, about thirty new countries have appeared, essentially because of the fall of communism. But also, and more fundamentally, cities and regions have emerged as autonomous actors and decision-making centres throughout the world, even in some of the original supranational organizations, such as the European Union. What is more, the progress of democracy and the tendency to turn inward should intensify the quest for greater political sovereignty by minorities in existing countries. Because of the integration of economic spaces, the continentalization of the economies themselves, and the globalization of businesses and markets, this quest for increased political sovereignty is accompanied, paradoxically, by a loss of substance, or at least a loss of scope, in that coveted political sovereignty.

Political spaces are becoming increasingly narrow, while economic spaces are becoming broader. As a result, the congruence between economic space and political space has broken down. Not to mention that there is, in addition, a corresponding break between political and economic times, or, more precisely, time periods.

States now have to consider human rights and, increasingly, consult with minorities and interest groups in every region of their territory. They have to carry out these consultations even before getting together to coordinate their actions and policies. Now an integral part of what was already a complex decision-making process, these rounds of consultations take a lot of time. Political time, state time, is very much slowed down. The state's capacity to act is also slowed down.

Conversely, economic time is moving faster and faster. Technology and deregulation speed up innovation and shorten the life cycle of products—witness the computer sector and the unending succession of new software products. Capital moves around the world at the speed of light, and savers have to learn to manage the fruits of their labour quickly and flexibly, and to seek a return that is high in the short term but risky, rather than one that is more certain but lower in the long term.

Inspired by Kant's famous thesis,[6] the dream of the architects of the postwar world was to create a state of eternal peace and constant development through interdependence among nations. The economic institutions of Bretton Woods* thus aimed to promote the internationalization of economies. This vision was formed in a context in which they thought primarily in terms of trade. Today, production, technology, distribution, and finance are integrated as well as trade. The new world economy is made up of national and transnational companies, individual investors, trusts, and "traditional" capitalists, all seeking the highest and fastest profit possible.

Thus we see emerging a huge area of irresponsibility, one that is literally subject to no control. The global economy has never been held accountable for what it causes. Nor has it been made to respect any of the principles of legitimacy that apply to relations between individuals and the state. Hence a new strength has arisen outside the state's area of responsibility, anonymous and stateless, intoxicating but threatening.

---

* In July 1944, the governments of the United States, Great Britain, and Canada organized an international conference in Bretton Woods, New Hampshire, to discuss certain economic proposals for the postwar period. The agreements made at this conference led to the creation of the International Monetary Fund and the International Bank for Reconstruction and Development (the World Bank).

Chapter III

The Divorce of State and Market

SINCE THEY NO LONGER INHABIT THE SAME SPACE, AND SINCE THEY no longer operate in the same time frame or, especially, at the same pace, the state and the market must find a new basis for their relationship. They must do so because it is essential for the development of societies and personal freedoms.

The state is a construct of reason, an abstract thing, a Hegelian entity; as we conceive the state still, today, its essential question is legitimacy, that is, the deliberate search for the just, the reasonable, and the equitable. Its time horizon is the long term, that of laws, constitutions, and charters. The market, on the other hand, seeks, as well as possible and as quickly as possible, to fulfil the consumption and production needs of societies. The essential question for it is effectiveness and profit. Closer to instinct and desire, the market does not share the time horizon of the state. Its time horizon is that most demanding one—immediacy.

In this context, the new precariousness of the state is easily explained. Its capacity to fulfil its responsibilities has always depended on its vertical authority over all the economic and industrial forces in its territory. However, it is precisely this vertical authority that has been irreversibly eroded. Such a change, such a fundamental transformation, will inevitably have consequences whose scope is still beyond our comprehension.

Let us think about this a little. Whereas internationalization only increased the interdependence of national economies, globalization eliminates the reality of the national economy and even its very concept. In this respect, the effects of globalization do not end with the breakdown of the congruence between political space and economic space. Insofar as political spaces are tending to become fragmented at the very time that economic spaces are tending to merge, the result is a veritable revolution in relationships among the state, business, and the individual. In other words, the current upheaval calls into question the very role of politics in every society and in the world. The breakdown of the congruence between political space and economic space thus leads directly to a separation between the power of the state and the power of the market. Here is precisely where the revolutionary potential of globalization lies. The changes it is bringing about are forcing us to rethink, to reinvent democracy.

Not all revolutions are violent. It took less than fifty years for the French—who had thought like Bossuet—to come to think like Voltaire. "The hierarchy, discipline, and order that authority provides and the dogmas that strictly regulate life—that is what men of the seventeenth century liked. Constraints, authority, and dogmas—that is what men of the eighteenth century, their immediate successors, hated. The former were Christian, the latter anti-Christian; the former believed in divine right, the latter in natural right; the former lived a life of ease in a society divided into unequal classes, the latter dreamt only of equality."[1] That is a revolution, a profound one. Similarly, it took only some fifty years for the world—which thought in terms of the nation—to come to think in terms of the world. In each of these cases, the depth of the change makes it impossible to talk about mere evolution and forces us to acknowledge that, in the final analysis, we are here again talking about a revolution.

Power and Strength

Power is the capacity to act. In addition to the natural ability to act, it involves a legal or moral faculty—and thus the right—to do something. The word power in this sense always conveys the idea of activity or action. It is synonymous with authority and is used regularly in lieu of the word *state*, which is, so to speak, the human incarnation, the institutionalization par excellence, of power. There is a transitory quality to this kind of power. It takes its logic from reason, and its place in the human body, as in the social body, is consequently "cerebral." It is "more airy, closer to heaven," to use the language of the ancient Greeks. The essential question for this kind of power is legitimacy. As it is for the state.

Strength is something durable, permanent. It is in the realm of possibility, *potentiality*. Aristotle described it as more ambiguous and less well defined than an action. When one has the strength—the potentiality—to do something, one may or may not exercise the power—the capacity—to do it. In this sense, the power to act is only an expression of that potentiality. One attains the power to act, but one possesses the strength. In the human body, the place of potentiality is the abdomen, which the ancient Greeks considered more material, closer to the earth, than the head, and its logic is that of instinct, of desire.* Its essential question is that of effectiveness. As it is for the market.

All the forces on the world stage represent strength in the sense of potentiality, which can thus be positive or negative, constructive or destructive. Strength is brute vitality, undifferentiated energy. It is essential to the world system, of which it is the basis. How it is directed by the power to act will determine its impact, good or bad. Because in itself strength has no moral value.

Condillac's definitions of power and strength offer food for thought: "It seems that [strength, potentiality] is associated with force, and [the power to act] is associated with freedom, that is, with the reasonable use of force, and this is why the just man uses his power to act while the unjust man misuses his strength."[2] The same applies to societies and states. The relationship between the state and the market determines the capacity to make reasonable use of the market. Left to themselves, market forces lead to great disorder and do not allow the human purpose of the economy to be fulfilled. On the contrary, the strength of their instincts and desires reduces human beings to their roles as consumers and producers.

Although they were clear and precise throughout the Cold War, the meanings of fundamental concepts such as *enemy* and *threat* have been weakened. In the international world of yesterday, a strong vertical bond existed between strength, especially in the form of military and nuclear might, and power, which was still essentially in the hands of the state, the only legitimate user of force. Vertical bonds, in which strength is under the authority of a legitimate power to act, are losing much of their significance because of the reduced importance of military and strategic issues since the end of the Cold War. Who is the enemy of the West? NATO does not have an answer; that strategic alliance is even questioning its identity and trying to redefine its mission. What are the threats facing humanity today? Some people point to the diffuse dangers of drugs, AIDS, global warming, terrorism, the spread of nuclear weapons, all of which are transboundary dangers. The vertical bond, in which military power is under the state's power to act, is thus far less strong.

The same is true for economic strength. The top-down vertical bond between the state and the market was also very significant. The state asserted its power to act through the regulation and control it continued to

---

* The novel *Narcissus and Goldmund*, by Hermann Hesse, clearly shows the fundamental distinction between power and strength. The monk Narcissus in his quest for knowledge is all power to act, in contrast to the artist Goldmund, who in his quest for the eternal Eve represents potentiality (strength).

exercise over the national economy and the companies located in its territory, including the subsidiaries of multinationals. However, it has gradually lost its traditional tools of management, in particular the ability to
establish customs tariffs, to grant subsidies, or to control monetary policies.
Every company and every subsidiary of a multinational had an interest in
informing the state of its exact needs, and the state could, through its decisions, help business, but now the connection between business and the
national state no longer has the same importance.

The Firms: From Multinational to Global

Successful businesses have already benefited from this situation and, at the
same time, accentuated the change in the power relationship between the state
and the market, a change that is at the core of the current historical evolution. By carrying out each one of their functions in the economic space
best suited to the requirements of performance and profit, global companies have outclassed the multinationals, which have been losing ground
for some time. And now those global firms are seizing the opportunities
offered by globalization, and at the same time helping to move the process
forward.

Globalization, as we have seen, is revolutionary. It is a more advanced
and more complex form of internationalization that involves a degree of
functional integration of economic activities dispersed over various spaces.
It is a recent phenomenon, one that merges economic spaces and ignores
political borders. This merits repeating because it is key: whereas internationalization simply increased the interdependence of national economies,
globalization entails the elimination of the concept and then of the actual
reality of national economies. We no longer think of the economy in the
same way. Hence the breakdown of the congruence between political and
economic space.

If the distinction between internationalization and globalization is
clearly understood, this is quite simple to explain. In the era of internationalization, a company had to be quite large and powerful to develop a
network throughout the world, since it had to repeat from country to country the model of the head office in all its aspects and all its functions, with
the possible exception of research and development. Only multinationals
had the means to do this; thus they benefited the most from internationalization. In the era of globalization, the company that performs best is the
one flexible enough to integrate its various industrial functions as efficiently
as possible while carrying out each one in the economic space that is most
productive and profitable for it. This is possible for a company that has

developed a substantial strategic capacity and a high level of intelligence that enable it to take full advantage of the powerful telecommunications and information networks now available. Very big companies are often penalized because of their size, which deprives them of the flexibility that would enable them to participate in strategic alliances that favour the integration of industrial functions independently of economic and political borders.

Avoiding the Fate of the Dinosaurs

With change occurring at an increasingly rapid rate, management gurus have for some time been telling companies that they must find different ways of doing things if they are to avoid the fate of the dinosaurs, who became extinct because they were not able to adapt to the upheavals in their environment. This applies to both big and small companies.

Many big firms have gone the way of the dinosaurs because they were unable to play by the new rules of the game. Of the twelve strongest firms in the world listed by the *Wall Street Journal* at the turn of the twentieth century, only a single one still exists today. In 1982, two American authors published a book entitled *In Search of Excellence*,[3] about the best-run American firms; eight years later, 50 percent of those firms had already disappeared or had major problems. Of the Fortune 500 firms for 1985,[4] 40 percent no longer exist today.

Big firms have had to carry out restructuring and downsizing, which is not unrelated to our current high rate of unemployment. According to *Fortune*, the top five hundred American firms of 1979 employed 16.2 million people, whereas the top five hundred in 1993 employed only 11.5 million.[5] This reduction of some 4.7 million employees represents nearly 30 percent over a period of fourteen years.

Globalization is certainly a strong trend, an inescapable force of our time. To some people, it is a positive development towards more widely shared universal values, a world that is less divided, better understanding of others, and competition that is finally free among the best in the world—a fast track to excellence and progress. To others, globalization is threatening, uncontrollable, and alienating at the local level, especially for institutions we are familiar with: local businesses, trade unions, municipalities, special interest groups, regions, and even national governments. In this view, globalization is seen as leading to a reduction of values to the lowest common denominator, the erosion of regional and national identities, the subordination of peoples to blind, distant, heartless forces—in other words, the prelude to some awful global melting-pot, with the bastardization that implies.

There is no point analyzing globalization according to moral criteria.

It is a process that in itself is neither good nor bad. What is certain, though, is that it is not neutral in relation to society's economic and political structures, and that it will produce winners and losers.

Globalization is, among other things, a product of the new information technologies that have resulted from the combination of two of the most powerful innovations in human history: microelectronics, which makes it possible at minimal cost to process huge volumes of data; and telecommunications, which makes it possible to transmit those data instantaneously around the world. We are talking more and more about telematics. Globalization above all affects activities that have an important information content.[6]

Economic spaces now compete to have the highest functions in the hierarchy of the technological industries established in their territories. The importance of business is constantly increasing in the new world geography. The state, less and less the manager of its economy, is rapidly being transformed into the partner of business, becoming a mere actor on the stage of industrial and commercial competition instead of its regulator. This is a far cry from the prestigious role of the single, sovereign actor in international relations.

The Emergence of a Global Civil Society

Although we speak mostly about the globalization of markets and economies, an increase in the number and strength of non-governmental organizations, or NGOs, is also at the centre of globalization. The influence of NGOs is based essentially on the technological progress that has also made the global market possible. A striking illustration of this is the Internet, which makes it possible to disseminate a vast amount of information to a great many individuals or groups for the cost of a telephone call. This circulation of information, which is constantly expanding, systematically ignores traditional borders.

The immediate result of this situation, combined with the loss of autonomy by national governments, is, for better or for worse, a sharing of powers between governments and a large number of NGOs. Indeed, NGOs have come to play a decisive role on a global scale. The aid NGOs provide to people in need, wherever they are in the world, exceeds the aid given to them by the entire network of United Nations institutions, apart from the World Bank and the International Monetary Fund (IMF).[7]

Such transnational groups play an increasingly large role in the international agenda, through their expertise and their capacity for direct action in countries experiencing environmental disasters, political crises, or epidemics. Indeed, there has been an astonishing increase in NGOs in the area of the environment. In 1993, 726 organizations were members of the United Nations' environment program, and 450 were members of the World Conservation Union. When the African NGO Environment Network was formed in 1982, it consisted of some 50 NGOs, and by 1990 it had 530 members in forty-five countries.

The numbers of people who belong to these organizations and the funds they control have likewise grown substantially, which gives them an ever-increasing political independence. The revenues of the World Wildlife Fund of the United States went from $9 million to $53 million (US) between 1980 and 1993, and the number of individuals belonging to Greenpeace went from 1.4 million to 6.75 million in the same period. Friends of the Earth began in 1969 with an office in San Francisco; it was then quickly established in Paris and London, and in 1992 it affiliated with twenty-five other groups all over the world.

This new involvement of NGOs in global problems goes far beyond environmental issues to deal with the survival of indigenous peoples, social justice, human rights, and the economy. For example, the Coalition for Justice in the Maquiladoras (Mexican plants for producing parts to be shipped duty-free to the U.S. or Canada for assembly) is made up of more than eighty organizations concerned about transboundary economic problems in the region of the United States–Mexico border.

NGOs in Africa, Latin America, and Asia still depend a great deal on government funding. Thus the credibility and capacity for independent action of many of those in the South are open to question. Those organizations that are independent of governmental funding, though, are beginning to offer serious criticism of government policies. NGOs have made harsh judgments on the issues of global debt, trade, and the role of banks in global development. The negotiating strength of the largest NGOs is beginning to have a significant impact on government actions in many areas.

Contributions of the World Wildlife Fund to projects in developing countries reached $62.5 million (US) over the last decade. Even larger amounts have been redistributed from the OECD countries to international cooperation organizations through NGOs. Some 10 to 15 percent of all development aid is controlled by NGOs. The perspective of NGOs differs greatly from that of governments, which are viewed as conservative and administratively paralyzed.

The experience of the NGOs enables them to take part in the ratification and application of international treaties. The Convention on International Trade in Endangered Species was initiated by NGOs, and they monitor its application. Similarly, environmental organizations, led by Greenpeace, have played a key role in the banning of prospecting in the Antarctic. On the recommendation of these organizations, France and Australia supported the Antarctic Treaty, which made the region a scientific research zone.

The shortcomings of states and of the current international system create the opportunity for independent organizations to play an increasingly significant role in the management of our common assets. The importance of these new organizations is such that many experts have come to feel that the intergovernmental structures of the United Nations are outdated. A reform of the UN to promote the development of true world democracy is now strongly supported by the day-to-day practice of groups that are independent of governments.

The globalization of NGOs follows the trend in markets for goods and finance, towards the gradual elimination of borders. The state still has a role, however, because of the existence of illicit trade, such as the drug trade, and the proliferation of increasingly diversified criminal organizations that take advantage of the disappearance of barriers.

Some people go so far as to conclude that the environmental movement today is the only vital force challenging capitalism, denouncing its negative effects—the "negative externalities," as the economists say—especially on the environment, and proposing forceful united action to counter these effects. In many ways, it is a modern throwback to the old idea of a planned economy. Traditional socialism sought to act by positioning itself upstream, so to speak; to prevent the pollution characteristic of the capitalist economy, it advocated a complete change of economic engine. More modestly, the environmental movement seeks to act downstream, and to improve the performance of the engine instead. According to Jacques Julliard, environmentalism might even be the only credible form of socialism in the post-Communist era.[8]

There is nothing surprising about the increasingly important role played by independent organizations. After all, information is power, as we all know. And states no longer have control of information. Therefore they no longer have a monopoly on power. A decisive phenomenon is the new information technologies, which make it possible for individuals to join groups and movements of their choice. Networks of membership and allegiance develop that not only are independent of states and their borders, but that are more meaningful for their members than states are: this is the difference between a group one chooses and a group one belongs to automatically.

This unprecedented situation clearly has a lot of advantages, but it also

poses problems. Make no mistake about it—NGOs act in their own interests, just as any other organized body does. The fact that members of
NGOs generally do not profit financially from their activities, which are
essentially voluntary, does not preclude their getting other satisfactions from
them, such as working to promote their values and their vision of the world.
We are clearly dealing here with a new type of transnational actor and with
new kinds of stakes.

The international order is not equipped to deal with these new stakes
or to organize these new actors. Being essentially state-based, it has not even
begun to reflect the shift in favour of civil society at the expense of the public sector. Marked by its Western history and its formation during the European Renaissance, the international order is a prisoner of international law,
which, while still uncertain and fragile, is already out of date. Hence the
following question: although a true world community does not yet exist,
can we begin now to think about world law? Not only can we, but we must.
We quite simply have no choice.

In fact, with the affirmation of civil society and the circumvention of
the state, we sometimes witness a kind of societal revenge. This is not without dangers; it could lead to great disorder. With more and more actors
involved, the international system is losing its capacity to manage power
relations and thus to maintain order. It is less and less a real system and
more and more a simulacrum of a system, which we almost expect to dis-
appoint us. Thus there is little surprise at the failures of international
mediation, the crises, or the blunders in the management of interdependence today.

As much as internationalization depended on, adjusted to, and encouraged the vertical bonds between the two kinds of power, power and
strength, globalization reinforces strength and frees it from its subjugation
to power. The power to act is to internationalization what potentiality is to
globalization. It follows that strength that is not subject to the power to act
is dangerous, and may be revolutionary in both a positive and a negative
sense.

The international order is thus marked by the coexistence of two
worlds linked by bonds that are becoming increasingly loose and even conflictual. The first is the world of the state and of intergovernmental organizations, a codified, ritualized world comprising a finite number of actors
who are known and more or less predictable. This world, which is coming
to an end—at least as the *only* system—is the one in which the power to act
resided and in which legitimacy still resides. The second is a multicentric,
diffuse world with an infinite number of participants whose capacity for

international action is increasingly independent of governments, to which they are nevertheless supposedly subject.[9] This duality has prevented the emergence of a new world order. The hope of 1989 has given way to uncertainty, confusion, insecurity, a world of upheavals.

Citizens' Allegiance to the State

The psychosocial mechanisms that go with the transformation of the international order are pushing individuals towards both supranational identification and subnational communities, two movements that undermine citizens' allegiance to the nation-state. The world of states is based on the exclusivity of the citizens' state allegiance, and the international system is based on the capacity of the state to act by totally committing a certain number of individuals and subjects.

The multicentric world, on the other hand, is based on networks of allegiances that are hardly codified, whose nature and intensity depend on the free and momentary will of the actors concerned. It strives to broaden its autonomy in relation to states, and therefore to increase challenges to political borders and official sovereignties. Bertrand Badie even speaks of "the end of territories."[10]

The world of the state, the world of the power to act, emphasizes the use of coercion, and its essential question—we should never forget—is that of legitimacy. The multicentric world, the world of strength, gives priority to informal relationships among individuals, and its essential question— this bears emphasis—is that of effectiveness. This constitutes the strength of the market. Transnational relationships can thus now be defined as relationships that are formed in the world space beyond the framework of the national state and that are at least partially free of the control or mediating action of states.

The citizens' state allegiance, already shaken by the failures of the welfare state, does not, however, gain anything from the change imposed by the market. Seeing themselves confined to their roles as consumers and producers, individuals realize that their identity is being completely redefined. This is where "Marx's revenge," which I mentioned earlier, comes in.

The Tribulations of the Market

The fact remains that, for the moment, the key factor in this multicentric world is the market. Supported by the emergence of a powerful transnational world economy, it imposes its own laws. Even states are subject to its discipline when they want to finance their deficits or attract investment to create jobs. GATT, and then the World Trade Organization (WTO) and

the International Monetary Fund (IMF), instruments of inter-state cooperation, have also brought about an *economic disarmament*, depriving the
state of major tools for accomplishing the tasks we have become accustomed
to entrusting to it. The state has thus surrendered a large part of its jurisdiction to the market, and now the transnational actors are the ones controlling the key elements of strength: access to financing, to the market, to
technology, and to information.

The triumph of liberalism and the establishment of capital as the main
factor of production will not last long if capitalism is not able to resolve the
contradiction between its two fundamental tenets, political democratization
and economic liberalization. Liberalization deprives the state of means,
tools, and resources, which prevents it from meeting the needs and demands
of citizens and interest groups, those needs and demands that democratization tends to increase and legitimize. Thus the redistribution of wealth is
increasingly difficult to achieve, while at the same time the gap between rich
and poor is widening, inspiring legitimate political demands and giving rise
to social imbalances. This is an essential philosophical question that will
become increasingly pertinent as the logic of globalization takes us towards
what Bertrand Badie calls the tribulations of the market.[11]

Chapter IV

Confidence and Development

IN A BOOK WITH THE EVOCATIVE TITLE *TRUST*, AMERICAN SOCIOLOGIST
Francis Fukuyama attempts to determine which societies will adapt
harmoniously to globalization. According to him, these societies share one
central feature, the level of trust that exists among their members, which
strongly influences the performance of their economy.

The degree of trust is expressed in what Fukuyama calls "spontaneous
sociability," the social propensity to form or join groups outside the family.
The effect of this sociability is to prepare people psychologically to work
autonomously but cooperatively in the private sector. It leads to a high level
of participation by shareholders and to German- or Japanese-style trade
unionism, a trade unionism of cooperation rather than demands. This kind
of sociability is essential for large companies, which accumulate capital and
develop key technologies more effectively than small family businesses. But
it also encourages volunteer activity, philanthropy, and community action
by private citizens. To illustrate his thesis, Fukuyama discusses three "low-
trust" societies, China, Italy, and France, and three "high-trust" societies,
Japan, Germany, and the United States.

Low-trust societies are fertile ground for family businesses. Without
substantial assistance from the state, however, they have a great deal of difficulty reaching a higher level of economic activity. For a long time, as we
will see in Part Three, Quebec was, on the whole, this kind of society.

High-trust societies, on the other hand, have cultivated a strong community life much earlier, and include many groups that have arisen spontaneously out of civil society. These groups, which are situated between the
family and the state, are active in the economy. They increase the social
capital that alone makes possible the creation of businesses that are able to
compete globally.

The ability to create, produce, and assimilate new technology is more

than ever essential for development, and it determines positions of dominance and dependence on a global scale. Insofar as companies are no longer
content with merely exporting—in which their interests coincide with those
of the state—their logic is becoming increasingly dissociated from the logic
of the nation-state. Companies seek productive investments abroad as
needed, and relocate readily as required. Business in low-trust societies is
penalized in this new economy, because the state, which is essential to them,
no longer plays its traditional role, and, worse still, the interests of the state
and business no longer coincide.

The Logic of Integration

From an economic point of view, the creation of a large regional market
often appears to be the only way to overcome the handicap of a limited
domestic market and create the conditions necessary for investment in
research and development. It is crucial that a large country with a significant domestic market be part of this regional market. But for all countries,
building a regional market is still a defensive strategy *against external forces*.
The increasing number of regional free-trade agreements means simply that
their members are seeking protection against competing blocs. As Bertrand
Badie and Marie-Claude Smouts aptly state:

> It remains to be seen under what conditions these more or less nat-
> ural solidarities appear in a region and for what purposes. . . . The
> image of the world as comprising three blocs—the famous triad of
> North America, the European Community, and Japan/NIEs
> [newly industrializing economies] of Asia—is both reassuring and
> disquieting. In the face of world disorder, it introduces a certain
> rationality. . . . But economic integration, assuming that it exists,
> eliminates neither nationalisms nor cultural boundaries. At best,
> it muddles them. The cost of changing economic strength into a
> political strength capable of reducing regional differences by
> imposing a kind of "peace through empire" has become prohibi-
> tive. The time is ripe for imperialism. But as an editorial in the
> *Financial Times* commented, though the times may be ripe for
> imperialism, there is no longer the vocation among imperialists.[1]

A more positive view of this phenomenon would establish that the tendency to create continental free-trade zones constitutes an attempt by the
state to continue to manage the increasing interdependence of the postwar
system that was institutionalized at Bretton Woods. Indeed, it is an attempt

by the state to ensure its long-term survival. The fact remains that many countries in southeast Asia, Latin America, and, more recently, central Europe have taken advantage of this logic of integration and embarked on ambitious programs of industrialization, opening markets, and development. This is also true of individuals in both industrialized and developing societies; many are taking full advantage of globalization and integrating well into transnational networks. Many others, however, are being left behind, and are becoming less and less capable of remedying their situation. This is the case for many whole societies, particularly in Africa, and it is also the case for large segments of the population even in the industrialized countries.

The Logic of Exclusion and the Emergence of a Marginalized World

Globalization thus also entails conditions of exclusion, marginalizing those who are not able to take part in transnational networks. The result is the emergence of a fourth world made up of immigrants and the new poor who are directly experiencing the pressures of the new world order.

The logic of exclusion accentuates the international division of labour and sometimes gives it a dramatic, dangerous aspect. It leaves to the countries of the South all the activities the countries of the North want to get rid of. Jean-François Bayart speaks of these countries as "states for sale": countries used as dumps for industrial wastes or testing grounds for everything from nuclear weapons to pharmaceutical products, places of perverse pleasures such as child prostitution, refuges for drug traffickers, havens for terrorists.[2] The excluded countries are powerless, if not docile; there are many societies in the South that are in danger of sinking into such an abyss. With an international drug trade that appears to be bigger than the trade in automobiles, there are false states that form within official national spaces;[3] the Medellín cartel in Colombia, for example, possessed most of the instruments of state power, even for a time controlling its own air space.

This logic of exclusion makes it more necessary than ever to find new means of integration and to develop solidarity. Since the state no longer has the capacity to regulate the economy, creativity is required. Societies, businesses, and individuals must now all show the imagination, flexibility, and courage to reinvent themselves and find ways to become part of political, economic, technological, industrial, and cultural networks and alliances. In this world of great changes, originality is still possible; indeed, it has become indispensable.

Fukuyama's thesis regarding the societies that will win and lose in this era of globalization is all the more interesting in that it seems to be corroborated by the views of Alain Peyrefitte. Peyrefitte's conclusions on the causes of economic development over the last four hundred years are strikingly similar to those of Fukuyama, to the point that the same word, "trust," is used in the title of his book.[*][4]

The Human Purpose of the Economy: The State and the Miracle of Development

The history of humanity is essentially one of deprivation; development is the exception to the rule. Thus Alain Peyrefitte speaks of the "miracle" of development.[5] Like Max Weber,[6] he attributes development not to traditional factors such as labour, capital, or climate, nor to the relative scarcity of natural resources as postulated in the theory of initial disadvantage; he attributes development to a collective attitude favourable to economic activity.

This attitude, typical of certain societies, is part of what Peyrefitte calls an "ethos of competitive confidence," which has given rise to three miracles of development: the Dutch miracle of foreign trade, the British miracle of industrialization, and the American miracle of economic innovation and high technology. There is an ethos, a pattern of behaviours and attitudes, that is the mark of modernity. Individuals who share this ethos create institutions—state, nation, market, business—in which it is reflected. New relationships are then established between public authority and these individuals, relationships that transform the political framework of the economy. These new relationships accentuate the role of tolerance in economic, social, and religious harmony. They involve the autonomy of economic activity and they encourage innovation. They are based on the shared conviction that the freedom of the market is in the general interest. All these attitudes are essentially related to confidence or trust.

Unlike Weber, who established a causal relationship, Peyrefitte observes an "elective affinity" between spontaneous socio-economic behaviour and religious affiliation, both of which arise out of the human propensity to escape traditional authoritarian controls in favour of a personal commitment to activities that change the community. It is this propensity that led certain societies in northern Europe to choose *both* Protestantism and capitalism. It is this desire for freedom that distinguishes them and that leads them to take risks.

---

[*] The French word Peyrefitte uses is *confiance*. It is an especially useful word because it actually means two things: it means confidence, of course, but it also means trust, and as we know, confidence leads to trust.

There is a significant correlation between the religious map of Europe —the south Roman Catholic and in decline, the north Protestant and burgeoning—and its map of literacy, that is, of *intellectual autonomy*. This religious map also correlates with the progress of democracy, modern urbanization, low interest rates, advantageous commercial credits, and ease of investment. There is also a direct relationship with the distribution of Nobel prizes in the sciences and social sciences, and with high per capita incomes.[7] The ethos of competitive confidence makes itself felt in every area: encouragement of reading and writing;[*] the discipline of individual initiative and a sense of responsibility; constant striving to adapt; the progress of reason and the reduction of the domain of irrationality; openness to economic modernity in the form of innovation, operational research, marketing, and distribution; and finally, rejection of monopolies in favour of the competition of ideas through freedom of expression, the competition of individuals through elections, and the competition of products through markets.

Reconciling Economic and Social Concerns

What is striking in Peyrefitte's observations is, first of all, that the success of a society and the takeoff of its economy go hand in hand. Everything holds together, everything is integrated. Economic development does not take place in a vacuum. Not only do social development and economic development go together, but they reinforce one another. In the emerging knowledge-based economy, business needs a skilled labour force and people capable of initiative, autonomy, and entrepreneurship. Education, which is largely a responsibility of the state, is essential to the confidence individuals and societies need to effect economic development. Knowledge and skills are essential for the creation of wealth, and the market and business need a public system of education. If businesses are more mobile, they will go where people are better educated. They will also increasingly be able to bring in people where they are needed. In this sense, business will play a larger role than the state in the new world geography. And access for the greatest possible number will ensure that everyone with talent will take part in development, as long as they too are very mobile.

Another thing that is striking in Peyrefitte's analyses is that these miracles of development have occurred in societies where respect for the

---

[*] My father, a Catholic but whose first language was English, told me about a fundamental difference he observed during his childhood: his Protestant friends had to read the Bible, while he was forbidden to. The intermediary of the priest, and he alone, had to interpret it. We will look later at other consequences of the crucial role of intermediaries in Catholic societies.

authority of the state coexisted with respect for the autonomy of the market. Globalization will thus have to permit the establishment of a new balance between state and market. The history of development shows that the state has played an essential role, guaranteeing the economic rights of the individual and establishing a framework in which the market could grow. Moreover, it has always been by giving them new rights that the state has won the loyalty of individuals, who have become, first and foremost, citizens.

Chapter V

The State and the Conquest of State Allegiance

THE STATE IN ITS ESSENTIAL FORM CAME INTO BEING AS AN instrument of political society in 1648. That year, the Peace of Westphalia marked the end of the Thirty Years' War, which had arisen from the antagonism between some German Protestant princes and the Catholic emperor. The state was born out of the transition from a horizontal division of power between the nobility and the clergy of medieval Europe to a vertical division of power based on control of territory. From that time on, the newborn state forced people to integrate into society by means of citizenship. France is certainly the first and most striking example of this. The conquest of people's allegiance as citizens led eventually, through various stages over the last three hundred and fifty years, to the state's monopoly on personal identity through citizenship.

This is why globalization, which represents such a profound and formidable challenge to the state, is causing an identity crisis. And the crisis is all the more intense because it is the state that is largely responsible for the incredible progress of humanity in terms of both the economy and freedom. We risk misinterpreting history and taking the wrong actions should we ever forget that it is the marriage of state and nation that permitted the formation of markets—precisely, national markets—and the birth of industry, of business. Now all this is being challenged by globalization. While no organizational model has yet been found to replace it, we must recognize that the state—crippled by transnational and horizontal flows, bypassed by sophisticated communication technology, unsuited to the new economic realities—is clearly not up to the current challenge.

Citizenship in the Traditional State

The fact remains that the state has served us well. It is the state that gave people their rightful place in politics,[1] though admittedly, in terms of the social contract, the individual remained subordinate to the state's collective goals. The primacy of the group over the individual/citizen was clear: political institutions existed—and continue to exist—to promote the public good.[2]

With a propensity to trade and to seek wealth, individuals, on the other hand, have been able to reach their full potential in the economic sphere. In this one particular area, they have achieved autonomy with regard to the state, insofar as the state, as a general rule, refrained from any intrusion that might slow down economic development. An area of activity reserved for individual initiative, which thrives and finds its fulfilment there, the economy at the same time contributes to the common good. This new relationship between a political sphere centred on the collectivity and an economic sphere centred on the individual is based on a social ethic that is seen as natural.

There are good reasons why the state has won people's loyalty and allegiance. In addition to giving them an identity as citizens, the state, through its monopoly on the legitimate use of force since 1648, guaranteed them—and still in principle guarantees them—physical security. This was the first manifestation of the state's vertical authority over its territory, and it proved a success. In the Middle Ages, highway robbery had made travel dangerous and hampered trade and commerce; this led to a broadening of the contract between the state and its citizens. In giving itself the means to fulfil its ambitions, the state was only responding to the growing expectations of its citizens.

In domestic politics, then, from 1750 on, power became centralized in the form of the national state, and any intermediate or regional representation was eliminated from the central authority. When monarchies came under attack in the eighteenth century, the state saw this as an opportunity to complete the consolidation of its domestic political power, an opportunity it eagerly took advantage of. It identified itself with the nation because of the emotions and the instinctive sense of belonging the nation inspired. This transition was necessary, since a state based only on each citizen's calculation of benefits received and costs incurred would surely not have been very effective.

The nascent nation-states used various means to assert themselves, in particular, their monopoly on the "legitimate" use of force. History has shown that these means were effective, even though they were not always particularly noble. Who ever said that in these matters nobility and effectiveness had to coincide? Speaking of the collective crimes committed by groups in the process of constituting themselves as nations, didn't Renan say that "nations cannot have memories"?

The Nation-State and the Market

Subsequently, the nation-state offered the individual a modified version of the original social contract, one that in addition to physical security provided economic security, through the establishment of national markets. In the mid-eighteenth century, the factory took the place of the craft workshop.[3] This new mode of production disrupted social relations, transferring work activity from the family setting to the factory. Property quickly replaced the family as the principal means of social identification, and societies in which people were trusting and confident enough to establish bonds with individuals outside their families had a great advantage. The insights of Peyrefitte and Fukuyama have shown how essential this is for the miracle of development, for it enables the establishment of a market economy that, instead of being based on the exchange of existing production, adapts to industry and the division of labour.

Political leaders in England established the first national market, standardizing production and building a merchant fleet. This joining together of the mechanisms of politics and economics in a large territory spread throughout Europe. It is interesting to note that the formation of national markets was a reaction by political leaders to the dynamics of a market that ignored the "prenational" borders of the time. By forcing the unification of politics and trade, England created the conditions that allowed political and economic spaces to coincide perfectly in the same territory. As in the political sphere, there was a transition from horizontal to vertical management of the economy.

It is thus in England that the modern economy first came into being. Indeed, "the development of a market economy and then of an industrial economy required the establishment of communities of an intermediate size between cities, which segmented economic flows, and empires, which stifled them."[4] Economic modernity also involved the weakening of traditional allegiances that hampered the logic of the market and the establishment of a social division of labour.

And as always in the great upheavals of history, technology played a role: "The intensification of trade created a communications community that developed its language, its symbols, and thus the actual conditions of its cultural unity, whereas traditional communication strengthened small groups and thus tended to reproduce solidarities at the micro-community level."[5]

The conditions now existed for the birth of citizenship, and then of capitalism. This all-too-brief history makes it clear why globalization represents such a huge challenge to this organization of social relationships:

by re-establishing horizontal economic relations, it fundamentally undermines the balance of the market that was created through the vertical intervention of the state.

The Firms

Although it is today one of the driving forces of globalization, the firm came into being in the space of national markets. Moreover, it could not have developed in the traditional society of old, which was believed to be divinely ordained. The recognition of personal freedom was needed in order for the organization of the economy to be based on the market and the guarantee of property rights. In classical liberalism, the economic sphere is the arena of personal freedom, the freedom to develop and grow, whereas in the political sphere the public good takes precedence over the private good. In order to succeed, the individual had to move from a social order based on family relationships to a social order based on property. Francis Fukuyama has shown clearly that societies that have made this transition have been more successful in the capitalist economy.

In the mid-nineteenth century, the firm acquired a legal status. Along with the establishment of corporations with large numbers of shareholders, this new status protected business from most offensives originating in the political sphere, at least from the arbitrary use of political power. The autonomy of the economy gradually attained the status of dogma in the states of the West. These states then granted rights to firms to permit them to create wealth in the autonomous economic sphere. In practice, states have delegated to firms considerable responsibility for the collective future: firms have designed and carried out economic and industrial projects of their own choosing, thus orienting the general development of society and its technical content.[6]

With the state as guarantor of justice and freedoms on one side and an autonomous economic sphere on the other, the individual/citizen experienced a remarkable emancipation. And some miracles of development ensued.[7] The authority of the state in the political sphere and the autonomy of the market in the economic sphere became firmly established and won the respect of the societies in which they existed. In this we see that Peyrefitte is correct.

This being said, the return of horizontal management as a result of globalization presents a challenge to traditional firms. As we have seen, it will have to undergo substantial changes if it wants to survive the crucial transition from national markets to a global market.

The Welfare State

Following the Great Depression of the 1930s, the state adopted, in addition to physical and economic security, a third "chapter" in its contract with citizens. Though Carnegie, Morgan, Rockefeller, and other merchants and capitalists had managed to surmount the terrible economic crises of the late nineteenth century, business leaders proved incapable of resolving the crisis of the 1930s.[8] Politicians had to take the initiative. The welfare state became the response of the capitalist countries to the social crises caused by the failures of the free market. Individuals now obtained social security from the state just as they had earlier obtained physical security and economic security from it. The contract binding the state to the citizens became total.

In this way, the state completed its conquest of people's allegiance. The rational state met the individual's need for order. The nation-state satisfied the demands of the individual's heart and emotions. Through the consolidation of national markets, the state met people's vital needs and gave them a space for development and personal fulfilment such as humanity had never before known. Since then, identity has been defined, perhaps even exclusively, in terms of citizenship. People consider themselves citizens insofar as they possess rights and have a recognized role in democratic practices.

The Technocratic State

Just as the nation, and then the market, once helped the state in its conquest of people's allegiance, information technology and management science would allow it to extend even further its monopoly on identity through citizenship. It finally became possible for the state to establish controls over financial and trade flows, and it was able to broaden its jurisdiction in the economic sphere and make itself guarantor of the stability of markets and the material well-being of individuals. Contradicting the democratic model that sees personal responsibility to the community as the source of all social progress, this expansion of the role of the state has led to a reduction of the citizen's responsibility to the collectivity. The welfare state stresses the rights of citizens and increasingly disregards their duties to the community. This new type of state is technocratic, and it uses new techniques. Among other things, it undertakes to respond to the demand for fiscal and monetary policies, so much so that the moral aspects of mutual aid—such as charity and solidarity—are replaced by a vast insurance company in which risks, calculated by actuaries, are shared by all.

To its credit, this state provides people with stability and security. Its approach is rational and it appeals to people's heads. But at the same time it excludes feelings of compassion, and the entire emotional realm. This state reflects an ethic of justice, in which benefits are based on rights, rather than an ethic of care or consideration, in which people are granted a benefit if they are in need, regardless of whether they may demand it by right.

The military needs of World War II and the subsequent reconstruction of the postwar economies that were in ruins led to an additional broadening of the powers of governments. The incredible economic growth of the "thirty glorious years"[9] following the war inspired a great deal of imagination, enthusiasm, and generosity by governments and the governed in the creation of economic and social programs. Public spending, which had accounted for approximately 10 percent of total production before 1929, reached 30 percent in the 1960s, and by the 1990s it accounted for nearly 50 percent of total domestic spending in most of the industrialized countries.

For a while, the welfare state was able to obscure the natural insecurity the capitalist economy creates. But only for a while.[10] The state as provider of security achieved this only at the cost of huge deficits. This state is today being challenged.

Now citizens have an ambivalent relationship, a love-hate relationship, with the state, political leaders, administrations, and public services. "Love" because, given the mounting problems—persistent unemployment, the increasing disorganization of cities, the clash of different cultures—the state seems to be the only effective actor remaining, but also "hate" directed both at a technocracy that is seen as remote and at a political class that is unable to offer any new ideas or deal with the real problems and wastes its energy in pointless squabbles.[11] Concern is growing, especially when citizens consider that the state is no longer adequately fulfilling its traditional mission in the areas of education, health, justice, and security.[12]

In fact, as we have already seen, the less respect the state shows for the autonomy of the economic sphere and its rules and discipline, and the less attention it pays to the signals of the market, the more the society on which it is based declines in terms of both economic development and freedoms. On the other hand, it is becoming increasingly clear that when the market ignores the signals the state sends it, it allows private interests to encroach on the collective interest. This is true in the case of the environment and also with respect to freedoms. Now, when globalization challenges the state, it at the same time threatens the order guaranteed by the state, which the market requires to run smoothly. In these circumstances, certain questions inevitably arise.

Could markets and firms operate for long without the state that supported their development and expansion? Today's disordered world will have to be remade, taking into account two factors. The first is the state, an actor that is seeking to ensure its survival and that has been able to reinvent itself on a supranational level to partially recover its effectiveness, in order to justify its existence and its legitimacy. And the second is the emergence of a global civil society and new, very powerful actors.

Will people remain faithful for long to their allegiance as citizens? What affects them more deeply than anything else is the loss of cultural references in the era of globalization. This is the source of the current identity crisis. Caught up in an increasingly global market, people are experiencing great upheaval. There will have to be a remaking of the world, and it will be carried out by people whose freedom must constantly be reconquered and made stronger.

Chapter VI

Identity Crisis and the Pain of Loss

W̶E NO LONGER KNOW WHO WE ARE. THE PROFOUND IDENTITY crisis human beings are experiencing now, at the beginning of the era of globalization, has two facets. On the one hand, the sense of security the state has gradually provided over the last three hundred and fifty years has been shaken in every respect. The discipline the markets impose on public finances has forced the state to re-examine many parts of the social security system built up over the last half-century. In the area of economic security, businesses are less and less dependent on the rights the state originally granted them so that they might develop and thrive. Globalization offers businesses a degree of mobility that often makes the economic security they originally required unnecessary, and people are seeing major changes in the labour market.

Although physical security was the first element of their contract with the state, citizens in the industrialized countries are now forced to acknowledge that, while globalization has generally led to increased physical security by reducing the threat of war between countries, hidden violence still exists throughout society. In some countries, such as the United States, the private protection and security industry will soon be larger than the public police services, if it is not already.[1] In dealing with violence the state does not always do what people have come to expect. This is the case for international crime and terrorism, which affect many countries, as well as for the increase in crime and violence in our own cities, in spite of improvements in recent years. All this leads to a weakening of the Hobbesian contract between the individual and the state.[2]

In addition to all this, and at the same time, new actors are emerging on the international stage. Within societies, these new actors offer people new allegiances that are often transnational and closer to the new stakes.

In doing so, they make possible the emergence of a global civil society in which, for a growing number of people, identifications and solidarities are more intense than those in national societies.

The Shift from a Vertical to a Horizontal Perspective

While the whole Westphalian system enabled humanity to move beyond natural insecurity and instability by providing a huge contract under the vertical authority of the state, people today must relinquish the heritage of the Enlightenment and the extremely high value placed on human reason. The erosion of society that we are experiencing causes a high degree of insecurity, yet it represents an opportunity for historical progress. Beyond the institutions that have served it well—the state, the market, and others—society may perhaps be able, thanks to globalization, to regain its humanity in spite of the bureaucratic rigidities and the markets that tend to reduce people to their narrow roles as consumers and producers.

This is another example of the replacement of a vertical perspective with a horizontal one. How we define ourselves and others has changed profoundly, as Alain Touraine writes:

> Until very recently, in order to understand a society, we tried to define its social relations of production, its conflicts, its methods of negotiation; we spoke of domination, exploitation, reform, or revolution. Today we speak only of globalization or exclusion, increasing social distance or, on the other hand, concentration of capital or of the capacity to disseminate information and forms of consumption. We had become used to seeing ourselves in relation to others on social scales, scales of skill, income, education, or authority. We have replaced that vertical vision with a horizontal vision: we are in the centre or at the margins, inside or outside, in the light or in the shadows.[3]

Observing that personal identity is no longer based on social relationships of conflict, cooperation, or compromise, Touraine uses a metaphor for social life taken from astronomy, as if each individual and each group were a star or a galaxy defined by its position in the universe. Human beings every day experience an increasing dissociation between the world of objectivity and the space of subjectivity.

At the heart of globalization and the dissociation it entails is the replacement of industrial capitalism by financial capitalism.* In the era of industrial capitalism, the political sphere was monopolized by class conflict and negotiation. The stakes were domination and exploitation. In the era of financial capitalism, the stakes are quite simply the concentration of capital and exclusion.

Exploitation, Exclusion, and Loss

Exclusion carries with it risks that are obviously and radically more serious than those resulting from exploitation. After all, people who are exploited are in a social relationship. They can organize and make demands. They remain essential to the functioning of society and the economy. The situation of the excluded is much more serious, because it is possible for society to get along without them. The excluded do not exist in a social relationship, and therefore they can be ignored. They are simply not needed. This is why, in spite of everything, it is better to be exploited than excluded.

The question of who we are thus takes an extremely distressing turn. And this distress, which forces us to face certain fundamental existential questions, brings us back to the subject, the individual. As the objective, technical world deteriorates into a pure market, while the world of cultural identities retreats into an obsession with community, the concrete, specific human beings that we all are, the individuals that we are and want to remain, ourselves as "subjects," are being torn apart and seeing our world fall apart. The same is true of the sphere of institutions and the individual's representation of the world. People are deeply shaken by the loss of cultural references brought about by globalization. Today's forced transition from modernity to postmodernity stems above all from the fact that culture no longer has anything to do with the economy.

The Separation of the Two Worlds

We have already seen how cultural identities are being fragmented while markets are becoming global and the economy is becoming unified. People are also experiencing a dissociation between two worlds: that of technology and markets, on one hand, and that of culture, on the other; or that of instrumental reason and that of collective memory; or, in still other words,

---

* In order to clearly understand the problem of identity for millions of workers and trade-unionists, we simply need to measure their participation in the concentration of capital. Many of them are owners of this capital. Many of them are shareholders in global companies through their pension plans, whose managers have a responsibility to obtain the best return for them, which is their key to security in their old age. They have become actors in this financial capitalism. They are in fact capitalists.

that of signs and that of meaning. As the century draws to a close, the dissociation between the economy and culture, exchanges and identities, is at the heart of our experience.

Culture thus has less and less to do with the economy. The emergence of financial capitalism has completed the separation of individual experience from the creation of wealth. Industrial capitalism made the creation of wealth more perceptible to the individual. Globalization accentuates the distance separating the world of networks of trade from the world of actual cultural experience. For too many people, these two worlds are moving apart faster and faster. But not, of course, for the "cultural" industry of entertainment, which is an important element in the global economy.

Less and less directed by economic, social, and political centres of production, the flow of trade has become an end in itself, seeking immediate and strictly financial profitability. What is more, while historically investments have followed trade, now it is rather trade that follows investments. And the primary purpose of financial trading, unlike traditional trade, is no longer the exchange of goods and services. The capital available from pension funds or insurance companies, for example, simply seeks the best financial return. Financial capitalism goes further and further beyond industrial capitalism. Capital obeys its own logic. Because it is becoming dematerialized, the economy is moving away from people's lives, from their concrete experience.

The Media

Another important factor in the growing gap in people's everyday experience between the objectified world of public life and the space of subjectivity or private life is the ever-larger place given over to the media. Television has gained a central place because it creates a direct relationship between the most private experience and the most global reality, because it creates an emotional relationship with the pain or joy of another human being, using the most advanced scientific techniques. This is a direct relationship, one that eliminates mediation between the individual and humanity, and that, by decontextualizing messages, could play an active role in the general process of desocialization.

In the same way, the international media create or amplify trends in opinion that are further and further away from social movements in which real groups engaged in direct conflicts can at any time measure the expected costs and benefits of collective action. These opinion campaigns succeed all the better when they put aside any consideration of the actual political effects or significance of the facts they are reacting to. They refer to a global society without states, and to dangers, threats, or misfortunes presented with no concrete social or political context. As if the increasing expansion of the market of information commodities necessarily entailed their detachment from the social conditions of their production, and their reduction to the state of merchandise.[4]

It must be acknowledged that the emergence of financial capitalism, focused on the symbol of capital, and the growing place of the media in our lives both contribute to making people spectators and discouraging involvement. And without involvement, human beings lose their humanity.

To Change Life

If we are no longer defined by our social and historical situation, then so much the better. There will no longer be any limit to our creative imagination. We will be able to circulate freely anytime and anywhere. We will be postmodern. Indeed, since the dissociation between instrumentality and identity is at the very heart of our personal and collective experience, we *are* all postmodern in a way. Primarily because we believe less and less in the historical vocation of a class or a nation, or in the idea of progress or the end of history, and because our demand is no longer to live *better tomorrow* but *differently today*. In contrast to Marx, who wanted to change the world, Rimbaud's ambition was to change life. Could Rimbaud in his exuberant youth have imagined what awaited humanity? Creativity will prevail over strength.

Political Actors and the Desire to Be a Subject

The main political actors of our immediate future will essentially need creativity. They will not be creatures of traditional power. These political actors will be neither citizens, as in our entry into modernity, nor workers, as in industrial society. They will be—they already are—those individuals or groups who are working to combine cultural experience (private life) with participation in the economy, the world of instrumental action (public life). This is why youth, women, immigrants, members of minorities, and environmentalists have for more than twenty years been the most prominent historical actors, at least in the industrialized societies. It is they who are striving most consciously to act and to be recognized as subjects, to fulfil themselves as human beings. Some of the most visible and deeply affected are those young people for whom the transition to the labour market has become so difficult that they have withdrawn into themselves and retreated from asserting themselves as subjects.

But occupational problems and the absence of political activism have not meant a retreat into hedonism for young people in general. Their attitudes are influenced by music, movies, and television, but they also make themselves heard through participation in humanitarian action and environmental campaigns. They are moved by a desire to be "subjects," which is expressed as a desire for life and a defence of a personal identity threatened by the fragmentation of occupational and social experience. Young people have replaced the defence of the ideal society with the defence of personal life, which most of them do not reduce to a simple craving for consumption or a demand for help. This desire to become subjects, full persons, will enable young people to rediscover the central role of art and aesthetic experience, which will nourish their thinking about life and the world.

Chapter VII

The Subject — at the Centre
of a New Aesthetic Experience

Our pale reason hides the infinite from us.
— Arthur Rimbaud

THE STARTING POINT FOR MY THINKING, AS WELL AS ITS CULMI-
nation, is *the subject*, which is something all of us desperately seek to
become throughout our lives.

Political and economic activity should help us in our quest for fulfilment. I do not believe it is necessary to choose between the individual and
the collectivity. I believe we need to transcend both absolute subjectivity
and the focus on the roots of our identity. The dominant American culture leads to excessive individualism, but, as the poet said, no man is an
island. Human beings—we will come back to this later—are historical
subjects. They need their community, or at the very least a community, in
order to develop.

The subject's community of origin often provides the false security of
ethnic and cultural identity. This type of security is necessarily based on
the exclusion of difference, which too often means the exclusion of others,
who are frequently seen as a threat. But a community made up of individuals who have become subjects would not be stifling. On the contrary,
Charles Taylor has clearly shown that communities can welcome diversity.
Commenting on an aspect of Taylor's work, the political scientist Philip
Resnick writes:

> Taylor does not abandon the search for common moorings, but rec-
> ognizes the different building blocks that modern society contains.
> Thus, he is open to the cultural diversity of modern national com-
> munities, criticizing the advocates of homogenization on the one
> hand, and of ethnocentric self-immurement on the other. And he

looks towards a larger "fusion of horizons" in which alternative, nay contending, views come to be incorporated into our rethinking of our collective identities.[1]

Taylor seems to distance himself from the modern sensibility with his "participatory" model, in contrast to the "rights" model. Without denouncing the fashion for declarations and charters of rights that leads to a sometimes excessively legalistic approach in Western culture, Taylor acknowledges the possibilities for more direct participation by citizens.

It may be that the market has a tendency to reduce people to the roles of consumer and producer. But this market, though it often operates blindly and causes trials and tribulations, is still the product of an innate human reflex, and it offers the best possible arena for human fulfilment. Politics enables us to make it a place of freedom, where rights are guaranteed.

What I am proposing throughout this book is a strengthening of the subject, which I feel is an urgent necessity. Subjects who have thoroughly explored their identity and deepened their awareness of the world they live in will be better able to resist both the appeal of withdrawal into community and that of the reductive market. At the same time, such subjects will be able to contribute to building a community that is welcoming to others, a place of fulfilment. They will also be able to force the market to respect human autonomy, which will make it possible for human beings to develop their abilities and push back their limits.

I deeply believe that in order to become full subjects, people, sooner or later, must discover the aesthetic moment that will be the source of a new political vision. This will make it possible to move beyond today's upheavals and contradictions and remake the world, to create a world in which human beings can be at home. Following Aristotle and Thomas Aquinas, philosophers have long taught us that "man" is a rational animal. This celebration of reason as the principal, and even the sole, distinction between humans and animals was reiterated in 1636 by Descartes in his *Discourse on Method*, in which the well-known statement "I think, therefore I am" designates the mind, the "cerebral," as the primary value.[2] And the philosophers of the Enlightenment perpetuated this view of the supremacy of reason in human beings. It is a view that has never satisfied me.

I have long been grateful to Professor Julien Naud, S.J., for teaching me that the human being is, rather, a "historical subject,"[3] a concept I would now like to clarify. I realize today how well Professor Naud's teaching prepared me to understand my time, the era of globalization. While the necessary remaking of the world entails a set of principles for changing public life, it first of all involves the remaking of the individual, and thus of the subject with the desire and the capacity to combine instrumental action and cultural identity. Cultural identity includes interpersonal relationships and emotional and sexual life as well as collective memory and personal memory. It is because of this remaking that the personal subject is not merely a historical subject but is above all a tragic, dramatic subject.[4]

It seems to me that globalization, by undermining the "rational," inevitably leads to the end of modernity and the fall of the classical model that since the Enlightenment has given precedence to reason. John Ralston Saul, in *Voltaire's Bastards*, even speaks of "the dictatorship of reason in the West."[5]

The Historical Subject and Models of Experience of the World

The subject, of course, is an irreplaceable individual, a unique being. But as unique and irreplaceable as he or she may be, the subject is still a *historical* subject, because individuals exist in time and space, and thus are influenced by the societies in which they live. The definition of human beings as historical subjects rather than as rational animals makes sense to me because it allows us to account for the four ways people experience the world. The "historical subject" comprises these four elements, unlike the "rational animal," which focuses on the rational element alone. These four elements give rise to four patterns of experience of the world: *biological, aesthetic, intellectual,* and *dramatic*.

What really distinguishes humans from animals is not so much their reason as their aesthetic need. It is this aesthetic need that liberates human beings from their biological impulses and stimulates them to develop their intellectual capacities. Biological experience is characterized by a purely animal consciousness, but there exists in human beings an exuberance that transcends the biological purpose of pain and pleasure. Human beings do not want simply to satisfy their biological needs as all other animals do; they want to satisfy their needs "well," even those needs that are the most undeniably biological. It is this quest that leads to aesthetic experience.

This aesthetic moment provides the authentic joy of existence becoming conscious of itself. Its spontaneous authenticity is evident in the tireless play of children, the athletic fervour of young people, the joy felt on a sunny morning, or the soothing charms of a sweet melody. Such pleasures are not purely biological. There is something in human beings that goes beyond biological ends per se. It would be too restrictive, however, to claim that good meals and attractive people are the only sources of aesthetic experience. Let us recognize, rather, that aesthetic experiences may be sought purely for pleasure, that they can defy immediate biological needs, and that this liberation in itself gives rise to a spontaneous joy that is its own justification. Kant speaks of the beautiful as that which is pleasing for itself alone, that is, without being subordinated to any end other than itself.[6]

A comparison between the definitions of human beings as rational animals and as historical subjects, and an examination of love and sexuality allow us to glimpse something essential to an understanding of how people will make the transition from the world of yesterday to the world of tomorrow. The new world will have to be dreamed before it can take shape. The creativity of individuals and communities, a creativity that is full of memory, intuition, and imagination, will be called on to contribute to this.

Human beings, as I said, do not want simply to satisfy their biological needs; they want to satisfy them "well." This aesthetic quest prevents desires from remaining at the simple level of instinct, such as hunger for food or the sexual drive for intercourse. It is true that drinking and eating are biological activities, but people separate them spatially and psychologically from the farm, the slaughterhouse, and the kitchen; moreover, they decorate the dining room and impose table manners on children. Clothing does more than conserve heat; it adorns as it covers, so the human body does not appear simply as a biological entity. Sexuality is obviously, but not solely, biological. It can even become something mysterious in the context of human life; beyond mere coupling, people put a great deal of effort into creating a favourable ambience and context in which to exercise their sexuality.

The first work of art of human beings is their own lives.

Art and the Expression of Emotions

Contrary to widely held belief, the function of art is not primarily to communicate emotions but to give them form, to articulate them. Hence artists are extremely important in a society. The aesthetic need—and art in general insofar as it satisfies this need—involves a double freedom. In addition to liberating human beings from domination by biological ends, art and the aesthetic need liberate intelligence from the constraints of mathematical proofs, scientific demonstrations, and common sense.

Aesthetic liberation, which allows free artistic control of the succession of sensations and images, emotions and bodily movements, does not simply check the biological impulse but infuses it with a flexibility that makes it a docile instrument of the spirit of investigation. It is thanks to this aesthetic liberation that human beings have been able to attain intellectual experience of the world. In this sense, the aesthetic moment is what most clearly distinguishes human beings from animals. For it is the aesthetic moment that makes it possible for human beings, after having acquired the ability to reason, to develop their intellectual skill. What is talent but the ability to put experience, biological or aesthetic, into an intellectual mould? What is it if not an ability to respond spontaneously with ease and precision to the demands of the spirit? This is where intuition comes in. The exact formulation quickly follows. The senses are attentive to significant details. Memory brings to mind conflicting cases. Imagination anticipates opposing possibilities. However, even with talent, in science, knowledge is built up slowly, following a very gradual process of partial understanding, supplemented by subsequent understandings, until an entire field is mastered. True creativity needs all these elements to develop and take form in a particular life.

The fourth pattern of experience, experience of ordinary life, is dramatic experience. In ordinary life, it is quite clear that we are no longer dealing with the biological, aesthetic, or intellectual types of experience. There is, however, a current of consciousness in everyday life that gives it a direction, a purpose. Behind activities there are motives and goals. There is something dramatic, tragic, in them: human desires are not mere instincts, since, as we have noted, the first work of art of human beings is their own lives. This is first of all evident in people's activities; the style is in the person before it appears in the work of art. The activities usually reveal the depth of consistency in the individual, whether they take place in the political arena, in the economic sphere, or in interpersonal relationships, since they arise from the same consciousness and therefore from the same direction, the same purpose.

It is on this dramatic level of human experience that the need for recognition comes into play. This experience is tragic. It inspires intense emotion. It involves a situation in which the individual becomes painfully aware of a destiny or fate that weighs on his or her life or condition. Despite the fact that the expression of aesthetic values in their personal lives satisfies individuals, because their own creations are involved, they expect these values also to be recognized by others, that is, to be confirmed by the admiration, approval, respect, and affection of others.[7] Human beings are spontaneously inter-subjective beings. Each individual tentatively discovers and develops the possible roles that he or she may play, and under the pressure of artistic and emotional factors works out his or her own choices and adaptations. This is the process of developing a personality; it is ordinary life.[8]

Falling in Love

Writing these lines about everyday life, I cannot help thinking of *Falling in Love*, a book by Francesco Alberoni.[9] He writes:

> Falling in love challenges institutions on the level of their fundamental values. Its nature lies precisely in this, in not being a desire, a personal whim, but a movement that carries with it a plan for life and creates an institution. . . .
>
> To fall in love is not to desire a beautiful or interesting person; it is a remaking of the social sphere, a vision of the world with new eyes. . . . The person who wants to fall in love in order to enrich his existence, to add something marvellous to it, isn't able to do so. Only the person whose life is missing something approaches the door that separates the real from the everyday.[10]

The parallel with the message of Jesus of Nazareth on the importance of losing one's life is clear: "Except a corn of wheat fall into the ground and die . . . ." The identity crisis and the pain of loss so many people are experiencing today prepare them, and maybe even condemn them, to risk all. The subject is being challenged in the most profound way. Like Charles Taylor with his participatory model, Alain Touraine believes that, beyond the declarations and charters of rights, beyond the struggles for social and cultural rights, the issue of our time—and I would say of the next century—is "the recognition of the right of all actors, individual or collective, to assert themselves and defend themselves as such, as actors capable of participating in the technical world and, at the same time, recognizing and reinterpreting their respective identities."[11] Our time is not ordinary. It should therefore yield more.

Let us return to Alberoni. Ordinary sexuality, which is experienced in everyday love and which has something in common with hunger and thirst, accompanies us through life—uniform, like the linear time of the clock. On the other hand, Alberoni says, there is an extraordinary sexuality that appears when the life force seeks new and different paths. Sexuality then becomes the means by which life explores the limits of the possible, the horizons of imagination and nature.*[12] This is its nascent state. This sexuality is related to intelligence, fantasy, enthusiasm, passion; indeed, it is

---

* Rainer Maria Rilke, in his *Letters to a Young Poet*, writes, "And in fact the artist's experience lies so unbelievably close to the sexual, to its pain and its pleasure, that the two phenomena are really just different forms of one and the same longing and bliss."

inseparable from them. Its nature is "to subvert, transform, rupture previous ties. Eros is a revolutionary force, even if limited to two people. And there are few revolutions in life."[13]

This experience of the nascent state of love allows us to ignore social classes, to forget races and ethnic groups. It makes it possible to change life, to imagine a new geography, to change the world. Alberoni describes it as follows: "The nascent state is an attempt to remake the world, starting with this different way of thinking and living; it is an attempt to achieve in the world this experience of absolute solidarity and the end of all alienation and uselessness."[14]

The following passage by Alain Touraine touches on many of the topics dealt with here:

> It is not merely a question of desire, work, or will; it is also a matter of struggle and liberation, for the actor is not only desire for the Subject, he or she is first of all suffering-from-not-being-a-subject, loss, fragmentation, desubjectification. This is what gives the construction of the Subject the dramatic force of a social movement. What enables us to live together is neither the unity of our participation in the technical world nor the diversity of our cultural identities. It is the kinship of our efforts to join the two areas of our experience, to discover and defend a unity that is not that of a "me," but of an "I," of a Subject.[15]

If I have emphasized this distinction between human beings as rational animals and as historical subjects, and even allowed myself a digression on love and sexuality, it is because it seems to me that here, and in the very nature of love and its sexual expression, we find something essential to an understanding of how human beings will experience the transition from the world of yesterday to the world of tomorrow.

After the Dictatorship of Reason

Not everything is rational. Not even the most important things. Alain Touraine asks an eminently pertinent question: "How have we been able to combine in a single concept principles as different as popular sovereignty and human rights, whose juxtaposition rather than integration is so obvious in the Declaration of Rights of 1789?"[16] We have done so by regarding the individual as an essentially rational being and defining society as a product of reason. But this was possible only in the West, where the model of development has been based precisely on the separation of rational and non-rational, which are identified respectively with the modern and the old or traditional. "The boundary thus created between public life and private life has led, in keeping with the tradition of the Greek city-state, to the construction of society on the opposition between persons able to participate in public life and those who must remain limited to private life, women primarily."[17]

The opposition between individuals and their private experience, rational or not, on the one hand, and the social order and the "ordered" public life that characterizes it, on the other hand—or to put it another way, the opposition between pleasure and law—was first posited by Nietzsche and Freud. The establishment of this opposition makes it possible to experience a new aesthetic moment, a new experience, which is disturbing to human beings while at the same time it represents an opportunity to go on to another stage of development. This new aesthetic is marked by two great moments of evolution. First, and contrary to what was central to modernity, culture no longer has anything to do with the economy. Second, on a positive note this time, this aesthetic experience is not dominated by men; in order to succeed it requires a contribution by women, who, beyond their right to equality, must assert their difference and give humanity the benefit of it.

A political vision will emerge, sooner or later, from this new aesthetic. It will be based on a philosophical conception that is different from that of the Enlightenment, the rational premises of which have now largely been made obsolete by this new civilization. Because that is what it is, a new civilization. I have always been struck by the way everything holds together in a society. There is always a consistency in the choices, the approaches adopted from one area to another. Thus a new appreciation of the value of the aesthetic in human experience will lead to new social relations and new political visions.

I first became aware of the internal consistency of societies by observing gardens. Gardens are an excellent reflection of a society's relationship to aesthetics and to reason. The traditional French garden is an anthem to reason. It completely imposes its order, its symmetry, on nature. The German garden is romantic, defying the classical rules of logic and aesthetics and making room for passion, freedom, and spontaneity. The English garden is pragmatic; it may leave a big rock in the middle and put a bench there or make a path around it. The Japanese garden is all in miniature; this art of miniaturization has been the strength of Japanese industry, especially in automobiles and electronics.

The connection to politics is equally easy to establish. Given the relationship between reason and nature in these societies, is the reader surprised that the environmental movement first emerged in Germany and that it is still much stronger there than in France? In France, nature is to be conquered and dominated, but not in Germany or England. The reader should not be surprised by the dominant role of the state in France in comparison with the less interventionist role it plays in Germany and England. Thus, the importance a society puts on reason is reflected in the type of state it develops, the strength of its ecology movement, and its artistic creations.

The political vision of modernity, which is perfectly in keeping with its source in the philosophy of the Enlightenment, involved the domination of power as the capacity to act: the rule of the state, law, the legal system. The next political vision will have to concern itself primarily with strength. This will be the specific, and essential, contribution of women. The new aesthetic, as I have said, is marked by two things: the separation of culture and the economy, and women's right to difference. There is a deep connection between these two phenomena, and that is the change in the boundary between public and private life, a change that is full of significance in many ways.

I would like to touch again on the transition to postmodernity. Postmodernism, a current of thought that originated in literary theory and that favours the mixing of genres, has become quite the fashion, especially in the United States. It is very difficult to apply it to political activity, as I am doing here, but it seems to me that it aims to challenge the political being constructed by the Enlightenment, an abstract being answerable to universal reason. For postmodernism, the subject is socially constructed at a multitude of precise points in time and space.

I espouse the positive aspect of the attack against the tyranny of reason while rejecting the radical aspects that would lead us to deny the very possibility of a rational view of the world. This means the reintroduction into public life of as many facets as possible of the multiple human identities that the abstract rational being denied; it means acceptance of femininity, first of all, but it also means responsibly embracing the full diversity of human identity.

Diversity is an irreducible characteristic of the human condition today. The discourse of postmodernism is right in attaching a high value to true pluralism. One of the effects of globalization is precisely this fragmentation, even disintegration, of cultures, this constant mingling of races, languages, and even eras (these days, even the ancient rubs shoulders with the ultramodern—cellular phones are proliferating in the farthest reaches of India and Africa). This seems to me to be a very useful development. Obviously, insofar as the discourse of postmodernism claims to base a new politics on rampant subjectivity, it leads to a disturbing form of intolerance—political correctness—and it is frankly seditious. Or it leads us towards universal indulgence, which, according to Raymond Boudon, has become the cardinal postmodern virtue. The principle that "everything is a matter of opinion" that characterizes democratic society may also lead to what Tocqueville called the tyranny of opinion and to "anything goes."[18]

Several points discussed here are of the essence of postmodern thought: the end of ideologies and the transition from the political passions of the last two centuries to the ethical passions of the next century; the evolution from an ethic of justice to an ethic of care; a politics in which there will be more room for commitment than for demands, and a greater importance placed on individual responsibility than on rights.

Chapter VIII

Remaking the World: Politics, Ethics, and the Common Good

THE INTERNATIONAL ORDER IS BECOMING DUALISTIC IN ITS MAKE-up, with two worlds coexisting in it. I have already briefly discussed these two worlds as described by James Rosenau:[1] the world of the state, codified, ritualized, consisting of a finite number of actors who are known and more or less predictable; and a "multicentric" world, consisting of an almost infinite number of participants who, it should be noted, have a capacity for international action that is relatively independent of governments, to which they are supposedly subject. The juxtaposition of these two worlds results in a very complex configuration of allegiances. The world of states is based on the exclusivity of state allegiances, and depends on the capacity to act (power) by totally committing a given number of individuals/subjects. The multicentric world, on the other hand, is based on a network of allegiances that is hardly codified, the nature and intensity of which depend on the free will of the actors involved.

This duality of worlds is accompanied by a duality of dynamics. The world of states acts in the international system in order to consolidate and legitimize its existence. The aim of the multicentric world, however, is to broaden its autonomy in relation to states, and thus to downplay state borders and sovereignties. The world of states favours the use of coercion, while the multicentric world puts a premium on consensual relations among individuals. The essential question for the former is legitimacy, and for the latter, effectiveness.

It is clear that the world of power—traditional states—and the world of strength—the multicentric world—will continue to coexist for several generations. But even as they compete, they will have to learn to live together. And it is up to individuals to carry out the remaking of the world that is required in this context, a fundamental task if ever there was one, and one that is existential in nature.

The inter-state order will endure for a long time. The state will want to ensure its survival. It is already reinventing itself; in recent decades it has been able to do so in many ways on a supranational level. But it is obviously going through a major change. And whatever it does, its world will be more and more deeply marked by transnational flows of all kinds.

Is salvation to be found in a new international order? Who knows? It was in this way that the state originally came to prevail, first in Europe, and then, with less success, elsewhere in the world. Perhaps through an analogous process the structures of authority will be able to change in accordance with the needs of a world that is rife with upheavals. The expansion of transnational networks is part of this: diasporas, migratory movements, economic and trade links have an effectiveness that blind admiration of the state too quickly obscured. The processes of integration seem to be going in the same direction. Instead of giving a narrow or polemical image of the European structure by speaking only of the transfer of sovereignty or demonizing federalism, it would be wise to assess the real innovation it brings: a composite political space.[2]

It is a safe bet that the future belongs to spaces of variable geometry, because they constitute an effective way to transcend parochialism and avert the threat of ethnic conflict in the world. This does not mean merely juxtaposing nation-states in new areas of integration, which would be equivalent to reproducing the model of the nation-state on another scale. It means conceiving states according to a new grammar and within the new context. In fact, we are already experiencing a post-international system, which is gradually replacing the system made up exclusively of nation-states.

Ethical Passions and the Common Good

The time of political passions is ending. A new period is coming in which ethical passions will be dominant. Behind the decline of political ideologies and the loss of trust in public leaders, there are upheavals in experience and collective action that are as important as the transition to industrial society and, before that, the formation of national states. The old forms of collective action are in decline; they have ceased to be movements of social liberation and have retreated into the corporatist defence of vested interests or outdated ideologies. Meanwhile, new voices are speaking out with emotion and passion about crimes against humanity, the threat to diversity by cultural homogenization, social exclusion aggravated by an economic system that is hostile to any political control, and cross-border plagues such as AIDS and the exploitation of children.

To the democracy that dreamed first of direct participation and then of equitable representation of social interests, there is now being added a democracy of guarantees, protective of the freedoms, diversity, and dignity of human beings. And it is human beings who, more deeply than citizens or workers, are defending their right to be full subjects. This new relationship between ethics and politics reintroduces into international discourse the old Aristotelian-Thomistic concept of the common good. Because the internationalization of trade and the rise of global financial capitalism have brought about structural transformations of power on a global scale, there is now a subtle jockeying between state authorities (who have yielded a large part of their jurisdiction to the market) and transnational actors (who control key elements of strength: financing, markets, technology, etc.).

The traditional modes of regulation based on cooperation among states have become inadequate. Must we now leave everything up to the free play of the market, and let the strongest win? The free play of competition would then be a transposition into the economic sphere of power politics, with different actors. Should we not, on the contrary, transpose the concept of the common good to the international arena, and consider peace, development, the quality of the environment, and world financial stability as collective goods that it is important to produce and preserve? In theory, the only clear answer to such a question is a philosophical one, which varies according to a person's values. In practice, answers and behaviour are ambiguous, and individuals support neither ultra-liberalism nor distributive justice. They try, more mundanely, to maintain the purpose of the market by containing competition within a "law of economic war" that is reduced to the bare minimum and thus acceptable to all.

In this post–Bretton Woods period, the construction of a stable economic order requires that related problems be negotiated together: trade, debt, currency, the price of raw materials. The game of negotiation consists in limiting one's own contribution to the collective effort while pressuring others to increase their contribution. This approach gives rise to many speeches and joint media releases, but these result in very few freely accepted restrictions.

The Juxtaposition of the Two Worlds

Given that the two juxtaposed worlds, the world of the state and the multicentric world, will continue to coexist for a long time yet, we must work to improve both worlds and try to reconcile them for the good of human freedom.

Attempts at supranational integration of various territories, in which states choose to share their sovereignty with their neighbours in order to be better able to confront the power of the world market as well as any attempt at international financial regulation, are examples of efforts to reconcile the two worlds. Even though they obey opposing logics and often conflicting dynamics, the fact remains that the two worlds need each other and must come to terms with each other in order to find their own balance. The state needs the signals of the market and of civil society to fulfil its role. The reverse is equally true.

The Strength of Women

The voices of women are among the new voices expressing ethical concerns. Women are playing a more important role than ever because they have learned, through successful struggles, to combine their professional and personal lives in a single vision, and thus to merge their instrumental world and their cultural world. In a word, they have learned to act as subjects.[3] Women's consciousness has kept on becoming stronger, defining itself in terms that go well beyond the demand for mere equality or identity. Indeed, insofar as women, much more and much better than men, define themselves as subjects wishing to combine professional and emotional life and capable of doing so, they have moved beyond the contradictions of today's world.

The existence of the subject is very deeply involved in intimate relationships. The women's movement has put an end to the identification of one particular category of human beings—men—with the universal. It is no longer possible now to give a single face to the human subject; there is no category above the duality of man and woman. At the same time, the subject shows both rationality and specific cultural experience, since men and women are both similar—as beings that think, work, and act rationally—and different—biologically and culturally, in the formation of their personalities, their self-images, and their relationships with others. Women's liberation and the destruction of men's monopoly on meaning and power are major achievements. The philosophers of the Enlightenment excluded women from modernity, identifying them with the irrational and thus with traditional society.[4] The liberation of women—who, in addition to equality, have been demanding the right to assert their difference—will be at the centre of the new experience of humanity; it will affirm the necessity and the possibility for everyone to combine professional and personal life, to lead a "double life," to connect the world of instrumentality with that of identity. This does not mean opposing female values to male values; that would be confusing and dangerous because it would fail to recognize their irreducible complementarity.

Women and the Remaking of Life

It is not the dominant actor but the dominated one who plays the principal role in remaking the world. This is shown in the fact that it is women, more than men, who are working out a model for remaking life. Because masculinity was built on the domination of femininity, men have great difficulty inventing a specific form in which to remake their personalities. Either they try to imitate women, or they have a hard time and are unable to understand their own difficulty in adopting conduct whose positive value they acknowledge while failing to grasp its meaning, because they are prisoners of their former dominant position. Whereas industrial society was a society of men, the contemporary world is developing into a society that gives femininity an important place. In the case of the former, historians of both political life and private life have shown that it is based largely on the opposition and hierarchical relationship between men and women. As for the latter, it is emerging, and not only in the industrialized countries, because women are working more actively than men, and despite strong resistance, to create a new relationship between the two hemispheres of human experience, the private and the public. The distinction itself is disputed by certain feminist critics. And it is no coincidence that many new social movements are led by women, whereas the labour movement and the national liberation movements were and still are run primarily by men. Not only have women wanted to abolish or reduce the inequalities they have suffered, and to gain the right to freely decide how to live their lives, but they have also revealed to all of us problems and a field of social and cultural conduct that are so new that it is impossible today to define the contemporary world without placing women's thought and actions at its centre.[5]

What is called women's liberation obviously is not reducible to the destruction of a hierarchical social order in favour of the laws of the market. Rather, it leads to the discovery of a female culture and to communication between that culture and the culture of men. Unlike humanism, which is dominated by masculinity, the recognition of the differences between the sexes leads to the remaking of the world so that men and women will be able not merely to remain distinct or merge, but to go beyond the traditional oppositions of private and public, authority and affection. This fundamental dialogue is needed to enrich the quality of all other dialogues, including cultural dialogue. The idea of a multicultural society is incompatible with identity politics, since multiculturalism is based on communication among cultures, like democracy itself, which implies a recognition of the plurality of interests, opinions, and values. In other words, in the absence of multiple interests and values, there is no point to democracy, just as multiculturalism is impossible in the absence of a variety of cultures.

The Ethic of Justice and the Ethic of Care

Let me recapitulate. Internationalization is giving way to globalization. The power to act is giving way to strength (potentiality). The state is being challenged by the market. The power to act and strength must be reconciled in order to humanize globalization. Men's power to act, or "power over," must come to terms with women's strength, or "power to." The historical subject is becoming less historical and social, and much more personal. This new reality cannot fail to have an effect on ethics.

And, indeed, a new ethic is emerging. This change could be described as a shift from an ethic of justice to an ethic of care.* For a long time, we believed we could not go beyond the horizon drawn by the Enlightenment, that of a commutative justice focused on retribution, redress of wrongs, and punishment of crimes. Postmodernism urges us to think beyond that horizon.

A striking illustration of the new perspectives that are opening up comes to us from South Africa. The work of the Truth and Reconciliation Commission, and the very fruitful process of thought and discussion that preceded it and that continues around it, has shown that the justice of the Enlightenment is not the only kind conceivable.** Comparable experiences on a lesser scale have been tried in recent years in Czechoslovakia and Chile. We may wonder whether France might have been spared the profound malaise caused by the trials of Barbie and Papon if, instead of those successions of expeditious trials and punishments, it had chosen another method, one similar to what we have seen in South Africa.

In any case, the participation of women in the emerging society will inevitably strengthen the ethic of care, because over the last centuries men have been more responsive to the ethic of justice.

---

* Jennifer Nedelsky, in an article entitled "Embodied diversity and the challenges to law," tackles this question and asks, with certain American women writers, if the ethic of care might supplement the ethic of justice. The answer is not obvious, since the ethic of justice concerns commutative justice whereas the ethic of care belongs rather to distributive justice and is based on altruistic considerations of the following kind: "You do not have a right to such-and-such. But you are deprived and vulnerable. I will therefore give it to you anyway." [6]

** The Web site of the commission (http://www.truth.org.za) provides a great deal of useful information. I found it revealing that on his last visit to Canada Nelson Mandela, who initiated this new form of justice, encouraged Canadians to give a greater role to women in settling the differences between anglophones and francophones.

The Common Good

Let us return to the concept of the common good. In its original meaning, the common good was the ultimate achievement of human beings and of human society, the highest degree of both personal and community development. For twentieth-century Catholic social doctrine, the common good is the overall social conditions that allow both social groups and their members to attain their highest good as fully and naturally as possible.[7] For American liberal doctrine, the common good means the public good and the improvement of the human condition throughout the world through the virtue, creativity, and entrepreneurial spirit of free citizens. In its most recent version, the essence of the common good is to guarantee the benefits of voluntary cooperation in social life.[8] Inherited from this double tradition—Catholic and Roman on the one hand, and liberal and American on the other—the concept of the "global commons" allows us to imagine all human beings as connected to each other and sharing similar circumstances and a common vulnerability.[9]

Today's decisions involve a spatial and temporal horizon of unprecedented scope. They involve not only relationships among states, societies, and individuals, but also the relationship of human beings with the rest of the world and with future generations. There is such a thing as a tragedy of the global commons; it occurs when the common good is sacrificed because no actor will engage unilaterally in policies of prevention when only concerted world action has any chance of success. If only for this reason, the responsible behaviour that is required in our current situation necessitates an ethical renewal. Unlike economic development, the new ethic cannot be based solely on individual interest. Another level of awareness will have to emerge. The situation we currently face differs quite substantially from what Ricardo observed in his time. He showed that a country benefited from practising free trade even unilaterally, since it introduced the benefits of competition domestically.[10] We need to establish new altruistic values, but we have to recognize realistically that free trade will not be much help to us in doing so. Why? Because in this case there is no objective connection with financial advantages as there is in the case of the establishment of free trade.

The scope of the challenge is immediately apparent. Free trade has been able to establish itself in large part thanks to the extraordinary and extremely rare convergence of the demands of self-interest and generosity. The pursuit of the common good will be successful in large part if generosity is strengthened and is capable of ignoring or at least dominating the claims of self-interest.

Part Two

The Canadian Exception

Two roads diverged in a wood, and I—
I took the one less travelled by,
And that has made all the difference.

— Robert Frost, "The Road Not Taken,"
Mountain Interval (1916)

Chapter IX

The Country That Refused to Become a Nation-State*

CANADA IS A VERY ORIGINAL COUNTRY COMPARED TO OTHER WESTERN countries formed in the eighteenth and nineteenth centuries. Canadians themselves have not always recognized or admitted the profound originality of their country. The traditional, conservative elites have fought it, and are still fighting it. However, this originality is at the heart of both our identity and our advantage as we enter the era of globalization.

The states that formed in the West starting in the seventeenth century made it possible for our societies to enter modernity. By creating favourable political conditions, they actually made it possible for freedom and democracy to develop, they made possible the creation of markets that were increasingly broad geographically and reached increasingly large populations, and they thus made possible the emergence of industry. In short, the West experienced unprecedented economic development thanks to the role played by the state, in particular, its role as arbiter of the rules of the game and guarantor of property rights and respect for the law.

From the Original State to the Nation-State

The state, however, eventually moved beyond this original function. As it evolved historically, almost everywhere in the world the state became the nation-state.

There is a fundamental difference between the state and the nation-state. The former, the original state, consists essentially of the political

---

* While reading John Ralston Saul's *Reflections of a Siamese Twin* in December 1997, I realized I had to finish writing this book, which I had started before entering the Canadian government. Readers will notice certain important influences in the opening chapters of this part. Having read the first part, they will understand that I feel a kinship with Saul's critique of the dictatorship of reason in the Western world. I realize we have both been sensitive to the same particular and original characteristics of our country. I would like to compliment him and thank him for his work.

framework adopted by a broad geographical area with a large number of inhabitants belonging to a variety of different social groups. The nation-state that developed in the eighteenth and nineteenth centuries, on the other hand, grew out of the marriage of the state with a nation, that is, with one of the member communities of the original state, usually the strongest one.

The price of such a marriage was not insignificant. Nation-states always arise in the same way: one community manages to impose its will on the others by using the apparatus of the state. France, Germany, Italy, and Great Britain all have one thing in common: in each of these countries, a single language—French rather than Breton or the Provençal spoken by Henri IV, or Piedmontese rather than Lombard, or English rather than the Celtic languages of Scotland, Ireland, or Wales—became dominant over the other languages, and a single culture—the Prussian one, to cite a famous example—prevailed over the other cultures. In this sense, the nation-state arises initially through the imposition of sociocultural uniformity, which is later embodied in institutions that are also made uniform: the same law everywhere, the same education system everywhere, and so forth.

This traditional nation-state is exactly what Canada refused to become, right from its birth in the nineteenth century. Too often Canada is not given credit for this original choice. On the pretext that Canada is a young country, we refuse to see the pertinence, lucidity, and courage of the choice it made at that time.

The Originality of the Canadian Choice

A brief look at history suffices to show that Canada's choice was very original for the time. German unity finally took shape only in 1870, under Prussia, with Bismarck, and with the help, it might be said, of the war against France. It was only in 1871 that Italy was really unified, by Cavour, under Piedmont. The Canadian federation dates from 1867. In other words, at the same time that Canada was making an unusual choice, other countries were taking a direction that was already traditional. Admittedly, Canada at the time of Confederation maintained its status as a British colony, but the political system established in 1867 was the culmination of much thought and discussion, and the result of agreements among Canadians right here in North America. The United States of America at that time chose to create a conventional nation-state. Our neighbours adopted the approach of integration through uniformity, and uniformity through assimilation. The most notable illustration of this orientation is the imposition of a single language on everyone. Successive waves of immigrants had to fit into the common linguistic mould of the United States, just as they had to fit into the common mould in so many other ways. The Americans created a country on the well-known model of the melting-pot, in which people of every origin and nationality are dissolved.

In Canada, the country was built on two languages from the very beginning. In itself, this observation is not very significant. But when we consider the whole *attitude of accommodation* that it implies, we see some of the social and moral provisions of those Canadians who conceived a model other than that of uniformity through the domination of one group or through assimilation, as in the melting-pot. The Canadian model is the mosaic.

What explains this original choice by Canadians? It must have something to do with the absence of clearly defined borders. We all know the borders of France; it is called "the Hexagon" precisely because of its shape. Similarly, we all learn in elementary school about the "boot" of Italy, a clearly defined image of that country's borders. Canada, on the other hand, does not bring to mind any precise territorial demarcation, if only because its northern boundaries remain quite vague for most of us. In terms of the imagination, this absence of a clearly defined perimeter corresponds to a kind of symbolic openness, leaving a certain amount of room for escape.

Without getting into what might be an unworkable psychosocial analysis, we have to acknowledge that this perception of Canada is shared by a great many people throughout the world. For them, as for us, to think of Canada is to give free rein to hope, to allow oneself to dream, to believe that one has finally found the place where the noblest individual and collective ideals have a genuine chance of being realized. It is not surprising, then, that the French writer Michel Tournier has one of his characters say that Canada cancels out all the misfortunes he has suffered.[1] In the depths of their misery, the prisoners at Auschwitz called the place holding the personal effects that had been stripped from them "Canada," a name that to them represented a place of infinite riches.[2] In their own way, the thousands of children who every year write to express their wishes to Santa Claus at "the North Pole, Canada," are demonstrating the same thing. And Canada honours the trust of those children; they receive answers thanks to the generosity of the employees and retirees of Canada Post. In other areas, too—immigration provides many examples—Canada honours the trust and confidence of the adults who come with all their plans and hopes to settle here.

A Pluralist State

Canadians have thus refused to create a traditional nation-state, and the country they founded has invented itself gradually according to a decidedly original model, culminating in the well-known Canadian "mosaic." In Canada, then, there is no *one* language that relentlessly supplants all others, there is no *one* culture that is imposed on everyone indiscriminately, there is no *one* religion that replaces all others. From this point of view, Canada is not a conventional country, but an exceptional country.

I like to think that the desire for accommodation we see in Canada already figured prominently as early as the seventeenth century. François Bayrou, in his biography of Henri IV, points out how much that king already lived in modernity. "Should we see this as a trait of a Protestant mentality?" he asks, and adds, "This Protestant spirit would lead to one of the first modern forms of economic voluntarism."[3] It was during the reign of Henri IV that Champlain founded Quebec City in 1608. In any case, Bayrou emphasizes "the originality of Henri IV's colonial plan, which reflected a very coherent vision of economic development . . . of profound respect for local populations. . . . The latter undoubtedly marked French colonization in Acadia from the beginning, a unique instance of osmosis between the indigenous populations and the colonists."[4]

Even before Canada existed as such, Canadians already showed a unique sensibility. Let us take the Durham Report, for example, written in 1839 following the Rebellion of 1837. Let us leave aside the report's recommendation for the union of the two Canadas of that time and its introduction of responsible government. In ethnic and linguistic terms, Durham, to all intents and purposes, recommended that French Canadians be anglicized. In this, he was simply proposing to do what had already been done by all modern countries—that is, countries in the vanguard, such as France and England—and was about to be done by Germany and Italy. Durham indeed reflected his era; he was a thinker of his time. However, this recommendation—which, it should be recalled, came from a non-Canadian—was rejected by French Canadians and, remarkably, found little support among English Canadians. Even more significant is the fact that English Canadians in reform, liberal, and progressive circles preferred to form alliances with their French-Canadian counterparts rather than endorse the Durham Report. They rejected Lord Durham's proposal, a rejection whose significance becomes very clear when we read his original text: "I expected," he stated unequivocally, "to find a contest between a government and a people: I found two nations warring in the bosom of a single state. . . . It is to elevate them from that inferiority that I desire to give to the Canadians our English character."[5]

Canadian identity was developed by leaders, on both sides of the linguistic divide, who shared the same views. The Rebellions of 1837–38 clearly show the starting point in the development of this Canadian identity. Louis-Joseph Papineau and William Lyon Mackenzie and their partners in the reform movement were in contact throughout the 1830s, and their objective was to obtain from England greater democracy and responsible government. They were both opposed to the conservative elites of their respective societies, and wished to replace them. This attempt at an alliance by the liberal leaders of Lower Canada and Upper Canada did not have sufficient time to take form and thus was unable to withstand British repression. But it marked the beginning of a tradition, a Canadian approach of accommodation, and a political leadership that reflected this Canadian sensibility.

Barely three years later, at the beginning of the 1840s, a new generation continued the work for democracy. Louis-Hippolyte LaFontaine and Robert Baldwin, both in their mid-thirties, assembled a complex coalition in favour of reforms. They knew that if they remained isolated, their efforts were doomed to failure; 1837 had clearly demonstrated that.

In the parliament of the United Province of Canada in Kingston, LaFontaine and Baldwin became the best of friends; they would remain so for the rest of their lives. A significant detail about their relationship is provided by John Ralston Saul: Baldwin immediately sent his two daughters and two sons to study French in Quebec City.[6] Their friendship, born out of shared liberal values, was demonstrated early in one of those moments that reflect Canada at its best. The governor, Lord Sydenham, the bishop of Montreal, Ignace Bourget, and the elite of Montreal had prevented the election of LaFontaine in Terrebonne. Baldwin, who had been elected in two constituencies, resigned in the fourth riding of York, asking the farmers there to support LaFontaine and the reform coalition in the by-election. LaFontaine won a landslide victory. The following year Robert Baldwin was beaten by the Orangemen and the Family Compact, and LaFontaine supported him in the riding of Rimouski, where the voters sent the same message.[7] In 1848 Canada finally obtained responsible government. LaFontaine wanted joint leadership, but Baldwin insisted that LaFontaine be named head of the government. He remained at his side. LaFontaine became, in a sense, the first prime minister of Canada.

But in Quebec, it is Papineau who is remembered as a hero. I remember being surprised to learn that the rebellion had a counterpart in Upper Canada, led by William Lyon Mackenzie, and that some of the leaders in

Lower Canada, such as Dr. Wolfred Nelson, were anglophones. Papineau had been presented to us so much as an ethnic hero and the sole leader. We have even forgotten his battles in favour of seigneurial rights after his return from exile, and his position on the Church, which had begun to assert itself under the leadership of Bishop Bourget. Is this because Papineau lost, whereas LaFontaine finally won? Do we prefer victims? It is true that LaFontaine, and then George-Étienne Cartier,* strongly resisted the leadership and power of the Catholic Church, which was now dominated by the ultramontanes.

It is also true that Canada adopted a model of development that was fundamentally different from that of any other country, a model based on accommodation, which led to Confederation in 1867. If Canada had adopted the traditional American way of uniformity through assimilation, Canadians' relationship to immigration would have been different. Canadians also avoided internal wars such as the American Civil War. Although this policy and this desire for accommodation are characteristic of Canada, perhaps even to the point of constituting one of the main elements of its identity, they do not preclude errors or resistance. The Manitoba school laws in 1890 and Regulation 17 in Ontario in 1912 limited the rights of French Canadians and contributed to containing them within the boundaries of Quebec.

Whether they had to contend with Orangemen or ultramontanes, reformers and liberals encountered opposition and resistance. But if there is a lesson to be learned from this, it is the following: united across the country, they were able to make a difference and contribute to the country's progress.** What the French and English Canadians of the time

---

* Rightly or wrongly, they used to insist in school that there was no *s* in the first part of his given name, which made him dangerously like an anglophone! So there is nothing new about the interest in the first names of federalist leaders such as Trudeau and Charest. I have never had this problem with the ethnic nationalists, since my surname already betrays my nordic (Scottish) origins—that unfortunate little *w* that says so much! Let me quote here the entry on the letter *w* in Albert Jacquard's *Petite Philosophie à l'usage des non-philosophes*, which is presented in the form of a dictionary: "According to the *Larousse* dictionary, 'the letter *w* is characteristic of the languages of the North and it is used in French only in words borrowed from languages that have it.' It is so ambiguous that it may be either a vowel or a consonant. In words that come from German, *w* is equivalent to a *v*; it acts as a consonant. In words from English, Flemish, or Dutch, it usually has an "oo" sound and acts as a semi-vowel. To defend the French language, it would be best to avoid using words starting with a vowel that behaves so wantonly." (Translators' note: Our translation.) By the way, the "S" in my name is for Stewart!

** Manning, Harris, and Bouchard, three politicians who are increasingly being compared, are a real threat to Canada's personality, to its identity: everybody in their own back yard, each minority abandoned to its regional majority, the end of Canada-wide equal opportunity and public services. As we have seen, there is nothing new in regional leaders taking these more traditional positions.

rejected was the assimilation of one culture by another.* They rejected the goal of creating a *single* nation to coincide with the state. This choice would make possible a form of pluralism that "normal" states do not tolerate, one that gives Canadians a head start in the era of globalization.

Canadian Values

From the outset, Canada refused to found itself on a single language, a single religion, a single culture. Instead it developed a form of citizenship that was political rather than ethnic. Canada has chosen to define itself in terms of a shared belief in certain fundamental values: respect for every person's unique qualities, a common concern for justice, a sense of proportion in the use of power. In short, we might describe the Canadian spirit as marked by a *passion for balance*—rather paradoxically, since passion involves a certain extremism whereas balance seeks a happy medium. This passion for balance is expressed in an uneasiness with radical ideologies and an active concern to find a middle course in human affairs. For Canadians, prosperity without equity makes no sense, coexistence without solidarity makes no sense, power without any counterbalance makes no sense, riches without generosity make no sense, and diversity without sharing makes no sense. Pluralism, a spirit of accommodation, the mosaic, solidarity, and the quest for balance are the watchwords, the key ideas that sum up the Canadian ideal.

Indeed, that first accommodation between English-speaking and French-speaking Canadians promoted the development of a spirit of accommodation that was to lead us to adopt a very different attitude to many major aspects of life in society—to immigrants first of all, but also to social questions. Pluralism is the very basis of this country. And this pluralism embraces not only French and English Canadians, but also the native peoples, who have helped us to adapt to our nordicity and given us a sense of community without which our country would not be what it is. It also embraces immigrants, who, because they are respected for themselves, have given us something irreplaceable that has enabled the creation of a rich cultural mosaic instead of a melting-pot. All these groups have taken part in the creation of this "abnormal," exceptional country that is Canada, and they continue to take part in its ongoing creation, providing the necessary adjustments to the many profound changes that are taking place. They

---

* In a letter dated May 18, 1942, U.S. president Franklin Delano Roosevelt explicitly recommended to Canadian prime minister Mackenzie King that he take measures to assimilate French Canadians into the English-speaking majority.[8] As pointed out by none other than Jean-François Lisée, in his return letter Mackenzie King completely ignored Roosevelt's suggestion. Roosevelt's letter to Mackenzie King is reproduced in Lisée's book.[9]

contribute in a remarkable way to making Canada a country that is well equipped and well prepared to benefit from globalization and to play a role in remaking the world.

Canada is not defined by any status quo. On the contrary, it is viscerally unfit for the status quo, as its history demonstrates, and that is precisely what gives it the flexibility for adaptation that is so envied. In this respect, Canada is indisputably exceptional: exceptional in the standard of living Canadians have attained, which very few peoples in the history of humanity have experienced; even more exceptional in the freedom and justice that prevail; and perhaps most exceptional in the respect and tolerance that reign. Freedom, justice, respect, and tolerance are cardinal values the various minorities in this country subscribe to and share, these minorities that have chosen together to form a majority precisely on the basis of shared values.

Such is Canada, in essence: a pluralist country defined in terms of its values, and not a nation-state that is relatively incapable of dealing with diversity or welcoming immigrants. Unlike France and Germany, for example, Canada shows an openness to immigration that bodes well for the future, because we feel the need to have other people come and share our values and our ideals, and help us continue to build them and foster their progress.

Canada must be reinvented with each generation. Canada is an ongoing project. It is up to us as Canadians to carry on that project, as our predecessors did and as our successors will have to do.

Chapter X

The Country of the Third Way, or the Passion for Balance[1]

A COUNTRY THAT IS A GENUINE EMBODIMENT OF PLURALISM, AND one that even finds much of its originality and its identity in pluralism, Canada has been rated by the United Nations as one of the top countries of the world in terms of human development, an assessment that takes into account both economic and social factors.

One thing is certain, a fundamental experiment is taking place in Canada that is an inspiration to all, and it is important that it be successful. Otherwise, what message will be sent to humanity at the dawn of the new millennium? What would it mean if Canada proved incapable of renewing itself and modernizing when it is considered by everyone to be such a great success in so many ways, a country with such enormous potential? What would be the impact of such a failure precisely during this time of globalization? Just as Canada found an original response to the challenges of the nineteenth century, it should be able to meet the challenges of globalization in a creative way. Canada can offer an exceptional solution to problems related to globalization and, in particular, to those related to the economy.

Canada, a "Political" Country Par Excellence

Canada is a "political" country. It has often been said that, with its movement from east to west, Canada went against history, since the natural economic flow should have given it a north-south orientation. This idea was the basis of the analysis and the diagnosis presented by René Lévesque in his 1968 manifesto, *An Option for Quebec*, in which he first worked out his thesis on sovereignty-association.[2] And more recently, Bernard Landry has attacked Canada's protectionist policy since the last century for having "cut us off from our north-south links that are so consistent with common sense and geography."[3]

In his discussion of this view, John Ralston Saul asserts, contrary to widely held opinion, that this east-west orientation is not an artificial thing resulting from initiatives of the central government, such as the railway across Canada and national policy. According to him, these policies of the last century only put a nineteenth-century face on what existed already. What created this east-west flow were the alliances with the First Nations established in the seventeenth and eighteenth centuries, initially by the French and French Canadians, and then by the English. These alliances were based, among other things, on the nordicity of the place and everything that implies.[4] Thus, to see Canada purely as an artificial creation is to reduce history to mechanisms, to economic factors only, and completely ignore geography, anthropology, and culture.

In this age of globalization, when there are many who would like to make everything subject to the laws of the market and the flows of the economy, in spite of the fact that this implies exclusion for so many, the very existence of a country like Canada, which is objectively one of the greatest successes in the world, represents a hope, a path, a model of resistance against current forces. Canada has never been a "normal" country; it has always been an "exceptional" country. Now, at the dawn of the third millennium, it must, more than ever, be that. And this is one of the reasons why Canadians must resist Quebec sovereignism, which represents an abdication of politics in favour of economics.

From the beginning, therefore, before it was an economic country, Canada was a political country. In a sense, its way of being political was oriented by the alliances with the first inhabitants of this territory, the native peoples, who also helped the newcomers adapt to the north and, especially, to winter. John Ralston Saul goes even further. He feels that Canada is such an inclusive country because it has been marked by the animism of the First Nations.[*5] This way of being political has led to the greatest possible inclusion of the various linguistic communities and immigrant communities. By trying to avoid exclusion, and largely achieving this, Canada has been a success in terms of human development. It is a country of inclusion. Its *political* nature has prepared Canada and each of its parts extremely well to meet the challenges of globalization while resisting the excesses that lead to exclusion or to a concept of society that reduces everything to a mere mechanism of the market. It is not surprising that the party that is most critical of the Canadian experiment, the Parti Québécois, is unreservedly in favour of free trade agreements and, especially, of north-south flows on

---

[*] Animism, the belief that things have souls similar to the human soul, gives rise to a respect for nature and for other people.

the North American continent. In keeping with its right-wing ideology and its still-regional position in Alberta, the Reform Party is not far behind.

The Development of Human Resources

To subordinate everything to economics on the pretext of globalization is not a panacea. I am therefore opposed to what the French are calling "la pensée unique," the only acceptable view in economics. Rather, it seems to me that the most valid human development will come through the search for a new balance between the role of the state, of politics, and that of the market, of economics. We must not forget that we are rapidly entering a knowledge-based economy. However, knowledge is held first and foremost by human beings, who are—or should be—free to come and go as they please.

Under these conditions, devoting the resources required to human development can no longer be seen merely as social spending, as it still was not long ago. We can no longer consider education and health, for example, mere commodities. The resources allocated to these two aspects of our lives are, rather, investments in human development—investments that will generate high-quality economic growth. Exactly the same thing can be said about social programs. Traditionally, they have been regarded as costs. The theory was that the more substantial and generous they were, the more expensive they became, and that this led to uncompetitive or less competitive prices on world markets—first, uncompetitive or less competitive labour costs and then, as a result, uncompetitive or less competitive prices for our goods and services. For a society as dependent on world trade as Canada, this is no small matter.

Closer scrutiny of the data, however, leads to very different conclusions. Even in the case of health services, which are so often decried as a source of additional costs for employers, we need to re-examine the prevailing views. A recent study by the international consulting firm KPMG compared ten Canadian cities and thirteen American cities with respect to the costs of doing business in seven manufacturing industries.[6] In every case, the total costs were systematically lower in Canada than in the United States. One of the factors in this comparative advantage is the fact that fringe benefits related to health services cost Canadian employers less than American employers; with no universal system of health insurance in the United States, employers there are disadvantaged in relation to their Canadian competitors, who have to assume only a part of those costs, that part not covered by our universal system.

What this example shows is something Canadians have always felt:

there can be no real, sustainable prosperity without solidarity. In other words, the economy takes on its full human meaning only within an appropriate political framework. In one of those remarkable ironies of history, Canadian values, which initially were intuitively felt to be essential to the quality of life in our society, have now been empirically confirmed as the basis of that quality of life. This has perhaps never been as clear as it is now when we are making the transition to a knowledge-based society, because the knowledge-based society by definition, and more than any other form of society, depends on individuals, on the country's population—which, we too often forget, is its most important natural resource.

Experience has already corroborated this view. For example, while the Auto Pact of 1965 guaranteed Canada a share of manufacturing activity in proportion to its demographic importance, which is about 10 percent of the North American market, the automobile industry has in fact carried out 18 percent of its operations on our side of the border. Why? One reason is that the big North American car manufacturers pay a lot more in the United States than in Canada for everything to do with their employees' health. To understand why this is an important factor, we need look no further than the fact that car manufacturers in the United States spend more on health insurance premiums for their employees than they pay for the steel that goes into making the cars. This is extremely significant, and it shows the direct positive effect that shrewd social investment has on economic growth.

Between the Anglo-Saxon type of liberal capitalism of the United States and Great Britain and the continental European model, which is sometimes too rigid from a social point of view and thus incapable of making quick adjustments when circumstances require, there is another model, a third way. And Canada could very well become the leader in this approach. Politically, too, there is a third way beyond the models we have seen until now. In one area or another of the country, there are political parties that appeal primarily to regional majorities. These parties are of no help to Canada since they do not hesitate to pit one region against another, Quebec against the West, or the West against Quebec. On the contrary, Canada must be able to count on majorities that are drawn from the various regions of the country on the basis of a common conception of the country, that is, on the basis of values and not of geography.

To Govern Is to Make Choices

That said, political activity is first of all the art of governing—not managing, but governing. And to govern is to make choices. The ability to make choices is essential to the integrity of people, institutions, and societies.

Sometimes we take our power to make choices for granted. Canada is privileged among nations. We Canadians have the good fortune of being able to make all kinds of choices regarding our way of life, our place of residence, our travels, our diet, and so on. Canadians appreciate being able to choose. How else can we explain the extraordinary sacrifices they have accepted in recent years in order to strengthen their financial sovereignty? It is clear that many psychological, political, and economic factors came into play when we needed the discipline to clean up our finances.

Canadians have always been a people that looked more to the future than to the past. A future with no choice is unacceptable to them. The possibility of choosing freely is a key element of the democratic process, and the most stable and harmonious democracies are those in which the highest percentage of citizens are able to benefit from the country's economic and social resources. It is the role of a government to make choices, and what has really enabled us to achieve our goal is our determination to exercise our capacity to choose.

As I stated at the beginning of this chapter, Canada usually comes first on the United Nations' human development index. More that just providing a handy federalist slogan, this is particularly significant in this time of remaking and rethinking. As Alain Touraine states:

> In industrial society, development has been reduced to the effects of growth on the improvement of the standard of living and living conditions. . . .
>
> The time has come to reverse the roles attributed to growth, culture, and social organization, and to propose a new analysis of development in our "low-modernity" societies.
>
> The UN and UNESCO have played an important role in this area. After the idea of development had been put aside for a long time in favour of that of dependence, we now see the idea of human development introducing a radically new definition of modernity. This concept was developed by the UNDP (United Nations Development Program) in its Human Development Reports from 1990 to 1996. Beyond the right to life, knowledge, and adequate resources, these reports place a special emphasis on political freedom, creativity, and personal dignity. This reversal of perspective concerning modernization is of the same nature as my effort to replace society with the Subject as the focus of thought. From this point of view, development should be seen as the increase in the capacity for choice for the greatest number.[7]

Canada is thus an advantageous place for the development of the individual, beyond the citizen, as a subject heralding the remaking of the world.

We face a double challenge: to protect and to improve our ability to eliminate exclusion and obstacles to equality. When we look at certain basic indexes—for example, those of child poverty, native people's health, or unemployment among Canadians with disabilities—we see that the fight is far from over. We must strive daily to achieve equality. However, in today's world, financial stability cannot in itself guarantee the ability to choose. There are powerful forces that pose a real challenge to Canada's autonomy. With the rise of globalization, or at least the most recent form of globalization, which is marked by the mobility of capital and the development of a global market, countries' ability to choose has been reduced.

At a time when the choices offered to consumers seem unlimited, some people consider the inability of the nation-state to be master in its own house a disturbing paradox. To others, it is a very small sacrifice to make in order to tap the market's potential for growth and win a piece of that potential. The truth is probably somewhere in between. I believe globalization has enormous possibilities for Canada. As a trading country, though not sufficiently a country of traders, Canada is eager to open new markets throughout the Asia-Pacific region and in the rest of the world; this is even one of its priorities.

In a book entitled *The State to Come*, the English journalist Will Hutton discusses the capacity to make national choices. He maintains that national autonomy can still be exercised, even though globalization sometimes restricts possibilities for action: "Strong communications and transport systems, a well-educated workforce and networks of publicly funded universities and research institutes are attractions not just to domestic business but also to multinationals. They too benefit from public initiative, even if they try to escape paying for it."[8] We should not be afraid of broadening our perspective; it will increasingly be accepted that investments in the human factor are part of any clear-sighted policy. For example, it will be accepted that investments to keep our children in good health and prepare them to learn are essential elements of any industrial policy.

Thinking about the Economy and Society Together

For too long, we have maintained a distinction between economic policy and social policy. We have to place them both in a single framework. How can a country hope to be a player in the new economy, an economy that depends on knowledge workers, if it does not give priority to human development? Clearly, the challenges and possibilities arising from globalization force us to recognize the importance of investing in early childhood development, education, and knowledge, and of making the investments needed to develop the productive potential of all our fellow citizens, including those with disabilities.

With the failure of communism in the planned economies of eastern Europe, capitalism found itself the undisputed, though not absolute, winner in the ideological Cold War on economic doctrine. But it is important, extremely important, to remind the proponents of free enterprise and capitalism at all costs that, while capitalism has won the war, it has yet to restore peace and harmony. As Will Hutton points out, "the operation of the unchecked market, whatever its success in sending effective messages about what is scarce and what is abundant, has an inherent tendency to produce unreasonable inequality, economic instability and immense concentrations of private, unaccountable power."[9] All things considered, if we want the market to be able to meet the considerable expectations of society, society must create mechanisms that reduce its negative repercussions while maintaining its productive capacities.

It would be useful here to remember a phenomenon that in itself is highly significant. While the Communist economies of eastern Europe were collapsing, the limits of laissez-faire economics were becoming apparent in Reagan's America and Thatcher's Britain. In both of these countries, widening economic disparities led to the increasing isolation of less-well-off citizens. Thus, according to John Kenneth Galbraith,[10] American democracy became first and foremost a democracy for the "haves." Lester Charles Thurow[11] devotes a chapter of an excellent book to democracy in relation to the market. His comparison of these two elements of our public life, their great defining principles, and the way they interact reveals their incompatibility in some cases but, more important, it also makes clear the need to bring them together.

Canadians' view of the United States is tinged with both envy and contempt. All over the world the United States projects the image of a country where everything is larger than life, the image of the American dream, all loud and colourful, that springs to life in the spotlight of Hollywood. But, as we all know, this dream can turn into a nightmare for people who find themselves on the wrong side of the spotlights. Canada has a very different social ethic, a more balanced one, and one that may even be seen as the opposite of the diehard individualism that characterizes the United States. We try to reach a balance between our rights and our responsibilities. This approach has served us well in the past. It made possible the creation of national programs such as medicare, old age security, and employment insurance. More recently, our new national child benefit was added to those great national programs we are so proud of. This has not prevented us, at the same time, from building a society in which individual initiative is rewarded and encouraged, and so is leadership.

Leadership, Citizenship, and Culture

What do we expect from the leaders of tomorrow, and what should we expect from the citizens who grant them the privilege of governing? When people speak of leadership of any kind, the word *vision* is often used. What path does this person want us to follow? And where do we as citizens want to go?

A glance at Canada today shows a country in the midst of great upheavals. And these upheavals, which give rise to a deep unease about the future, make us see how entrenched the fear of the unknown is in our country. All true leaders must be able to neutralize this fear if they want to fulfil their responsibility to contribute to the progress of their society. They have to establish a climate of confidence, to get people to believe in their own abilities and their collective capacity for social progress. In the last American presidential election, President Clinton and Senator Robert Dole each had a vision he hoped to share with the voters. In both cases, this vision aimed to inspire confidence and to touch the hearts and minds of Americans. The two men shared the desire to make the United States a great country, or perhaps we should say an even greater country, a common refrain in American elections. Dole called for a return to a time when there was no doubt about the greatness of the United States, when life was simpler, when values were more clearly defined; by reconnecting with their past, Americans would ensure a better future. President Clinton, on the other hand, looked in the opposite direction, promising to build a bridge to the future, a bridge that would take Americans across the river of their anxiety to the other side, where a better life for themselves and their children awaited them. We all know the outcome of that election. I do not want to overemphasize the importance of the bridge metaphor in Clinton's victory, but the fact is that citizens do rely on their leaders to reassure them about the future. This brings us to the very heart of the question of confidence and trust that was discussed above.

Leaders would be well advised to resist visions that are too grandiose to be achieved. "If there is one lesson to be learnt from the great ideological battles of the past," states Will Hutton, "it is that political projects informed by some utopian vision . . . are doomed." The true role of government must be "the business of argument; initiating processes; building institutions; creating a culture; putting in place obligations to balance the privileges of the various interest groups that constitute society; delegating, as much as possible, decisions to the local arena; and building a consensus for action."[12] Thus the political leaders of the twenty-first century will have to act as intermediaries. One of the sources of discontent described by Charles Taylor in his book on modernity is the powerlessness people experience when faced with decision-making processes that are increasingly technocratic.[13] As John Ralston Saul points out, technocrats are eliminating decision-making processes based on common sense and moral principles.[14] Modern leaders must therefore be able to manage the flow of information from citizens to technocrats as well as in the opposite direction. If leaders are too technocratic, they risk losing a clear perspective on reality. Conversely, if they deny the importance of technical knowledge, leaders may undermine their ability to communicate the essence of government decisions to the general public. Once again, balance and judgment are required.

Citizens usually get the government they deserve. In a democracy, the voters are always right. But it goes without saying that democracy is never as well served as when voters are able to make enlightened choices. *Making Democracy Work*, the well-known book by American political scientist Robert D. Putnam, demonstrates extremely convincingly that the solid civic traditions of collectivities are essential for a responsible government that wants to make the right decisions. If there is now one fundamental role for politicians, it is that of intermediary between citizens and the apparatus of government: meeting with citizens, knocking on their doors, in short serving as an interface between them and the big institutions that make up the public service and the government.

On this point, Christopher Jencks gives us something to think about: "We will surely need to change our institutions and attitudes in hundreds of small ways and not in one big way."[15] It is up to all of us now to do everything in our power, every day, to establish a climate of confidence, to protect choices, to seek ideological balance, and to humanize leadership. It is thus impossible to eliminate the cultural element from political life. Values are at the heart of culture in the broad sense. And it is their values that deeply define Canadians—liberal values, of course, but liberal values tempered with a great concern for others. For liberal values must be modernized if we do not want them to lose their appeal and their capacity to bring out what is best in people. In this area, too, Canada has what is needed to become a leader of a third way. In a world that regards economic laws as absolutes, there is a danger of neglecting or even of eliminating the weak. Globalization carries that risk. We must avoid that trap if we want to be able to take advantage of globalization without denying a share of its enormous benefits to anyone, in any society or in the global community. It is typically Canadian to counter the law of the jungle with a conception of the world that attempts to combine the social, economic, and political aspects of the lives and the development of peoples. It is thus equally impossible to eliminate the cultural element from economic life.

The Passion for Balance and the Third Way

The passion for balance that marks the Canadian spirit is also shown in the development of a feeling of regional identity, insofar as it provides a counterbalance to the increasingly universalizing trends in our world. This feeling, which has been evident primarily in Quebec for quite a long time, is becoming stronger throughout the country. By way of illustration, let us recall that twenty years ago 5 percent of citizens in Manitoba defined themselves first and foremost as Manitobans; the proportion now exceeds 20 percent.

I am not one of those who deplore this phenomenon. On the contrary. At a time when globalization of the economy is intensifying, citizens are realizing that certain powers are moving to other levels. When this occurs, they find they are better able to exercise other powers that have remained closer to them; thus their feeling of regional identity is reinforced, creating a new balance. This is perfectly understandable from a human point of view, and it has the effect of bringing people together across the entire country. As their feeling of belonging to their part of the country develops, Albertans, to mention just one example, are gaining a better and better understanding of the specific needs of Quebeckers and the importance they attach to Quebec. Reciprocally, Quebeckers are contributing to the development of other Canadians by asserting their differences with pride while at the same time sharing essential values.

Canada heralds the emergence of a third way. It is already a composite political space. Circumstances require it, and the country has a history and a flexibility that will enable it once again to find an original response to the challenges facing it and the other countries of the world. In order to do so, it will have to redefine certain roles and responsibilities. What now seems clear is that the federal framework our fathers passed down to us lends itself very well to the changes that the new context of globalization has unquestionably made necessary. But this is an issue I will deal with later. For the moment, let us simply recall that in our country the state has always played an indispensable role. The geographical vastness of Canada, the diversity of its regions, and its sparse population are some of the factors that have been most decisive in forcing our country to rely on the state. Balanced by a real concern for individual rights and freedoms, state intervention has usually been moderate in Canada. And on the whole, the results have been positive. This experience will benefit us as never before in the years to come.

Quite a study could be made of the causes of the generous attitude of Canadians. I believe that Canada's nordicity has something to do with it. The First Nations taught us how to cope with the country's nordicity, and in turn our experience of the North led us to discover the pressing necessity for cooperation and solidarity. Once we had tasted these, we began to value them for themselves. Finally, harmony between nature and human beings and harmony among human beings became our true second nature, giving us something we are known for throughout the world, which, for want of a better term, I will call Canadian civility.

Canadian Civility

Between the traditional nation-state and the usual international relations, on the one hand, and globalization and the new strategic alliances between the state and business—as well as between companies in various countries—on the other hand, is there room for a different way of doing things, a way suited to the new realities? Between the ideological dogmatism of the right and that of the left, both of which are obsolete, is there room for a reasonable, carefully considered attitude that will allow us to realize great social, political, economic, and even moral ideals? Between the hard-heartedness of unfettered capitalism and the destructive wastefulness of those who want us to give without first striving to produce, is there a middle ground? Between xenophobia, which is already too widespread, and forcing everyone to fit into one mould, is there a way of making immigrants feel welcome in our country? Between the brittle rigidity of overly strict rules and surrender to the law of the jungle, is there room for a measured flexibility? Between the ultra-legalistic spirit that is almost inevitably doomed to inaction and the reckless attitude that takes unnecessary risks, is there room for a creativity that is both bold and authentic?

There is indeed a positive answer to all these questions. That answer is to be found in the third way that Canada increasingly embodies in the eyes of the entire world. Not that everything is perfect here. Far from it. But Canadians have a healthy sense of responsibility that has led them to take the initiatives needed to solve their human problems insofar as that is possible. From the beginning of its history, Canada has rejected the model of the nation-state in favour of the model of respect for languages, cultures, and religions, a model that today is perfectly suited to globalization, which involves people as much as it does goods and services. Thanks to their pragmatism, Canadians have been able to avoid the traps of radical ideologies;

their sense of compromise has generally prevailed. Between xenophobia and forcing everyone into one mould, between hard-heartedness and ineffectual good intentions, Canada has chosen the middle ground of enlightened compassion and respect for differences in the sharing of fundamental values. Between rigidity and the market's law of the jungle, between legalism and the irresponsibility of "anything goes," there is flexibility, adaptation in fact even before adaptation in law, and ingenuity in making concrete adjustments while waiting for statements of principle—an attitude of accommodation, of give and take.

Canadian identity is based on shared convictions and values. Canadians share the same sense of responsibility and the same overall vision, because they have a balanced approach to their rights and duties. This view expresses an ideal more than a reality. But it is our ideal, one that distinguishes us from many other societies and, beyond our differences and disagreements, bonds the identity of all Canadians to a country that is exceptional. It is a political ideal that has been and continues to be embodied in the original and fair ways we have of dealing with social issues and managing the economy.

Chapter XI

A Status Quo in Constant Evolution

IN CANADA, THERE HAS NEVER BEEN A LASTING STATUS QUO. EACH generation of Canadians has had to reinvent the country. The Canada of today, in spite of its roots in the values Canadians have developed all through their history, is very different not only from the Canada of 1867 but also from the Canada that existed before World War II.

Each Status Quo Lasts Twenty Years

Following the war effort, which had led to an increase in the strength of the central government, Canada went through a period, between 1940 and 1960, in which the federal government emerged as the dominant power in the country. The effort of reconstruction, the building of a welfare state with many universal social programs, and megaprojects such as the St. Lawrence Seaway explain this.

The provinces gained prominence in the period from 1960 to 1980. Jean Lesage, who had learned to govern in Ottawa, where he was a member of Parliament from 1945 to 1958 and a Cabinet member from 1952 to 1957, led the Quiet Revolution in Quebec. This was a period during which the province established a modern state and a political power based on a skilled professional technocracy, which enabled it to carry a lot of political weight. Noting Quebec's remarkable successes with Lesage's "équipe du tonnerre," or crack team, who would arrive in Ottawa with well-prepared dossiers, the other provinces quickly followed suit and built up their own administrations.

The period from 1980 to 1995 was one of great federal-provincial tensions, a time of confrontation between the two levels of government over jurisdictions and revenue sharing.

With the globalization of the economy making borders increasingly porous, Canadian political leaders now have to realize that jurisdictions are not and cannot be rigidly separate. Children, for example, are neither a provincial nor a federal jurisdiction—each level of government has certain tools, and they have to learn how to work together for the well-being of Canada's young people. Canada now appears to be reaching a turning point, as globalization gives us an opportunity to redefine our country. The time is ripe for us to build a stronger partnership between the two levels of government in order to better serve Canadians.

In order to understand Canada and its potential, we must first look at the events that have marked its history and consider how it is distinctive. Indeed, as we have seen in the last two chapters, although Canada's history is relatively short, it has created something special that is worth further examination. But history does not tell us everything. We also need to review the current constitutional situation. What should we hope for from this last great debate that has been going on since the failure of the Meech Lake Accord?

The Sources of Canadian Identity

Canada as we know it today was formed in a little less than two and a half centuries on a territory first inhabited by the native peoples, a territory that the European newcomers must have found breathtaking. Although there were English possessions on the periphery of New France that would later become part of Canada, it is, in my view, in the St. Lawrence Valley that Canada began to take shape. Two factors were decisive in this. The first factor was the relatively early appearance of a European-style colonial society that was capable of opening up to modernity. By the mid-eighteenth century, there was a French-speaking population on the shores of the St. Lawrence, few in number but well rooted in New France, with a rural economy that encouraged interdependence and cooperation and a few traditional French institutions around which community life was organized. The population lived under the French *ancien régime* as it then existed in the Île-de-France.

The presence of a European colonial society in this part of the world is not unusual; there were others at various times throughout North America. But after the defeat of 1759, the population of New France faced a new situation: British occupation. This was the second decisive factor in the history of this country. Since 1763, when sovereignty was transferred from Paris to London, Canada has been the expression, first in its political life and then very soon after in its institutions, of a constant desire for conciliation between different languages, cultures, and traditions. The long tradition of representative government that goes back to 1791 has a lot to do with this. What was accomplished between people of French and English origins in the first decades influenced all subsequent relations among Canadians of all origins.

As we have seen, these same differences in language and culture were, for better or for worse, the basis of the nation-states that proliferated as a result of the great revolutions of the late eighteenth century. For many countries, as we have also seen, the entry into modernity came at the cost of forced assimilation, if not outright elimination, of linguistic, religious, cultural, and other minorities. Lines of national demarcation, generally based on the majority ethnic group, were established between states, and accentuated. When there was no way of reconciling ethnic differences in an elementary spirit of justice, these differences were exacerbated and became the main reason why groups of people made war with each other. This did not happen in every country, but history, even very recent history, is strewn with examples. As Stéphane Dion has put it, "The false idea of 'one people, one state' would cause the world to explode."[*][1]

Here in Canada, linguistic and cultural differences gradually developed and thrived while cohabiting in one country—but this "national" framework is unusual. It is based on simple legal citizenship, without any one ethnic group's characteristics dominant throughout the territory. It is the "political nationality" George-Étienne Cartier so aspired to. To me, this is a fundamental characteristic of Canada. It is inextricably linked to the Canadian identity today, and as we enter the twenty-first century, it is what distinguishes Canada from other highly developed countries, Canada's contribution to modern civilization. The reasonable and reasoned patriotism that is espoused here—which some people see as a lack of national fervour, and almost a flaw in our make-up—is one of Canada's strengths. It is based on shared institutions that respect the cultural backgrounds of all and that are designed to allow different communities to live together in close proximity without sacrificing too much of themselves. This *modus vivendi* among communities could serve as a model for a political system to deal with the changes that are coming all over the world. The Canadian model is clearly not the only contender, but it is one that could be tested elsewhere.

The Francophone Contribution

Of course, it took time for this characteristic to acquire the significance it has today. We must also recognize that it was partly a result of historical circumstances or accidents. For example, after the colonial war of 1759, the first British occupiers probably wished the French residents would

---

[*] There are approximately three thousand human groups in the world recognized as having a collective identity. This explains why nearly 90 percent of the 185 states recognized by the United Nations have multi-ethnic populations.

assimilate and disappear into the English colonial population. There had been a similar situation not long before in Acadia, and between 1755 and 1762 the English authorities had deported the French-speaking inhabitants. Dispersed through the English colonies in what would later become the United States, they were supposed to assimilate into the majority population. But the overall conditions—if only the number of inhabitants—would have made it difficult to carry out such a plan in New France.

Indeed, the determination to assimilate that may have motivated the military or civil authorities at the end of the eighteenth century diminished and finally disappeared as Canada's special nature took shape. While it still exists today in the minds of some Canadians, it has become marginal; it is a political anomaly in a country where we have never spoken of a national melting-pot, as they do in the United States. There, the very great diversity of origins, languages, cultures, and identifying characteristics of all kinds does not exempt anybody from a basic rule of behaviour: adoption of the dominant American language and culture in order to integrate. This is why the Canadian policy on official languages has been cited in the United States Congress as an example *not to follow*. This also explains, without necessarily justifying them, political measures such as the recent Proposition 227 in California, whose aim was to put an end to Spanish-language education in the primary schools of the state, and other proposals of its kind.

The evolution I am discussing did not take place without friction and confrontation. Canada's history is marked by political crises of varying degrees of seriousness in which linguistic differences, and for a long time religious differences as well, played a part, either explicitly or implicitly. This was the case in the rebellion of the Patriotes in Quebec in 1837, the Riel affair, Regulation 17 in Ontario, the conscription crises, the 1970 October Crisis, and so on. Some of these events—the Rebellion of 1837, for example—cost many human lives. Nevertheless, most of the great political controversies this country has experienced in the course of its history have been resolved peacefully. Canada has never had an internal conflict as bloody as the American Civil War, even in relative terms.

There is one constant in the history of this country that is a key element for understanding Canada today: the desire for collective affirmation of French-speaking Canadians, in Quebec and in the rest of Canada. This desire has deep historical roots that predate the creation of modern Canada. It is the reason why French-speaking Canadians will never be satisfied with the status of a mere linguistic minority destined for eventual assimilation, why they will continue unrelentingly to reject any policy that might threaten their collective identity and the institutions that embody it. Jean Lesage's slogan "Maîtres chez nous," masters in our own house, was a good expression of this enduring desire. At the same time, in spite of a great deal of resistance and some bitter failures, the country has continued to evolve in the general direction desired by a substantial proportion of these Canadians. And the willingness to accommodate them that has been shown by the rest of Canada is also clearly a constant in this country.[*]

What Lessons Can We Draw from This?

On one hand, we need to be aware of the past in order to prepare for the future. Although we always reinterpret it in the light of the present, we cannot change the past. And there is no use trying, as some people do out of ignorance of their history, or perhaps even deliberately, to deny the fundamental significance of the sometimes conflictual relationship between the two Canadian majorities since 1759. This relationship has gradually created a political culture of accommodation and reciprocity, and in doing so it has shaped the Canadian identity. Those who underestimate its importance in policy development risk strong resistance from French-speaking Canadians. Those who would simply reject its consequences put the country in danger.

On the other hand, the future has yet to be written, and as a liberal I am convinced that we are not prisoners of some kind of historical determinism that dooms French Canadians to assimilation in Canada. When some schools of thought imply the opposite, it seems to me that they are investing history with a meaning that it cannot really possess. This was the case not long ago for the Marxist critique of history, and it still applies to a certain nationalist critique in Quebec, despite its undeniable erudition.[2] The past is not the future. Deep and lasting changes have come about many times in the history of this country, often thanks to bold initiatives by authentically Canadian political actors. I am one of those people who without hesitation consider these developments positive and who see the future of Canada as extremely promising for all its citizens.

---

[*] When my friends in the rest of the country sometimes express weariness with the Quebec question, I remind them how much Quebec's demands have contributed to the development of Canada as we know it today. I am sure their ancestors also had moments of weariness when faced with the demands of my ancestors. This history of accommodation gave us not only our political identity but also a national anthem written by Adolphe-Basile Routhier to the music of Calixa Lavallée—which took a long time to supplant "God Save the King" in the rest of Canada—a more autonomous status in relation to Britain, and then the Maple Leaf flag, which is now a proud symbol for all. Quebec has prodded the country in the right direction. I tell my compatriots outside of Quebec that it is just as tiring for us to push as it is for them to resist.

No to the Narcissism of Small Differences

Meanwhile, we must beware, on both sides, of falling into what Freud called "the narcissism of small differences."[3] The original polarization between French-speaking colonists and colonists—and even soldiers—who spoke English cannot have fixed forever the terms of the discussion on the future of Canada. Quebeckers, in particular Quebeckers of French origin, have an indestructible attachment to their native soil, but they share with their Canadian compatriots a whole set of traits that make them immediately recognizable as Canadians as soon as they leave Canada.

In addition, the Canadian population is no longer what it was in the eighteenth or nineteenth centuries. Unless we define it in a way that I think would be most unfortunate, Quebec society is today made up of people of very diverse origins, including some English-speaking people, who choose to live in a society in which the French language predominates. Unless we define it in a way that is now completely obsolete, "English Canada" (which was established originally in Upper Canada) today comprises much more than English-speaking people of British stock—Canadians from central Europe, Asia, and many other places are just as much a part of it as the descendants of the merchants and Loyalists who came from 1763 on. The "rest of Canada" is therefore much more than the simplistic image conveyed by the term "English Canada."

If we want to see Canada in a way that encompasses its full reality, we cannot disregard the millions of citizens from backgrounds and cultures other than British or French who have come to enrich its population over the last century. These citizens from a variety of cultural backgrounds today represent nearly one third of the population of the country. In Saskatchewan, citizens of German culture constitute the second-largest group in terms of cultural background. In Manitoba and Alberta, citizens from a Ukrainian background are the second-largest group. In Toronto and Montreal, there are large Jewish, Italian, Greek, German, Polish, Hungarian, Romanian, Slovak, Haitian, Russian, Portuguese, Latin-American, and other communities. In Vancouver, the same is true of communities from Asian backgrounds. Finally, since the last major constitutional reform, the Aboriginal peoples have acquired legal autonomy, which also changes the original equation. While Canadian institutions are deeply marked by that equation, it reflects only part of Canada's history.

Chapter XII

One Constitution, Two Cultures, Four Myths

C ANADA'S SPECIAL NATURE HAS BEEN REFLECTED IN THE CANADIAN constitution at every stage of the country's development. As part of what were even then seen as its fundamental provisions, the Quebec Act of 1774 established a constitutional pact that has survived to this day, dealing mainly with the maintenance of French private law, partial legislative autonomy, and freedom of religion. Since then, this pact has undergone many changes, which we do not need to examine in detail. The essential events in this history are the division of Upper Canada and Lower Canada in 1791, their reunification in 1840, Canadian Confederation in 1867, and the repatriation of the constitution, with the addition of a Charter of Rights, in 1982.

Constitutional Culture Shock

Two conceptions of the constitution, from different traditions, have influenced the course of events from 1774 to today. There was, and there still is, for some French Canadians a tendency to want to make explicit in black and white in a document that is as complete as possible the main rules of the political game—a desire, in short, to reveal in the constitution the secret of the collective *modus vivendi*. This rationalist approach, which is often found in reform-minded political actors, assumes, essentially, that everything that exists is intelligible. In many ways it is quite Cartesian and French, but it was shared by the authors of the American constitution at the end of the eighteenth century, who were also heirs of the Enlightenment. The constitutional reform of 1982, with the inclusion of a Charter of Rights, was an opportunity to give it free rein as never before in Canada.

There is also another approach, one represented, at another time and in another country, by Edmund Burke, according to which it is preferable to leave things as they stand, to let the collective *modus vivendi* adapt by itself to the requirements of each situation, with the understanding that certain rights, by constitutional convention, are inalienable. The British tradition of parliamentary government and constitutional stability has long been marked by these values. Many eloquent voices, on both the right and the left, put forward this point of view in the months leading up to the constitutional reform of 1982, including Sterling Lyon, the former Conservative premier of Manitoba, and Allan Blakeney, the former New Democratic premier of Saskatchewan.

An important aspect of the British tradition, which served as the backdrop to the Canadian constitution for more than two hundred years, is the absence of a written constitution. The British constitution consequently has an immanent, diffuse quality, with custom, convention, and common sense as important as texts in regulating the art of governing. Today, certain important international agreements, such as the Treaty of Rome and the European Convention on Human Rights, compensate to some extent for this absence of basic texts, which is unique in Europe, but they do so only to a limited extent. The institutions of Great Britain, in their relationships with each other and in their most fundamental aspects, are still governed by an unwritten constitution that is one of the oldest in the Western world. The evolution of these institutions has continued uninterrupted since 1066, without any need for constituent assemblies to be convened.

Of course, this comparison and this argument cannot be taken too far. Great Britain functioned for a long time as an essentially unitary country with an absolutist régime; it went through a series of revolutions in the seventeenth century; some of its present institutions, including the monarchy, have undergone profound changes over the years. However, the idea of change within continuity has proven strikingly valid in this constitutional tradition in which *the facts precede the idea*. From the time of the French Revolution to the end of the twentieth century, the British constitution was modified little by little, through practice. In the long run, the cumulative effect of a series of initially imperceptible changes was great enough to make the political régime in Great Britain today profoundly different from what it was in 1790.

During the same period in France, a country of written law, the constitution went through more than half a dozen radical transformations, from a first republic to a first empire, then a restoration of the monarchy, then a second imperial régime, and finally a succession of republican régimes, each one attempting to distinguish itself as sharply as possible from the preceding one. In short, France experienced a series of desired but sometimes bloody discontinuities in its constitution. On the whole, France's constitutional history has been much more eventful than that of Great Britain, even though both have gone through periods of great political turmoil.

Something similar to British constitutional stability may be seen in the United States, where the constitution, although it is written, has undergone few changes since the Revolution. Some substantial modifications have been made to it at certain decisive moments in the country's history—the Fourteenth Amendment, for example, as a result of the Civil War—but never on a scale comparable to the changes made to the French constitution. The American constitution hardly changes because, as is generally the case in a federal system, the process of constitutional change is complex; this largely explains why only 26 of some 9,100 modifications proposed since 1789 have been ratified. This sometimes leads to great frustration for groups that are otherwise quite influential in society, as was the case when the Equal Rights Amendment failed. But the desire for change can be satisfied elsewhere than in the constitution. With respect to the equality of the sexes, for example, many laws adopted by the federal Congress and the state legislatures have already to a large extent implemented the policies sought by the proponents of the Equal Rights Amendment.

The Constitutional Question in Canada

Although in Canada, unlike the United States, the constitutional question is a constant subject of political debate, it seems to me that it has taken on a disproportionate importance here in the last twenty years. The real or alleged situation of francophone Canadians is the reason for this state of affairs. Of course, other concerns have surfaced in the last twenty years that deserve the utmost attention and that are also expressed now in the form of constitutional demands: the rights of the First Nations and the Western provinces' desire for greater autonomy, to mention only two. But only the situation of francophone Canadians, and in particular the Quebec question, at this time carries with it the danger of the break-up of Confederation. The fate of francophones outside Quebec—considered in the light of the rates of linguistic assimilation, which are still cause for concern—and the desire for affirmation of the francophones of Quebec give strength to the sovereignist arguments. Furthermore, there is no doubt that the constitutional reform of 1982, which was opposed by the Quebec government at the time, and the apparent reasons for the rejection of the Meech Lake Accord by the rest of Canada in 1990, and then of the Charlottetown Agreement by the whole of Canada in 1992, also helped the sovereignty movement. But this misunderstanding, which has persisted for nearly two decades now and which the sovereignty movement has maintained by cultivating various myths about Canadian federalism, divides and weakens French Canadians rather than serving our cause. It is time to turn the page and show the rest of the world what we have to offer as Canadians, because a great deal is expected of us.[*]

Four Constitutional Myths

There are several elements of information related to this complex question that make me optimistic and lead me to consider statements about an alleged constitutional impasse to be extremely exaggerated. There is nothing static about this country's constitution. There has always been a constitutional debate in Canada, and it will be productive as long as its purpose is something other than to inflame quarrels or jealousies among regions. Why am I so confident?

The Myth of the Status Quo
Recent experience continues to show that, when we make the effort, Canadian federalism is still a flexible and dynamic system of government. However, it requires cooperation between the levels of government. We need to practise not a federalism of perpetual tensions and confrontations, but an authentic, cooperative federalism in which federal and provincial partners are respectful of each other's prerogatives and jurisdictions. In fact, such a partnership is already functioning within the existing government structures insofar as we make an effort to treat our counterparts as allies rather than rivals.

An example that is already old comes to mind, one of many: the settlement of a dispute over immigration by a lasting agreement between the Canadian government and the first sovereignist government of Quebec, signed by ministers Jacques Couture and Bud Cullen. This was followed by a second agreement, the Gagnon-McDougall agreement. There are now approximately 450 bilateral or multilateral agreements between the Canadian government and provincial governments. More recently, we were able to modify the constitution to resolve the thorny issue of denominational school boards in Quebec and Newfoundland. The idea that these relationships are marked by permanent strife is a caricature. It is important to realize that federalism as it already exists, without any substantial constitutional reform, is a malleable system capable of adapting to the needs of all

---

[*] I cite the following observation, which is only one of many, because it has the merit of being concise. It is from the *Dictionnaire du XXIe siècle*, published in 1998 by Jacques Attali, an adviser to President François Mitterrand before becoming president of the European Bank for Reconstruction and Development. If Canada resolves its current misunderstanding, the author writes, this "wonderful land of immigrants will be one of the first examples of a successful multicultural, democratic country without borders, where everyone will be simultaneously a member of several communities that were formerly mutually exclusive." (Translators' note: Our translation.)

Canadians, including Quebeckers, even the sovereignists among them. Looking at the events of recent years, one is sometimes tempted to wonder whether the solution to this supposed constitutional impasse would be to replace the politicians rather than the constitution.

The Myth of the Impossibility of Special Status
Since 1995, tangible progress has been made in adjusting the division of powers in such areas as labour market training, employment support, anti-poverty measures, and environmental protection. These changes are far from negligible. But, as is often the case, those who once emphatically demanded them now seem to hope they will go unnoticed when it comes time to evaluate the progress that has been made. The Agreement on Internal Trade is another example of effective consensual federalism, as are, in another area, the foreign trade missions known as Team Canada.

The equality in law of the Canadian provinces is always accompanied by a multitude of situations that are equivalent to de facto special status. For example, Quebec, among other things, selects its own immigrants, has its own provincial police force, collects its own income tax, supports the funding of postsecondary education, has its own language legislation, and runs its own pension plan, while administering large sums of money through its Caisse de dépôt et placement (Deposit and investment fund). In doing all this, in areas of activity in which the federal government is much more present elsewhere, it already distinguishes itself in many ways from the other members of the Canadian federation.

To claim, as some do, that the Canadian constitution imposes an intolerable straitjacket on Quebec contradicts the views of the most reliable observers. In a detailed study of Canadian federalism in 1995, Claude Ryan examined the effect of the division of jurisdictions in eight sectors of activity in which he had previously been a provincial minister. At the beginning, summing up the judgment he was going to explain in depth, he wrote: "What I conclude from this assessment is that, in the sectors I was responsible for myself from 1985 to 1994, the government of Quebec had all the latitude needed to act in a free and responsible way. I also conclude that, where the constitution imposed restrictions on the capacity of the National Assembly and the Quebec government to act, they were correct and reasonable."[1]

The Myth of Centralization
It is still sometimes said that Canadian federalism is centralizing. With respect to the division of legislative jurisdictions, experts in comparative federalism have no difficulty refuting this assertion.

With respect to government policies, which is perhaps more significant, people who support this view are living in the wrong century. At the birth of Confederation, when huge infrastructure projects would occupy the federal government for years, when that same government was taking on the debt of the Canadian provinces, and when the doctrine of laissez faire exempted the provinces from the heavy obligations that they would have years later with the emergence of the welfare state, it was normal that the main fiscal resources would go to Ottawa. That is what the constitution provided for, giving Parliament jurisdiction over customs and excise taxes. In fact, the taxation of 1867 is in no way comparable to what we have today, and these duties were at the time the main source of revenue for the state. The federal government of the time was responsible for two thirds of public spending in Canada, and the provinces received two thirds of their revenues from it. Later, the Depression and World War II also had a centralizing effect. But this relationship was subsequently altered substantially.

Since the beginning of the 1950s, the proportion of federal employees in the work force has decreased by practically half. Federal revenues, which in 1950 were more than three times higher than provincial revenues, had by 1993 fallen to $1.20 for every dollar collected by the provinces. In terms of spending, for every dollar spent by the provinces, the federal government spent $2.46 in 1960 and only $0.67 in 1993, which represents a drop of 76 percent.[2] This evolution coincides with the extraordinary growth of the provincial governments since 1960; in Quebec, for example, the Quiet Revolution was also a revolution of the state, a period of building a modern state. Finally, I would like to point out that the spending power of the federal government—a power found in Canada as in the United States, Australia, and all the large federations—is subject here to limitations that do not exist anywhere else, which the federal government imposed on itself in February 1996 and which are more generous towards the provinces than the formula proposed in section 7 of the Meech Lake Accord.

The Myth of Duplication

As for people who criticize the Canadian federal system for its size or the supposed overlapping and duplication that occurs, they are ignoring the obvious way in which federal and provincial services complement each other, which is quite visible in areas such as health and social affairs. Moreover, figures published by the OECD clearly show that public spending in Canada, in all categories together, is substantially less than in unitary countries such as France, Italy, Norway, the Netherlands, and Sweden; Germany is the country most similar to Canada in this respect. Data from the same source show that Canada is about average in the size of its public sector, and that the tax burden, or the share of government revenues in the GDP (gross domestic product), compares favourably with that of many unitary countries. I do not see any point in providing a technical proof here; there is already an ample bibliography on this subject. It is clear, however, that charges of inertia, ineffectiveness, or uncontrolled growth made against the Canadian federal system are consistently contradicted by the facts.

The Constitution of 1982

The conception of federalism expressed in the constitutional reform of 1982 did not abolish the previous conception, which was the basis of the constitution of 1867. Without stating it explicitly, the earlier constitution, almost all of whose provisions remained in force in 1982 alongside the additions made, was permeated with the theory of the "two nations" or the "two founding peoples." This theory is no longer adequate to explain Canada today, a pluralist society, much broader and more populous than the Canada of 1867. But it contains guarantees for the French fact in Canada, placing this characteristic of the country on the same footing as the other values to which the constitution gives the highest priority.

Because it was carried out in spite of the opposition of a sovereignist government in power in Quebec, the reform of 1982 to some extent offended public opinion in Quebec. Nevertheless, it cannot be denied that it was opportune at a time when a great number of countries were becoming increasingly aware of the fundamental nature of human rights and choosing to provide legal protection for them. This reform thus gives priority in principle, for certain purposes and in certain kinds of situations, to individual rights, or to put it another way, to individuality in certain of its manifestations. This important change in the Canadian constitutional system did not alter the balance between federal and provincial governments. It simply means that *all* governments, in their legislative and executive bodies, must now take these guarantees into account and submit to court decisions that ensue from them. In fact, if there was any transfer of power in 1982, it was not at the expense of provincial jurisdictions and in favour of federal jurisdictions, but rather at the expense of governments and in favour of the courts. Moreover, there is a striking resemblance in content between the Charter of Human Rights and Freedoms that has been in effect in Quebec since 1977 and the Canadian Charter of Rights and Freedoms, which came into effect throughout Canada with the reform of 1982.

In terms of its substance, therefore, and with one reservation, this reform was indisputably a major improvement. The reservation that I would add concerns the repatriation of the constitution with the introduction of a new amending formula that the government of Quebec had refused to agree to.[3] This change is still controversial for some confirmed Quebec federalists. For my part, I believe that repatriation, which finally made it possible for Canadians to take charge of their constitution and removed it from under Westminster's trusteeship, should be seen, after more than fifteen years, as a gain, not a loss. I am still sympathetic, however, to the arguments of those critics, and it seems to me that the Constitutional Amendments Act assented to on February 22, 1996, which provides for regional vetoes, including one for Quebec, is a step in the right direction. If this formula were integrated into the constitution, it would undoubtedly satisfy many of these critics.

Furthermore, the Constitution Act of 1982 did not change the essence of federalism, which has always been to allow the fulfilment of distinct collective interests, even collective rights, by establishing distinct governments under a single constitution and distributing legislative jurisdictions among them according to these collective interests. Certainly the reform of 1982 represented a change of direction towards a less parliamentary form of government and one giving a bigger role to the courts. But it affected only a fraction of the Canadian constitution, which prominent political figures at all times in our history since 1867 have seen as comprising much more than a grouping of governments jointly exercising their authority on behalf of citizens who are equal under the law. I am thinking here in particular of former prime minister Lester B. Pearson, who had a very sophisticated understanding of the Canadian constitutional system and whose practice of federalism was always very respectful of the special nature of Canada that I discussed at the beginning of this chapter. We owe to him the Laurendeau-Dunton Royal Commission on Bilingualism and Biculturalism, whose work led to a radical transformation of the language situation in Canada. We also owe to him the federalism of accommodation that contributed greatly to the rise of the Quebec state, beginning with the Quiet Revolution.

The rest of Canada is currently rediscovering this aspect of Canadian federalism, or at least that part of it that is consistent with Canada's special nature.[4] There is also a better idea of what was left to be done after the last major constitutional adventure, the repatriation of 1982. And there is no reason to believe that was the end of the story. The legitimate aspirations of Quebeckers who are attracted by the sovereignist positions have to be recognized. On the other hand, to suggest that only a new series of major changes to the constitution can satisfy their aspirations and allay their fears for their identity is only to mislead them.

Federalism and Globalization

Globalization leads not only to the reaffirmation of civil society and to a salutary rollback of the state, but also to the development of a de facto federalism, created by the most varied groups of people and interests, transcending borders, and absolutely outside the framework of sovereign states. Why reject the huge network already in place since 1867 only to re-establish, often with the same players, forms of partnership that already exist within the Canadian federation?

Unlike some people, I do not believe that the next century will see the collapse of the nation-state. On the other hand, I do not believe either that this form of political organization has a brighter future than federalism does. Since World War II, there have been signs that the nation-state has had its day, or at any rate that its days of glory are past. The way of the future seems to me to be the gradual absorption of nation-states by new structures that are better suited to globalization: spaces of variable geometry. This is shown in such strong recent trends as the initially functionalist and now federalist path taken by Europe. It is also shown, in reverse, by other recent trends that, one hopes, are marginal, such as "ethnic cleansing" in the former Yugoslavia, Rwanda, Iraq, and elsewhere—events that go against the tide of history.

Renewing the Canadian Social Union and Canadian Federalism: A Twofold Project[1]

RENEWING THE CANADIAN SOCIAL UNION CONSTITUTES A HUGE project for the country. The Canadian concept of social union is far from simple. It involves a complex system in which social programs and underlying shared values are interwoven. This relationship between action and values is a fundamental part of the Canadian identity.

The Canadian government and the governments of the provinces are negotiating an agreement governing their overall relationship in the vast sphere of the social union. This negotiating table reports to the Ministerial Council on Social Policy Renewal that was set up in June 1996 by the First Ministers' Conference. The work of the other issues tables—those concerning child poverty, persons with disabilities, health, and other issues—is continuing. As chair of the Ministerial Council on Social Policy Renewal, I am working to achieve the goals that led me to become involved in politics. I entered active politics, in January 1996, to take part in modernizing Canadian federalism. To modernize it in a way that will meet the expectations and needs of Canadians in general and Quebeckers in particular. To modernize the country so that Canadians can benefit from the extraordinary potential of globalization while ensuring that its opportunities are shared by all, in accordance with the Canadian model.

By putting its public finances in order and thus regaining some room to manoeuvre, Canada has recovered its capacity to make major choices for society. The country, overall, is ready to make some significant changes, changes that are needed to meet the economic, political, and social challenges of this era of globalization. Like all countries in the world, Canada must adapt. Canada must change, and it is changing.

In terms of employment and labour, Canada compares favourably with the twenty-nine member countries of the Organization for Economic Co-operation and Development (OECD). This is first of all because the economic and social situation in Canada is something that impresses all observers; some even speak of it as the "Canadian miracle." But it is also because the other countries are too often wrestling with ideologies concerning government intervention, which is advocated by the left and rejected by the right. In contrast, Canadians and their governments tend to look for practical rather than ideological solutions to their problems. Quebeckers are in agreement with Canadians in general, favouring a third option that lies somewhere between the American laissez-faire approach and the social model of continental Europe. Indeed, they have profoundly influenced Canada's choice of this pragmatic middle ground.

Economic development does not take place in a vacuum. There can be no true, solid economic union unless there is also a sound and vital social union to support it. The Ministerial Council on Social Policy Renewal has achieved spectacular progress that benefits children in low-income families and persons with disabilities. This progress also contributes to a more harmonious, more constructive federalism, with a clearer delineation of the roles of each level of government.

The Era of Partnership:
The Striking Example of the National Child Benefit

The National Child Benefit is the most recent example of this relationship between our social values and the concrete action we are taking. In the Ministerial Council, all levels of government and people of every political stripe are working together without squabbling. This is an example of federalism that works, federalism that is modern, efficient, and based on the concept of partnership among governments.

One thing is unfortunately true: children who come to school hungry and cold are in no condition to learn. And this is not fair. In Canada, it does not make sense. Children are our future, the future of our economic development. A good start in life ensures that children become healthier adults who are better able to find their place in the labour market. The National Child Benefit is the most important social program to be brought forward in the last thirty years. It is as important as the Canada Pension Plan and the Quebec Pension Plan, which were established for our senior citizens in the 1960s.

The mechanics of the National Child Benefit are simple: the government of Canada will increase the child tax credit, thus increasing the incomes of low-income families. The provinces and territories will take the savings they achieve in social assistance and reinvest them in programs and services. As things stand now, too many parents cannot move from welfare to work without penalizing their children—moving off social assistance can mean losing up to three thousand dollars a year. With our benefit, we want to help those parents get out of the welfare trap and get back to work.

The National Child Benefit gives every province increased room to manoeuvre. For Quebec, for example, this means a savings of $150 million per year, beginning in July 1998. Each province is thus able to offer programs and services that are specifically tailored to meet the needs of its citizens. Is it interference by the federal government when income-based tax credits are paid out to individuals and the provinces are able to offer more programs and services that are better suited to their population? No, it is federalism at its best. It is simply a matter of clarifying the roles of each level of government. How can the government of Quebec oppose this approach, as Lucien Bouchard did in St. Andrews? How can it be so dogmatic? After all, the government of Canada's policy and Quebec's family policy share the same goals and are mutually supportive.

Moreover, the governments of all the other provinces, from the most conservative ones—such as the Harris government in Ontario—to the most progressive ones—such as the Saskatchewan government—including the most independent-minded—Alberta and British Columbia—have reached a consensus to work together in the best interests of children. This is a far cry from authoritarian federalism: each party is accountable to its citizens and not to the other level of government. That is real partnership.

The Labour Market Agreement

It is always possible to agree if we want to, as we proved when we negotiated the labour market agreement between the federal and provincial governments. That went far beyond training to provide a new way of managing all the active measures under the new Employment Insurance Act, including targeted wage subsidies, self-employment assistance, and measures to facilitate labour market integration—at a cost of $500 million a year. Agreements have been reached with nine of the ten provinces, in a spirit of solidarity and respect for the specific characteristics of each of them.[2] Each labour market agreement is custom-made to meet the specific labour market needs of the provincial partners. Several provinces, Quebec included, have opted for full devolution, while others have chosen co-management with the federal government. This is yet another illustration of the kind of modern, flexible federalism I like: federalism that responds in different ways to different needs.

From Unemployment Insurance to the Pension Plan

Canada is an ongoing project. Each new generation of Canadians has had to reinvent this country to make its policies, programs, and institutions ever more responsive to the changing needs of citizens. And our generation cannot escape its responsibility. Now it is the baby boomers' turn to reinvent the country. And Quebec must contribute to the modernization process.

Being the minister responsible for the Canadian social union and being from Quebec is both a blessing and a curse. A blessing because of Quebec's long tradition of innovation and progress on social issues. A curse because the current government of Quebec says that the federal government has no role to play in the social sphere, that social matters come under provincial jurisdiction alone. However, Quebec has always participated in the evolution of Canadian social policy. A quick look back at the not-so-distant past provides evidence of many cases of mutually advantageous cooperation between the different levels of government in Canada.

Before the stock market crash of 1929, health, education, and social assistance were essentially left to the private sector, especially charitable and religious institutions. But since then, much has changed. The Great Depression led to a consensus between the federal and provincial governments to amend the constitution to set up a Canada-wide unemployment insurance system in 1940–41. Of course, hard-line proponents of Quebec autonomy were fiercely opposed to this change, although it was a real step ahead for Quebeckers—a rather incredible position to take, according to a recent biography of Adélard Godbout, the premier of Quebec at the time.[3] Fortunately, the vision and pragmatism of Godbout's Liberal Party won out over ideological dogmatism, giving the people of Quebec access to a major new social program for workers. Other partnership ventures were to follow.

Canadian federalism is characterized by experimentation and competition as well as solidarity. The Canadian federal system provides a flexible framework for trying out good ideas in one province and eventually implementing them across the country for the greater good of all Canadians. These ideas have included hospital insurance, which started in Saskatchewan and was extended across the country in the early 1960s. Healthy competition between levels of government and among the provinces means that each tries to surpass the others and all Canadians benefit.

In social matters, Quebec's successive governments have always practised a healthy pragmatism. They have, of course, insisted on the primacy of the provinces in social matters, but they have always tempered this approach with a large degree of openness and willingness to enter into partnerships. They have placed the best interests of Quebeckers above all other considerations. Premier Paul Sauvé took this pragmatic approach and declared that Quebec had no constitutional objection to the introduction of a Canadian hospital insurance plan. Jean Lesage, in turn, implemented the plan in Quebec in partnership with the federal government.

The Liberal governments of Jean Lesage and Lester B. Pearson took this same pragmatic approach to providing income security for seniors through the Quebec Pension Plan, which parallels the Canada Pension Plan. A not insignificant corollary to this, and one that provides an excellent illustration of the benefits of partnership, is that the Quebec Pension Plan gave rise to the Caisse de dépôt et placement, a key tool for economic development in Quebec. The Caisse de dépôt has been so successful that the Canada Pension Plan is about to institute something similar for the rest of the country.

It was Robert Bourassa who said that Quebec recognized the federal government's essential role in ensuring that all Canadians have an acceptable standard of living. He also maintained that the administration of social programs should be shared, depending on the type of management required in each case—sometimes centralized, sometimes decentralized. Under his premiership, health insurance, a major social initiative and one that is the envy of many countries in the world, was introduced in Quebec, and Ottawa and Quebec reached an agreement on family allowances that clearly recognized Quebec's uniqueness. Whenever social innovations were introduced at the federal level, Bourassa took part on behalf of the people of Quebec.

Renewing the Social Union and Federalism

In an article in *La Presse* in the fall of 1997,[4] Claude Castonguay, considered the father of health insurance in Quebec, and certainly not a person one would call a centralizing federalist, urged Premier Lucien Bouchard to view the renewal of the Canadian social union as an opportunity rather than a dark plot hatched by ill-intentioned federal forces and the other provinces to divest Quebec of its authority and control over social matters. Referring to his own experience as minister of social affairs in Bourassa's Cabinet, Castonguay described the approach of that government as aiming to clarify the division of powers, and not attempting to claim a special status for Quebec or force the federal government to withdraw from the field of social programs such as old age security. In other words, they tried to move ahead on issues instead of merely making demands or crying humiliation. Castonguay made two more important observations. He pointed out that Quebeckers have benefited from these programs, which in many instances have a redistribution component that has been to Quebec's advantage. Second, he shrewdly noted that if both parties in a negotiation truly want to reach an agreement, a solution can usually be found, even for issues that at the outset appear impossible to resolve.

The Ministerial Council on the Social Union is an outstanding forum for moving ahead on issues. As Castonguay recognized, it is not a place of authoritarian, intransigent federalism. And even though it would be difficult to find a more flexible federal system, there is clearly still room for improvement. We must keep working to build a modern and effective federalism for the twenty-first century.

While the Godbout, Sauvé, Lesage, and Bourassa governments participated in every major step in our country's social development, the current Quebec government refuses on principle to have anything to do with the monumental task we have undertaken for the benefit of our children. In practice, Quebec's family policy has the same objectives as the federal benefit and, indeed, the federal benefit is advantageous for Quebec. But orthodoxy, or perhaps even dogmatism, dictates that the current government reject a progressive program that reflects a new style of federalism and that a large majority of Quebeckers clearly want.

Quebec's Traditional Approach and a New Partnership

Premier Bouchard's claim that his approach to the social union is based on the traditional approach taken by his predecessors is, to say the least, a distortion of reality, although perhaps convenient. The "empty chair" approach has never been that preferred by Quebec governments.[*] And for good reason; it is completely contrary to the best interests of Quebeckers.

We have to understand that the time is right for the renewal that everyone wants. Globalization is making it necessary to redefine the relationship between the state and the marketplace, between the state and the community, and between the state and the individual. Canada has no choice. We have to redefine, to reinvent the relationships between Ottawa and the provinces, and we have to innovate. The needs of our citizens must take precedence over any other considerations. The step-by-step and case-by-case approach is very promising; it has already borne fruit in the labour market agreements, the federal withdrawal from the areas of forestry, mining, and social housing, and the limits on spending power.

My vision is that of an increasingly vital Quebec that is a major partner in a modernized Canadian federation, a society that benefits from Canada and, as recognized in the Calgary Declaration, is essential to the vitality of Canada. The Canadian social union is an excellent avenue for renewal of

---

[*] This was written before the Saskatoon meeting in August 1998, in which Premier Bouchard finally took part, but he still seems to be interested only in Quebec's right to withdraw with full financial compensation, and not at all in the Canadian social union as a whole.

the federation. No one wants continued counterproductive and costly quarrelling when a real partnership that is imaginative, based on respect, and tailored to meet the challenges of the twenty-first century is entirely possible within our federation.

Sovereignists who claim they want an economic union with other Canadians but not a social union should look to the European experience. The European Union shows that there cannot be an economic union worthy of the name without a social union. As the Europeans have developed their common market and their economic union, they have felt the need to considerably develop what they call "l'Europe sociale," Europe as a social entity.

Canada is a model for many Europeans. In a recent interview, French political analyst Alain Minc said that many Europeans, at least those of a certain political persuasion, dream of the European Union becoming what Canada is for its provinces, and appealed to Canadians not to destroy the model Europeans hope one day to replicate.[5]

Chapter XIV

Canada's International Personality

E XPERIENCE SHOWS THAT IT IS DIFFICULT TO SEE OURSELVES, AND that often the point of view of others helps us to see our own individual identity in a meaningful light. This also applies to groups of people, and Canada is no exception. Although we are barely aware of it, Canada does have an international personality. It is the product of our attitude of accommodation and the values it entails.

The Canadian International Development Agency (CIDA) sees evidence of this every day. Whether they are anglophone, francophone, or "allophone"— if I may be permitted to use that inelegant term—whether they are involved in La Francophonie, the Commonwealth, or elsewhere, Canadians are perceived as being respectful of others. This is the impression shared by all who come into contact with Quebeckers or other Canadians throughout the world.

With no colonialist past and no imperialist ambitions, Canada enjoys an enviable international reputation for respect, tolerance, generosity, and openness.* The recent treaty banning anti-personnel mines is one more example of the initiatives that have made Canada a model country for the whole world; not the least of these was the creation of the UN peacekeeping forces, instigated by Lester B. Pearson.

Canadians' civility is another aspect of their international personality. It is said that we lack aggressiveness in foreign markets. Perhaps. Our civility, however, that well-known Canadian quality, is a much more attractive trait than many of the characteristics considered typical of other nationalities. This Canadian personality explains why Canada's influence on the affairs of the world is so much greater than its demographic weight alone would justify—because, after all, there are only thirty million of us.

---

* I had the opportunity to see this for myself when I was minister for international cooperation and minister responsible for La Francophonie, and I was struck by it.

A Larger Role Than Is Justified by the Size of Its Population[1]

As a middle power in the hierarchy of international actors, Canada, in keep-ing with its personality, has taken the path of cooperation in order to pro-mote Canadian interests and values on the international scene.

At the end of World War II, Canada became a member of the United Nations and all its agencies. It is among the countries that have contributed the most to the process of internationalization, which has gone on for fifty years. As a neighbour of the United States, Canada has always sought to maximize its influence by participating in the greatest possible number of international organizations and by supporting multilateralism. No other country belongs to as many clubs. Multilateralism has become Canada's mantra. By taking part in the Bretton Woods Conference, Canada was among the countries that established the great economic institutions of the World Bank and the International Monetary Fund. And Canada is also among the twenty-three founding countries of GATT, the General Agreement on Tariffs and Trade, which recently became the World Trade Organization.

These international economic, financial, and trade organizations have been the engine of the internationalization that the winners of the war desired. They were convinced that countries that were more interdepend-ent would be better able to avoid war, which had done so much harm in Europe over the previous century. The European Economic Community was soon born out of the same inspiration, the same desire. The primary objective of economic interdependence was thus political: to prevent wars among nations. Canada was, from the start, among the creators of these new institutions, for it saw them as a way to promote both its national interests and its political values in favour of peace.

I am emphasizing this political will that emerged at the very beginning of the era of internationalization because too often people who plead the case of the state today do so in an overly narrow way. We have to break with the oversimplified view that sees the market, on the one hand, as subservient to private interests, and the nation-state, on the other, as the exclusive cus-todian of all the universal values associated with the idea of the common good. The state was at the heart of this commitment to economic interde-pendence through internationalization. Liberalism and the liberalization of trade that must accompany it emerge and thrive only once the state itself becomes liberal. Frédéric Moulène expresses this very well: "The Le Chape-lier law of 1791 that banned coalitions is evidence of this, as are the anti-union laws passed by the House of Commons under the impetus of Thatcher less than two centuries later: it is always the politico-legal authority that gives the market its full strength."[2] This trend was intensified in the era of internationalization. With globalization, technological innovation often permits the market and business to flout politico-legal authority or to circumvent it. But until very recently, the state and the political sphere actively supported economic and trade development.

If Canada plays a larger role than is justified by the size of its population, it is of course because of its special personality, but also because of the broad framework in which it has chosen to make its contributions. It has been very active in political and military affairs. At the United Nations, it has sat on the Security Council in every decade, and it has just been elected for a sixth mandate, outdoing all the other countries in its category. Canada has also taken part from the very beginning in NATO (the North Atlantic Treaty Organization), which was created during the Cold War. Canada introduced the idea of promoting economic and cultural exchanges among countries rather than limiting their relationship to military cooperation. At the Conference on Security and Cooperation in Europe (CSCE), Canada supported the creation of forums in which the countries of Europe, including Russia, could take part in security negotiations that would go beyond mere military cooperation.

In addition, Canada is a major partner in the Commonwealth, where its role as an intermediary is highly valued. It benefits from this preferential access to the many member countries whose common language is English or who at least share its use. Initially an economic and trade organization, the Commonwealth has reinvented itself in recent decades as a very important political forum on many issues. Canada is also a major partner in La Francophonie and the Agence de coopération culturelle et technique (ACCT), giving us access to another sphere of influence, that of the countries sharing the use of the French language. Quebec and New Brunswick, the two provincial governments that have adopted French as an official language, enjoy a special status as participating governments in these organizations.

More recently, strictly in terms of trade, most countries have added regional liberalization efforts to the multilateral arrangements agreed to through the World Trade Organization. This is a general trend from which Canada is not exempt. Thus Canada signed a free trade agreement with the United States, which was soon expanded to Mexico to become the North American Free Trade Agreement (NAFTA). Canada supports the extension of NAFTA to several other Latin American countries. As a Pacific Rim country, Canada is also involved in the Asia-Pacific Economic Cooperation (APEC) Council, the countries of which are working to increase trade and active cooperation with each other.

Canada is a member of the Group of Seven, usually called the G-7, the very prestigious club of the seven most industrialized countries. Canada also belongs to its political counterpart, the P-8, which includes Russia. It is a considerable advantage for Canada to sit at these tables with the Great Powers, and many countries in the world value the role Canada plays there.

Canada has systematically supported an international system governed by law and not power. The rule of law is the very essence of civilized conduct within and among countries. Clearly defined rules help restore the balance of power and prevent the strongest countries from subjecting society and the international community to their control.

Challenges and Opportunities on the World Stage: The Management of International Affairs

For the last fifty years, Canada has distinguished itself on the international stage by defending human rights, peace, disarmament, and development. Faithful to this tradition, Canada recently expressed its international personality again by leading the initiative for an international treaty on anti-personnel mines. But the world in which we have achieved such great things is disappearing. The end of the Cold War, the rule of technology, and policies of liberalization of the economy and trade, as well as the emergence of new world problems, are showing us a world that has little to do with the one in which we became a country:

• We are moving from a bi-polar international system to a multi-polar one dominated by a single superpower that has all the advantages: the United States.

• Traditional international conflicts have subsided, but we are witnessing outbreaks of new internal or ethnic conflicts.

• Computerization and globalization of the economy have broadened the base of the appropriate decision-making process, but they have also created the risk of marginalizing certain developing countries, or certain segments of the population in the developed countries.

• Population growth has created an opposition between the young, fast-growing populations of the developing countries and the aging populations of the developed countries.

• The increased exploitation of natural resources and the accompanying pollution that result from population growth are likely to cause conflicts over access to those natural resources.

• Massive migrations have become a worldwide phenomenon that has a direct impact on the fight against infectious diseases.

• Environmental degradation is taking place at a much faster pace than international efforts to stop it.

- International crime not only threatens economic balance but corrupts whole governments.
- Terrorism now strikes any time, anywhere, and for any reason.

All things considered, Canada's main problem now is dealing with the many changes that are forcing us to question policies established in another world order.

The New Face of Power: The Battle for Hearts and Minds[3]

With the end of the Cold War, the nature of relationships among states, like the instruments of power and influence, has profoundly changed. From a world dominated by geopolitical considerations, we are now moving to a "geo-economy." Indeed, we are leaving a world haunted by the threat of nuclear annihilation and entering a world oriented towards economic prosperity. Economic cooperation among the traditional allies of the Cold War period has given way to international competition. In a knowledge-based economy, this means that the lines of influence will no longer be determined solely by military or economic power. Economic expertise, ingenuity, and flexibility; the acquisition of knowledge; and information management are also factors.

This new state of affairs has various consequences. First of all, power will be less concentrated and more flexible, and cooperation among countries sharing the same ideology will be a necessity. Canada will have to find and maintain new partnerships outside the North American continent. Coalitions around issues will become important instruments for asserting our influence and managing our relationship with our imposing neighbour, as our current alliances do in many ways. Finally, these coalitions will not necessarily comprise states alone, but also other actors, whose cooperation may be vital.

Our ability to create these coalitions will depend in part on the exercise of "soft power," the power that is inherent in the new relationships brought about by the new global knowledge economy and the information revolution. Soft power is the art of communicating information to foreign observers, including the international media, in such a way as to achieve the desired results through persuasion rather than coercion. Soft power sets the terms of discussion and so influences the nature of the solution. From now to 2005, because of the increasing connectivity of information networks, the impact of soft power will only increase. New technological ecosystems will emerge. For governments, the implications of soft power are enormous: they will no longer be the sole holders of interactive power. In other words, states will not have a monopoly on the advantages of soft power. Governments will be expected to manage through information rather than through coercion.

In the international context, the control of soft power will have the following effects. First of all, the dissemination of information on the negotiation of international trade agreements will be crucial. The protection of national interests will have more to do with the projection of information than the projection of military power. And to succeed, diplomatic activities will have to focus on the exchange of information rather than on the protection of information. Finally, the collection of information will be broadened and the dissemination of information will be targeted.

Military power will continue to play an essential role in certain situations; sometimes there is no substitute for muscle when it comes time to defend vital interests. In what circumstances would we consider the use of military power? In the event of a war among Persian Gulf states, or the collapse of a régime with an immediate and dramatic impact on Canadian interests in the global energy market. A major conflagration on the Korean peninsula might also draw us in, not to mention other possibilities that are more remote but no less fraught with consequences. We cannot avoid preparing for conflicts in which our vital interests are endangered. In addition, there will be many more conflicts, mostly internal and of lower intensity, in which Canadian interests are not specifically threatened; our obligation to contribute will be largely humanitarian in nature, and will perhaps be driven by the population as a result of the "CNN effect" or by immigrant communities in Canada.

Canada's Role in 2005

Canada is particularly well equipped to play an international role that is in keeping with the promotion and protection of its interests in a changing world system. We will, however, have to fight to maintain and improve our image and preserve our special nature in a more fluid international context where influence is based on expertise in and control of soft power.

In 2005, Canada could manage its international image using means that will make those it uses today seem simple. First and foremost, it will be able to go beyond merely formulating messages to fighting for space for dissemination, or "bandwidth." Soft power will thus be crucial to allow us to use international resources not only to meet our national objectives, but also to promote and protect our vital interests, including prosperity and unity. With respect to international questions, Canada in the year 2005 will be faced with strategic choices it will be unable to ignore.

Globalization with a Human Face

Countering the destabilizing effects of economic globalization and protecting the emerging economies, while trying to make sure that less-developed countries benefit from the knowledge economy—these are not only crucial objectives for Canada in terms of security, they are also measures that could open up immense possibilities for trade and investment. In this respect, Africa could very well be our main challenge. First of all, we could plan to develop better means to foresee, follow, and prevent the bloody conflicts and catastrophes that are decimating African populations. Second, it would probably make sense to create new mechanisms for the transfer of knowledge and to adopt better practices and standards that are more suited to developing countries in order to make Canada a "knowledge broker." Third, it would likely be advantageous to focus our development assistance policy and the activities of our international development organizations not on programs, but on the creation of institutions that encourage the autonomy of the people concerned and help reduce poverty.

To Ensure Human Security: A Global Civil Society

The emergence of a global civil society motivated by common interests must govern the quest for the necessarily complex solutions to the worldwide challenges that have so far resisted inter-governmental approaches. Without a community of interests and values on an international scale, any effort to solve these problems will lead to a sterile confrontation between rich countries and poor countries. Various elements of our foreign policy—development, human rights, good management, systems governed by rules—could be put towards the creation of a global civil society. In the next ten years, we could, first, define the concept of "global civil society" and make sure we integrate it into our international program. We could then incorporate our objectives in the areas of the environment, good management, labour, and social policy into the objectives of short-term economic growth of the appropriate international institutions. Finally, we could strengthen the links between international and regional organizations in order to improve our ability on a national scale to fight new infectious diseases, cross-border pollution, international crime, and uncontrolled migration.

Soft Power: Developing Our Potential

Canada has an enviable image on the international scene, which makes it an influential and credible player. But to get the full advantage of this, it will have to master the use of soft power. Our capacity to participate and make our influence felt in coalitions depends on it. Canada will have to acquire the means to gather, process, and disseminate strategic information, and establish coordination mechanisms or synergies among various actors—states and others—at home and abroad. It will have to emphasize its distinctive character and the quality of its image and its cultural products on the international scene.

As in all great periods of transition, the challenge we face in this period of globalization is not so much to foresee the future or preserve the past but to conceive the present. This is one of those rare times when history permits considered choices. But we need the courage to make the necessary decisions. We need to know how to manage the contradictions, tensions, and risks associated with the great changes taking place in the international system. The most immediate task, the one that is most decisive for the future, is to fill the widening gulf between old and new players through the international or domestic redistribution of power and wealth among political and social institutions that often seem incapable of change.

During the past year, we reached a crossing of the ways. The financial crisis in Asia and, more recently, the nuclear tests carried out by India and Pakistan have created new circumstances whose effects could be crucial for the new international order to come. In the first case, there is a danger that a violent backlash against the rules and values associated with the globalization of financial markets could compromise what has been accomplished through the liberalization of trade. The potential consequences of such a crisis, not only regionally but also worldwide, show the vulnerability of our economies to the failures of a market left completely to itself. It is in light of this that we have to understand the meaning of the Canadian proposal for a monitoring and early-warning mechanism to deal with these potential crises.

The case of the Indian subcontinent is another illustration of this institutional deficit. Because we have failed to carry out institutional reforms—for example to the Security Council—that reflect the new aspirations and political and economic realities of the post–Cold War period, we are faced with a fait accompli. While most states have eliminated the threat of military force, and specifically of nuclear weapons, from their political repertoire, India and Pakistan are jeopardizing the possibility of a demilitarization of international relations. The recent tests go against Canada's policy on the non-proliferation of nuclear weapons and disarmament. It will certainly be as difficult to convince these two countries to give up nuclear weapons as to convince the five recognized nuclear powers to do so.

If we are not more attentive to the dangers inherent in the formation of economic blocs, something we have been able to resist until now, the combined effects of these crises could very well lead to the creation of new politico-military blocs. Furthermore, Africa provides an example of the dangers of marginalization that may result from globalization. Whatever new possibilities for accelerated development are offered by the new information technologies, it is still necessary to establish a political and institutional framework capable of taking advantage of this potential.

At a time when private capital is replacing official aid to development as the main engine of economic progress, the Asian financial crisis reminds us of the dangers of the mismatch between the rules or institutions for the public management of a state and the laws of the market. There does not yet exist a very precise model for how best to meet the challenges of globalization, but there are certainly lessons to be learned from the experience of some countries.

Canada has always been among the countries most exposed to the dangers of diversity, disparity, and complexity that go with openness to the world. It has clearly demonstrated that these risks can become true advantages for a country, although they very often result in a direct threat to social stability, and even to the physical well-being of its citizens, as is the case for organized crime, the scourge of drugs, terrorism, illegal migrations, and environmental degradation. But our prosperity is and has always been dependent on the free movement of goods, capital, services, people, and ideas. In fact, more than 40 percent of our GDP comes from international trade. While maintaining an open, multicultural, democratic society, we have been able to manage the risks and take advantage of the benefits of this openness and this diversity. This is why Canada can take a key position between the new world and the old one, between North and South, between Europe and Asia, between the old and the new culture.

Cities like Montreal, Toronto, and Vancouver are now crossroads of all the great cultures of the world. And that is where our strength lies. The Canadian family is so large and so diverse that there is always somebody who can draw on his or her culture to offer a solution to a new problem, or who can look at a new challenge and see a possibility to be exploited. The Canadian experience is one of many cultures, many peoples, two languages, and a single voice. In Vancouver, the Sikh, Hindu, and Pakistani communities live together in harmony and thrive, while their subcontinent of origin is on the brink of a dangerous confrontation. Tolerance of diversity is the ingredient that makes the difference for Canada. Our country was founded by two peoples, and from the beginning this has marked its life and constantly forced us to question our respective attitudes.

In the global village of the twenty-first century, good neighbours will be those who show the tolerance and spirit of compromise Canada has always been known for. These are the societies that will prosper; they will give all their members the possibility of realizing their dreams, and in return they will benefit from the realization of these dreams.

Part Three

Quebec: Towards a Postmodern Society

Chapter XV

A New Quiet Revolution: From the "Obelix State" to the "Asterix State"[1]

QUEBEC ENTERED MODERNITY FAR BEHIND MOST OTHER REGIONS of North America. But Quebeckers, like most societies in the world, finally made this transition by building a modern state—neutral, professional, based on expertise, and non-partisan—to replace the Church.

Even before it was given form by the Liberal government of Jean Lesage, the transition was desired and heralded. To draw a parallel with what I have said about the importance of aesthetic experience and its effects on social and political development, I would like to mention the *Refus global*, the famous manifesto published in 1948 by the Automatiste painter Paul-Émile Borduas and other artists. In it, Borduas rejected the narrow structures that stifled art and thought in a closed society. As historian Yves Frenette has observed, "The same year (1948), with less fanfare but just as much effect, a young playwright, Gratien Gélinas, subtly criticized the family, the Church, and the state in his play *Tit-Coq*, the story of an illegitimate child denied a normal life by 'polite society.'"[2]

So it was in the arts that criticism of the traditional values initially arose. It led to the creation of a Ministry of Education concerned with education for all citizens and to the deconfessionalization and laicization of social services and especially health care.[3] In short, all the elements of so-called traditional society disappeared. So much so that francophone Quebeckers, who had never been very involved in the economy, learned to use the public levers created by a government that had become skilled and professional, enabling them to gain access to many sectors of the economy and business.

Canada had established the apparatus of a modern state a few generations earlier, and during his thirteen years in Ottawa, Jean Lesage had in effect served his apprenticeship, learning to govern in a way that was not narrowly partisan, with the support of a public service based on skill and expertise. His experience in the federal government helped the Quebec Liberals achieve their ambitions. With a handful of enthusiastic technocrats, the Liberal Party accelerated and institutionalized the modernization of Quebec. It quickly built a complex state apparatus and adopted social measures that ensured a better distribution of goods and services and increased democracy by extending civil rights to the social and economic spheres, the sources of material well-being.[4] The nationalization of electricity under Hydro-Québec, which had been created by the last Liberal government of Adélard Godbout, became a symbol of Quebeckers' engineering skills and ability to control their natural resources. But above all, Hydro-Québec became a major school of management for many francophone administrators, who soon flooded into the private sector, where they would finally find a place.

Jean Lesage knew what the federal Liberals under Pearson had in mind for their eventual return to power, perhaps their intention to set up the Canada Pension Plan. The Liberals did not come back into power until 1963. Lesage was thus able to steal a march on them by preparing his plans—with the help of such people as Michel Bélanger and Jacques Parizeau—for Quebec's own pension plan and the creation of the Caisse de dépôt et placement to manage Quebeckers' pension savings and thus build up a substantial fund of financial capital for Quebec's economic development.

At that time, the "Obelix state"[5] was at its height: contractors were building large numbers of schools, hospitals, roads, and dams and developing expertise that would be exportable outside Quebec's borders. The Quebec state built by the Liberal government thus led to the emergence of a French-speaking business class, and an immense change in Quebeckers' attitudes towards the economy in general and to industry, trade, and finance. It also led to a change of attitude in the social sphere, in which charity, with its religious connotation, gave way to rights, with their civic connotation, so that making claims became legitimate and protected by law. The trade unions also gave up their religious affiliations at this time.

Canada would never be the same again. The Canadian government, until then the only really professional structure of government, had played a very large role in the country since the war. But Ottawa now had to deal with Lesage, who knew the central government well. The other provinces, in turn, seeing Quebec's successes at every federal-provincial meeting, soon built stronger governments supported by less-partisan public services.[6] Ottawa had until then tended to look down on the more amateurish provincial administrations, but there was now no longer a basis for this arrogance. Competence was now distributed more equally in the country, hence the importance of the current trend towards more partnerships between levels of government.

The first Quiet Revolution, that of the 1960s, took place when the Bretton Woods system was at its height, that era of internationalization that, unlike globalization, confirmed the role of the state in society.

The State in the World Economy

The strong central government that was necessary in the days of the entrepreneurial state is now a burden, a millstone. The state will remain a major player in our society, but it must now act as a catalyst and partner in economic and social development. It therefore must redefine its relationship with the business sector, in which companies that are more specialized are creating and managing value in a wider economic space and need to be more competitive and better strategists. It also must rediscover the meaning of community and the people who make it up, the meaning of civil society.

The Effects of Globalization on the Quebec Economy

The concept and the reality of a national economy are now things of the past; they have given way to the concept and, increasingly, the reality of a global economy. Denied its traditional means of intervention, such as tariffs and subsidies, the state must give up its customary role all the more quickly because of the disastrous state of public finances. The consequences, however, are not entirely negative. Like a person, the state often changes only under the pressure of unavoidable circumstances, and just as often, the change turns out to be beneficial—as if it were a law of nature that we surpass ourselves when we are forced to. In any event, everywhere in the world—in countries with a tradition of interventionism, such as France and Japan, as well as in countries with a more liberal economic tradition, such as the United States and Germany—the role of the state in trade and industry had grown, although in the case of the more economically liberal countries this was less obvious.

Quebec should not hesitate to adapt to the tide of change. In fact, it does not really have a choice. The economy of Quebec is undergoing massive restructuring. People who expected the end of the recession to bring back prosperity for all have been disappointed. Half—perhaps more—of the jobs lost have not come back in spite of improved economic conditions. Contrary to appearances, this represents an extraordinary opportunity for us to restructure our economy. The jobs lost will have to be created elsewhere, so we might as well create them in sectors with good prospects for the future. This is the only path to prosperity available to us, a path that requires major changes in labour market training in order to better prepare workers for the new industrial functions and, especially, for the knowledge-based economy.

A very large part of the Quebec economy has always depended on natural resources. There is nothing wrong with that, but it is no longer enough, and it makes Quebec vulnerable. Quebec is also vulnerable because of the importance of various traditional labour-intensive industries in which a score of countries are competing mercilessly. In both cases, fortunately, something can be done. Our traditional industries can be transformed into high-tech industries, but to do so, our companies will have to undertake further automation, especially in their factories. We will have to make significant efforts just to hold on to the favourable position we objectively occupy among the societies of the world and to maintain our standard of living. Things are particularly hard for Montreal, since its old industrial base is having great difficulty adapting to change at a time when it is necessary to turn towards today's leading sectors. But at the same time, more jobs related to the knowledge-based economy are being created in Montreal than anywhere else in Canada, which augurs well for the future.[7]

The triumphalist economic discourse from certain quarters leads to passivity and inaction. A more realistic economic discourse—admitting that Quebec's economy, if not in crisis, is at least not as powerful as that of the rest of Canada—has a better chance of mobilizing our energy and making us do what is necessary. In the period of internationalization when it was created, "Québec Inc." was able to help us, because, like internationalization itself, it was based on the existence of national economies. But that time is past. Quebec must now go beyond the stage of "Québec Inc." It must reject the corporatism of its elitist summits to which federal representatives are not even invited because "we have to decide things for ourselves." The federal government's weight and influence on the Quebec economy are decisive, just as its macro-economic responsibilities and its skills in technology, trade, and international development have proven to be. We have to become part of globalization, which knows no national borders or economies. The ramifications of this are many and complex.

A New Quebec State:
From the "Obelix State" to the "Asterix State"

With an enviable economic heritage, since it ranks among the industrialized societies with the highest standard of living in the world, Quebec must break with the type of state it has developed, which has become increasingly heavy over the years. Too many ministries have become dinosaurs, "states within a state" that, because of their vertical management, make bureaucratic decisions far removed from industrial and regional realities, about which they know little. What is more, programs and policies are too often conceived in a vacuum, with no coordination among ministries and no provision for their adjustment to particular circumstances. If the state, no longer able to fulfil the role of entrepreneur and engine of economic development, really wants to become a catalyst and partner in development, it must reduce its size and show greater flexibility, more intelligence, and a better sense of strategy. It must be less costly in order to free resources so that civil society and the private sector can take on entrepreneurial functions. In short, the "Obelix state," that muscular creature, must give way to the "Asterix state," a cerebral one.

Re-establishing the competitiveness of the state is an important objective for the years ahead. The state plays such a large role in Quebec that its economy has no chance of recovering its ability to compete unless the state regains its own competitiveness. We must therefore stay the course and continue to work to clean up public finances. But we have to go further. We must take the opportunity to reform the state. Until 1994, the Quebec government tended to avoid making budgetary choices, reducing all governmental activities equally without distinction. By doing so, it only reduced the *growth* in spending. The Parti Québécois government then proposed "a different way of governing." The budget for the first year was a referendum budget, and since then the government has avoided carrying out a practical and thorough review of all programs in the entire state apparatus. Typically, they chose the "Cartesian" approach of major reforms decided at the top and across-the-board cutbacks; the Rochon reform of health care is a good example of this.

And none of this takes into account the fact that the Quebec state costs us too much for what we get from it. For example, Quebec is among the societies whose governments invest the most in education. And we are justifiably proud of the fact that the entire population of Quebec has access to education. But with a school year of 180 days compared to 220 days in South Korea, a dropout rate of more than 35 percent before the end of high school, and a success rate of only 36 percent in CEGEP (community college), we are clearly not getting an acceptable return on our investment. And yet labour market training is essential for the development of an economy in which knowledge is fundamental.

Quebec also needs to make significant progress in the area of information management. It could do a lot to improve the quality of the information provided to business, particularly in the areas of technology and foreign markets. But there will be good results in this area only if the information is managed efficiently according to the clienteles concerned. And it would be to Quebec's benefit to do this in partnership with Ottawa, which already has the advantage of extensive worldwide networks in technology and science. Here, as elsewhere, there is no need to reinvent the wheel.

Government and business have to agree on trade practices that are consistent with their priorities for economic and industrial development. After the Team Canada missions, it was a good thing that Quebec decided to establish its own "Missions Québec." These trade missions in which government and business work hand in hand are definitely the way of the future for economic development. This is an area in which immigrants and members of cultural communities can play a decisive role in Quebec's economic development, because many of them maintain close links with other parts of the world.

Redefining Sovereignty: The Case of Education

Quebec would be well advised to adequately fulfil the basic functions it can exercise right now in areas where it has complete sovereignty. It would do well, for example, to devote the greatest possible resources to education. Like the other provincial governments, the government of Quebec has to understand that the exercise of sovereignty, even in the areas where it is enshrined in the constitution, must be rethought in terms of the new division of responsibilities that is needed between public and private sectors. The division of powers is being transformed not only by privatization, outsourcing, and deregulation, but also by the massive transfer of resources, responsibilities, and facilities from the public to the private sector. By better taking into account today's realities, the government can and must reinvent the role of the state and reach a new form of partnership with the private sector. It can and must do this in education, which is a key area for individual emancipation and collective identity as well as for competitiveness in the new world economy. The capacity of the state to bring together industrial, economic, and cultural functions at a high level in the technological hierarchy depends on this redefinition of the role of government.

True power in the new society comes increasingly from firms that are capable of high-quality initiatives and achievements *outside* public institutions. It comes from individuals and organizations in the community that show boldness and imagination in their efforts to improve life in society. But the political institutions have to keep pace with them. For example, in the next few years, the best pupils will be using computers to learn physics and chemistry, mathematics and music, French and English. However, our schools are too often under-equipped in computers, and our teachers, who have little familiarity with them, will need to be brought up to the level already reached by our excellent computer companies. Quebec has to be able to count on scientific institutions and entrepreneurs that will give the next generation real access to the best education possible. Since a remarkable pool of skills in computers and software design already exists in Montreal and elsewhere in Quebec, we will be able to offer the next generation true cutting-edge training, especially if we can also draw on what certain businesses are doing in education elsewhere in Canada. A few firms in "Canada's Silicon Valley," in the suburbs of Ottawa and Hull, have developed very significant expertise in this sector.

With the progress in new information and communication technologies, provincial sovereignty in education is being challenged much more fundamentally by the market than by the federal government. But the political debate has been so monopolized by the traditional vertical pattern between Quebec and Ottawa that this horizontal aspect of the situation, which is much deeper and more serious, unfortunately goes unnoticed.[8]

Annual spending on education by the member countries of the OECD totals $1 trillion (US). A market like this cannot fail to attract the interest of business at the very time when various employers' groups are seeking ways to ensure a better match between education and the requirements of industry, to provide suitable preparation for telework, and to reduce the cost of in-house training.

In such a context, there is a danger that education will be narrowly regarded as a service provided for the economic world, since even the OECD favours a two-tiered education system in which the state would guarantee access to education for those who will never constitute a profitable market.[9] However, since lifelong learning cannot be based on the permanent presence of teachers, it will have to be provided by educational services firms. Thanks to the new information and communication technologies, there is now a global market in the training sector. And the new possibility of providing educational programs in other countries, without students or teachers having to travel, could very well have significant repercussions for education and training worldwide, including in Canada, where the jurisdictions of the provinces and Ottawa would count for little.

Using distance education, industrialists are attempting to create a vast network of private education outside the public systems, which would be reduced to providing basic education.[10] But since the awarding and recognition of diplomas are in the public domain and are strictly regulated, a system for the accreditation of skills would have to be set up. In Europe, a commission studying the recommendations of the European Round Table of Industrialists has already looked at how such a system would work.

Let us suppose that a young person has access to several commercial suppliers of education through the Internet, and thus, by paying for courses, acquires various skills. Throughout the student's self-directed learning, the education suppliers credit him or her for the learning acquired. The credits could be entered on disk in the student's computer, which would be connected to the suppliers' computers. During a job search, the student would connect by computer to a job offer site, which would probably be managed by an employers' group. The student would transmit his or her profile, which would then be evaluated by a computer program, and if the profile corresponded to that sought by an employer, the student would appear on the list of suitable candidates. The employers would thus manage their own training system without having to worry about control by governments or universities.

On February 29, 1996, the commission on the recommendations of the European Round Table of Industrialists called for tenders for the implementation of the second phase of this program, which is known as the Leonardo da Vinci program. In the background document distributed to bidders, the commission states that the goal of the operation is to ensure the recognition of skills through a flexible system of accreditation of learning units that would make it possible to provide individual attestations of knowledge and skills in the form of personal skills cards. These cards would become veritable passports to employment.[11]

On May 6, 1996, the ministers of education of the fifteen member countries of the European Union decided to encourage research on products and processes for distance education and training, including multimedia educational software.[12] The OECD intervened, recalling that the Annenberg/CPB Project in the United States was working with producers in Europe, Japan, and Australia to design various types of new courses for distance education. The students thus become clients; as for the institutions, they become competitors fighting for market share and they are encouraged to behave like businesses. The students have to pay in full or in part for their courses.[13]

Meanwhile, the European Round Table of Industrialists wanted to make sure that educational software would be effective not only for vocational education but also for basic elementary and secondary education, and therefore for the major markets in terms of economies of scale. Petrofina and IBM Belgium/Luxembourg have already launched a project called the School of Tomorrow. Could such a project ever be compatible with the school's social role?

The European Round Table of Industrialists further defined its positions in a 1997 report in which it stated that the European population must embark on a process of lifelong learning, stressing that there was no time to lose. It also made clear that the appropriate use of information and communication technology in the educational process will require significant investments of financial and human resources but will generate commensurate benefits. The report concluded that it will be necessary for all learners to be equipped with the basic educational tools, just as in another time everyone acquired a television set.[14]

Some of the most astute observers in Quebec are also thinking about the school of tomorrow. For example, Jean Paré states that "the real question for the future of Quebec is education," and continues as follows:

> Should we choose a "system," with its organizational chart and its fiefdoms, or an education "market," an open, multiple structure capable of responding effectively to varied, changing clienteles? One whose scope is not necessarily local or national. Because work is now mobile. The challenge is to provide quantity, quality, and diversity at the same time.[15]

My intention in providing this brief overview of what is a genuine revolution in educational methods is simply to bring out the real issues in education, which are certainly much more crucial than the relations between Quebec and Ottawa in this area. We must not be Manichaean about this. The state will use public education primarily to confirm people's identity as citizens, and private industry will use it to make workers more productive. Education should help every individual become a whole, fully autonomous person. The state and the market should each offer what they do best to support the development of the person. It is the specific relationship between the state and the market that needs to be redefined.

Chapter XVI

Decentralization, not Provincialization

T HE QUEBEC STATE HAS TO CHANGE THE WAY IT RUNS THINGS. THIS is not so much a matter of less government as of *better* government. Top-down vertical management has to be replaced with horizontal management, lighter, more intelligent, better integrated, and more result-oriented. Quebec has to get away from solutions thought up by bureaucracies locked into across-the-board, standardized programs and technocratic approaches. The state built up in the 1960s by Quebec's first generation of university graduates has too often emphasized major reforms and the sterile intelligence of abstract solutions. It has to make a decisive shift to a pragmatic approach to problem solving.

The "Asterix state" of Quebec has to start working on three major areas: the relationship between the state and business, the role of the regions in Quebec in the context of a much-needed decentralization, and finally, the status of Montreal in Canada and in the world. The objective should be to free the energy and creativity of everyone everywhere in Quebec, because there is a great deal of potential there.

The Relationship between the State and Business

Businesses in the same sector have to learn to work together and develop cooperation, in order to exchange information and identify common needs. Occasionally, businesses may even choose collective ways of meeting certain of their needs in areas such as staff training, foreign market analysis, or research and development. When an industry has identified its needs and set its priorities, the state should coordinate its actions and tailor them to the industry. The days are over when business had to adjust as best it could to universal programs designed as if it were possible to regulate everything *a priori*. If government and industry are able to put such a policy into effect, they will be taking a big step towards horizontal management.

Many ministries, concerned more with protecting their power than sharing it, are still reluctant to embark on this path. However, we live in a world where power, like information, must be shared if we are to realize its potential. Former minister of industry Gérald Tremblay introduced the concept of industrial clusters in Quebec, a concept based on the theories of the American management expert Michael Porter, but in spite of its merits, it did not gain acceptance. Human Resources Development Canada, on the other hand, has helped establish twenty-three sectoral councils in which business, trade unions, and education and training institutions together plan the labour needs of the industry in the short, medium, and long term, and take appropriate measures. In general, these councils work very well.

The various industrial sectors also have to find ways to integrate Quebec industry into the North American and even the global economy. And government departments have to understand this reality, because all the industrial sectors in Quebec extend beyond the province's territory. This integration will involve the need not only for external markets for Quebec businesses but also for strategic alliances and partnerships in the areas of finance, technology, and production.

The aerospace sector, which is so important for the economy of Montreal, exists in Quebec, Ontario, and Alberta, and it is essential that all parties work together in this dynamic sector of the future. Similarly, the pharmaceutical sector exists in Quebec, Ontario, British Columbia, and Massachusetts. The situation is comparable for the urban transportation equipment industry, which is established mainly in Quebec and Ontario; companies in this industry have had tremendous success throughout the world as long as they have cooperated with each other. Quebec has a good start in this sector, with Bombardier and its Canadian partners UTDC and de Havilland as well as its companies in Ireland and Belgium.

A Broader Approach to Social Responsibility

In Canada, as elsewhere in the West, globalization has brought social policies to a crossroads. Where some see a threat to our social programs, I, on the contrary, see an incomparable opportunity to raise the issue of the social sphere again, and to formulate a response suited to the unprecedented circumstances in which we find ourselves today. Contrary to what too many people believe, deregulation and free trade do not lead inevitably to no-holds-barred capitalism. They can also lead to new kinds of action. The spirit of volunteerism, for example, finds expression not only in volunteer work but also in programs that promote a sense of social responsibility in business. We have to move beyond the era of social policy to adopt a broader approach to social responsibility. What does this involve?

If it is true, as is generally felt in Canada, that the state and the private sector are two essential pillars of economic and social development, then a third pillar is increasingly emerging. The government-market equation—more government, less market, or less government, more market—must be expanded to include the community, which involves the individual and the voluntary sector. At least the post-deficit period we are now entering allows us to reconsider our approach in the light of one essential fact that has become obvious: our country's economic and social development can no longer be the prerogative of the state. Nor can it even continue to be based on a partnership of the state and the private sector alone. New forms of social solidarity need to be established among Canadians. This is very fortunate, because new forms of solidarity have become necessary in order for us to adapt to the new society that is in the process of being built. The convergence of the economic and social spheres necessitates a renewal of solidarity. Quebec is particularly well placed to develop a policy on social responsibility because it possesses the principal conditions for it: a dynamic and expanding voluntary sector; a desire for involvement on the part of the citizens themselves, for whom passivity and blind trust in the state are things of the past; and finally, businesses that are taking more and more initiative in the area of social responsibility.

The state can no longer take sole responsibility for the needs of its citizens, even their urgent needs. It must therefore make its action in the area of social responsibility part of a much broader network of initiatives from various sources and of various kinds. In Europe, and more and more in North America, businesses are increasingly taking part in this movement. And for good reason, because the economic value of social responsibility is now being recognized. Businesses know that in order to differentiate themselves from their competitors they must increasingly rely on intangible factors, of which social responsibility is a prime example. This helps them both motivate their employees and gain market share. What is involved here is much more than corporate image; it is a company's real commitment to certain values, ignorance of which and, to an even greater extent, abuse of which are, for very serious reasons, no longer tolerated by Canadians. These values include not only respect for the environment but also, especially, respect for people, including the most disadvantaged, whether they are disadvantaged because they are young or old or vulnerable as the result of illness, poverty, or some similar cause.

Regional Strategic Planning

Relationships between the state and business are still too often the exclusive preserve of the central administration. The regions will have to take charge of them and shape them in accordance with the local business reality—a bottom-up movement that is the opposite of Quebec's current top-down approach. The region as a unique space has yet to be invented in Quebec. And it is urgent that this be done, because the region will soon become the main arena of a new synthesis of private and public, the place where the relationship between the economic and political spheres will be redefined. Today it is economic regions, not nation-states, that determine world development.[1]

Throughout the world, globalization is accompanied by regionalization and by subsidiarity, a practice and a principle involving the transfer of powers and responsibilities to the level closest to the citizen in order to minimize the cost of identifying needs and to cut transaction costs. In Quebec, up to now, relations between the central government and the regions have been primarily, if not exclusively, on a sectoral basis, generally involving central ministries and specific clienteles of individual citizens (such as farmers and entrepreneurs) or corporate citizens (such as municipalities). Such methods of operation inevitably result in a lack of coordination and a dilution of the effect of any actions. This is why I proposed, a few years ago, that corporatist socio-economic summits be replaced by rigorous regional strategic planning.* The socio-economic summits led to overly polite relationships and insufficient coordination among the regional players. Long lists of desirable measures were drawn up without any priorities being established and with no strategic orientation. The result was a useless scattering of public funds, something that has now, in any event, become impossible because of the precarious state of public finances.

It is not enough to spend in the regions; what is required is investment. The Bourassa government made substantial progress towards regional strategic planning. The aim of such planning is precisely to eliminate partisan politics from regional development by forcing the players to make choices according to objective criteria based on an assessment of regional

---

* I described this approach to the members of the Association des commissaires industriels du Québec (ACIQ) in 1989 at their conference at Lake Magog, and it was very well received. The Bourassa government then asked my team of consultants at Samson Bélair Deloitte and Touche to elaborate on the concept and write a regional strategic planning guide. I would like to thank my two associates in this successful project, my colleague Alain Trépanier and my client Jocelyn Jacques, secretary for the regions of the Executive Council of the Quebec government. This contribution was a fundamental element of the Picotte reform. The first application was in the form of a pilot project carried out in the Lower St. Lawrence region.

strengths and weaknesses and an analysis of the environment. The region can thus invest in its strengths and disinvest in areas where it is weak, which are often the areas in which its neighbours are strong. With each region investing in its strengths, all of them become stronger. The region thus defines its vocation, its mission; and, like industry, the state moves towards horizontal management if it tailors its actions to the needs of the client, in this case the region, rather than asking the client to adapt to standardized programs developed by provincial ministries. The regional actors, by working together to carry out this difficult exercise, put aside pointless parochial bickering to achieve solidarity at a higher level. In doing so, they are able to respond to the challenge of the new competition, which no longer comes from the neighbouring village but from South Korea, northern Italy, or Tennessee, and will soon—sooner than we might think—come from Budapest or Monterrey, Mexico.

Inexorably, the logic of politics and administration will finally be replaced by an economic logic. If the Bélanger-Campeau Commission showed one thing, it was that the regions are unhappier in Quebec today than Quebec is in Canada. This change is therefore essential. When and only when it occurs can regional businesses be expected to make an effective contribution, which will allow the regions to take control of their situation and play the role they should in the Quebec economy. If they are carried out well, these exercises in regional planning could lead eventually to the allocation of larger regional budgets. And since we cannot talk about budgets without talking about accountability, this will lead to innovations in regional democracy. Decentralization should lead to true autonomy. If the regions are properly understood and adequately supported, solidarity will develop between them and Montreal, which plays a crucial and irreplaceable role.

Montreal as a North American City

In this new configuration, Montreal will finally be able to focus its efforts on the special place it can occupy at the top of the technological hierarchy in the new economic order. Montreal cannot and does not have to content itself with its status as the metropolis of Quebec. It must once again become a great city of North America. It needs to be said long and loud that Montreal is a region unlike any other.

The more than 40 percent of Quebeckers of all backgrounds who are Montrealers must be regarded as an important asset that contributes to the personality and vitality of Montreal, and not as an anomaly in a Quebec that some people would prefer to be homogeneous. Quebec City must respect and value Montreal's "difference," perhaps by recruiting more civil servants from communities other than the francophone community, in order to better understand the situation.

The integration of recent immigrants and those who have been here much longer must respect the Canadian tradition of recognizing the value of different cultures and not aim for assimilation in the American style. The linguistic currents that meet in Montreal make it a truly international city: a city where it is possible in a few days to produce a Quebec-designed software program in fifty languages; a city where call centres function twenty-four hours a day with staff speaking dozens of languages to customers throughout North American and the whole world.* We should encourage our fellow citizens to preserve their transnational cultural and business networks and use them to benefit our economy.

Montreal is the international city par excellence because Montrealers have learned to deal with culture shock. There is no tendency towards homogenization in Montreal, nor towards American-style cosmopolitanism. This attitude is healthy, and it is a real advantage for adapting to globalization, to its migratory flows, and to the reception of semi-skilled workers from elsewhere, who nourish our economy, our society, and our cultural vitality.

If Quebec does not want to be condemned to the lowliest functions in the new world distribution of work and production, an industrial redeployment is required. Except with respect to the production of high-tech goods, Montreal can no longer and should no longer engage in manufacturing and assembly.

With two French and two English universities, two major schools (the École Polytechnique, a technical school, and the Hautes Études Commerciales, a business school), teaching hospitals, four hundred and fifty research centres, two hundred consulting engineering firms, a large number of private and public laboratories, and some eleven hundred companies in high-tech industries such as aeronautics, aerospace, telecommunications, pharmaceutical and medical products, computers and information technology, and biotechnology, Montreal possesses a pool of knowledge and researchers that

---

* A walk in the Park Extension neighbourhood, which is part of the Papineau–Saint-Denis riding I have the pleasure of representing in the Parliament of Canada, provides an excellent opportunity to see how much Montreal has been enriched by recent and older immigration. Another thing I enjoy is going up St. Lawrence Boulevard through the various areas of the neighbourhood populated by successive waves of immigrants. One can imagine them coming up from the port to settle among their compatriots who also discovered America here. These neighbourhoods are teeming with activity and offer an extraordinary variety of food products from culinary traditions of Asia, central Europe, and elsewhere. Two great ways to get your shopping done, on my honour as a member of Parliament.

places it on the leading edge among cities. Bilingual and multiethnic, Montreal can accommodate the foreign scientists we need to supplement our teams in order to design and develop new technologies and new products. Montreal will thus be less and less dependent on the pace of growth set by Toronto or Boston, as it unfortunately is when it limits itself to secondary functions in manufacturing and assembly. Montreal has to become more and more deeply involved in key sectors: information technology, terrestrial and space telecommunications, aeronautics and aerospace, biotechnology, micro-electronics, environmental industries, and others. The leaders in this technological shift are well known: Nortel Telecom, AES Data, Micom, Spar Aerospace, Marconi, CAE Electronics, Teleglobe, CGI, DMR, the Canadian Space Agency, Bombardier.

A high-tech service industry is also becoming increasingly important for an economy's competitiveness. Even manufacturers' competitiveness is increasingly dependent on access to the management services and information they need. Another key area for Montreal is the propulsive service industries: computers, engineering, management, finance, insurance, transportation, and communications are essential for the technological shift.

If Montreal rises to the challenge, a reorganization of the Quebec space will take place and there will be a renewal of solidarity between the metropolis of Quebec and the regions. The redistribution of activities and responsibilities will contribute to increased harmony and cooperation within Quebec and the improvement of its image and competitiveness outside Quebec. We will make progress in every respect.

After "Québec Inc."

Good strategic use of capital, which is increasingly hard to attract, is extremely important, if not essential, for the re-establishment, maintenance, and improvement of Quebec's competitiveness. The Caisse de dépôt et placement of the "post Québec Inc." period will have to re-examine its investment criteria and strategies. It must be sensitive to industrial and regional development and make its decisions according to economic and not political logic. Government intervention is no longer the name of the game; by internationalizing, the Caisse will simply be better able to carry out the second part of its mission, the economic development of Quebec, because investing shrewdly abroad will enable it to find partners for Quebec companies and interest potential investors in Quebec. While respecting NAFTA, it could, for example, invest in distribution networks covering certain parts of the United States that specialize in strategic products that could contribute to Quebec's development. It could also invest in networks that

are of interest to European exporters, which would finally give some substance to the old dream of making Quebec a hub between Europe and
North America.

Courage, clear-sightedness, and enlightened choices by the political and
economic leaders of the 1960s enabled Quebec to largely catch up with
Ontario and the rest of the continent. We have made considerable progress
in thirty years and have developed remarkable comparative advantages that
make it possible to view the future with optimism. Nevertheless, one thing
remains clear: the economic space and the political space of Quebec coincide less and less. "Québec Inc." is no longer enough. And above all, we live
in a very different world than that of the period from 1960 to 1985. The
world has changed in forty years, and it has been in upheaval in the past ten
years. This means we have to create a second Quiet Revolution. The first
one involved modernizing an antiquated society through the creation of
public institutions and the establishment of a modern state. The next revolution will involve opening Quebec up to the world and integrating it into
the huge global restructuring that has already begun. This revolution, which
will have to take into account the new economic and industrial geography
and the new world culture, will not catch us off guard. Quebec has what it
needs to succeed.

A Double Gamble

I am willing to bet that the elements of this second Quiet Revolution will
not depend primarily on constitutional renewal. Their implementation by
our political and economic leaders involves various administrative arrangements among the provinces and with the federal government, and requires
nothing more than a certain number of legislative measures. These initiatives are available to our leaders now if they take the trouble to look to
the future.

Facing a future that is filled with uncertainty, we cannot limit ourselves
to extrapolating from the patterns of today and the solutions of yesterday.
Only world-class government and business will enable us to have a society
that is itself world-class, one to which free, autonomous individuals contribute all they are capable of. Beyond the reappraisal of the first Quiet Revolution and the transition from the "Obelix state" to the "Asterix state," the
new Quiet Revolution must not be content with looking back to its modernity; it must be resolutely postmodern, allowing Quebec, this time, to lead
the march of history rather than follow it.

Chapter XVII

A Postmodern Quiet Revolution: The Strength of Quebec[1]

QUEBECKERS NOW NEED TO USE THEIR ENERGY AND THEIR INSTITU-
tions to strengthen civil society and help Quebec integrate into the
transnational networks, strategic alliances, and cultural coalitions that are
rapidly forming—all this so that free, autonomous individuals can fulfil
themselves and contribute all they are capable of. By embarking resolutely
on Quebec's integration into this new context, based on the transnational
horizontal model that is rising in importance rather than on the vertical
model of the nation-state that is rapidly becoming obsolete, Quebec society will demonstrate its maturity, its originality, and its distinct reality. All
the more so as the fragmentation of political spaces leads increasingly to the
weakening of the state and the domination of the market.

Quebec Society and the Transnational Economy

Although Quebec's entry into modernity came very late, it was finally so
successful that Quebeckers are now in a position to become one of the first
postmodern societies in the era of globalization. Such a political endeavour
could unify Quebeckers as a whole and provide a strong incentive for young
people who want to work to build the future. If it makes the right choices,
Quebec could even become a model for much of the world.

Richard Martineau recalls an idea expressed by Bernard-Henri Lévy:

> All border countries are rich lands, lands where people think more
> quickly than elsewhere, where their intelligence is extremely sharp,
> where cultures not only cohabit but jumble together. Communi-
> ties that doubt, fragile communities, communities that have to
> marshal themselves in order to exist are communities where the
> culture is more fertile than elsewhere.[2]

Martineau goes on to say that "Quebec is a fascinating laboratory" and that "our society is in a way a rough draft for the world of tomorrow . . . the trailer for the coming attraction."

I share Martineau's feeling. I would say that Quebeckers can make a unique, innovative contribution to the world to come, and in doing so influence the course of history. We are at a crossroads of the great trends of the future and our own destiny. Many, if not all, societies face similar challenges, but here in Quebec this issue has already been very well defined, and we are well advanced in our discussion of it. This gives us a great advantage. In this sense, the debate of the last thirty years around the idea of independence will not have been in vain. But only if we can leave it behind. So how can we get beyond it? What policies are required?

We can get beyond it by recognizing, first of all, that the world of states and the "multicentric" world obey increasingly contradictory principles: the "multicentric" world that is now taking root seeks constantly to free itself from the territorial framework that hampers its activity, which is based on transnational flows, whereas the world of states, which is coming to an end, functions on a territory that it makes the emblem of its identity and its sovereignty. Any political project that is really suited to the circumstances must take into account the juxtaposition of these two worlds we move in, and not only the world of states to which the current debate is limited, monopolized as it has been for thirty years by the question of political independence and vertical legal sovereignty.

I am proposing a second Quiet Revolution, one that frees itself from the first one, especially from its premises. The future of Quebeckers does not lie narrowly with the state and with Quebec government control of all powers. Our future does not lie there, both because government solutions are obsolete and have lost much of their influence in this period of porous borders and transnational flows, and because that state, which was created in the 1960s, must itself adapt to the needs of today and tomorrow. Quebeckers will be able to take advantage of the situation only if, at the outset, they accept one unavoidable fact: the transition to postmodern society will not be carried out by the state. There is no point beating around the bush—the next Quiet Revolution in Quebec should definitely not involve reinforcing the first one by strengthening the Quebec state even more.

Many commentators have observed that the creation of the new Quebec state led to the establishment of a new "clergy" during the 1960s. At the very least, I would say that this state was built on a rather unique foundation, one that drew on the Catholic culture of its society. Chantal Bouchard writes:

The Reformation, by profoundly changing the concept of the state and its role in social organization, is transforming the cultures that are articulated around the various forms of Protestantism, differentiating them from cultures that have remained Catholic. Even though Western societies have been substantially secularized during the twentieth century, they remain deeply marked in their political and social organization by the form of Christianity they practised for centuries.[3]

In the following chapters, I will look at the connection between forms of Christianity and economic development. There is also a connection between forms of Christianity and the political institutions a society establishes. As Chantal Bouchard shows, the state that arose from the Quiet Revolution reflects the Catholic form of Christianity practised in Quebec.

Relationships with the law, the state, the church, and God are profoundly different for Catholics and Protestants. For Catholics, the relationship with God is mediated by the Church, which is a structure of hierarchical powers. Temporal power, modelled on that of the Church, tends to be centralized and to manage the society through a large, highly differentiated bureaucracy. The Quebec state of the 1960s was clearly very much marked by this culture derived from the practice of Catholicism, which had until then been omnipresent in Quebec.

For Protestants, only the divine law is legitimate, and the relationship with God has to be direct, without any intermediary. Under these conditions,

instead of involving a relationship of individual constraint, power merges with knowledge of the law and the obligation that everyone obey it. Legitimate insofar as it is the expression of people's consciences, [the divine law] introduces self-regulation of civil society and of a limited state control into a culture and its practice of social control.[4]

The next Quiet Revolution must aim to allow all people to fulfil themselves, and it must also take into account the increased importance of transnational networks. Quebec will become a great postmodern society if Quebeckers are able to resist both the market's tendency to reduce them to the narrow roles of consumers and producers and the temptation to turn inward or withdraw into the community.

At the outset, I would like to make it clear that this new Quiet Revolution, like that of the 1960s, will bring profound changes for Quebec. Just as the society of 1960 broke courageously with its past, today's society will have to create a new fusion of general and particular interests and a new relationship between them. This new fusion will aim above all to eliminate exclusion as a social phenomenon; and this new relationship will aim to allow everyone in society to achieve fulfilment.

Women and the New Quiet Revolution

As Lise Bissonnette states, "Even the Quiet Revolution, which we thought we were part of, had conceived modernity without [women]."[5] It is clear to me that the contribution of women will be necessary and healthy for the creation of the new Quiet Revolution and for this new fusion and new relationship of general and particular interests. Already, women in Quebec, as elsewhere in the world, are at the heart of the change in values. One of the reasons for this is the realization that "the spotlight is moving, as we saw with the Bread and Roses march, towards poverty, where women are over-represented."[6]

The progress of women is very significant. In this regard, Quebec was for a long time, "under clerical influence, one of the most hostile places in North America to the advancement of women, denying them education, entry into the job market, and the right to vote or to exercise free speech."[7] The right to vote at the provincial level, let us remember, was granted to them only in 1940, by the government of Adélard Godbout, when they had already been voting for a long time at the federal level and their sisters in the other provinces had also been voting in provincial elections. The Quebec magazine *Forces*, in its issue devoted to Quebec women, showed how much progress has been made and provided ample proof of women's ability to contribute fully to the next Quiet Revolution.

The second Quiet Revolution will be postmodern if it allows individuals who belong to groups that are ready to do so to participate actively in the remaking of the world. As I have said, the experience of women, with their concern for combatting exclusion and poverty, has prepared them especially well to make a contribution that is not only important but essential to postmodern society. I also spoke of two other groups of people whose personal and collective experience has led them to play an essential role in the emergence of modern societies: young people and immigrants. Quebec can take pride in the energy and vigour of these groups as well.

The first Quiet Revolution promoted universal education for young people. These efforts have borne fruit, and the young people of Quebec are now well educated and skilled. Young people are also more advanced in the process of remaking their personal lives, given their more varied experience. They have lived in reconstituted, nuclear, or single-parent families, or, at

the very least, they have had friends who have lived in very different family situations. Moreover, with the job market having become more difficult,
they have the feeling of being close to exclusion. Their contribution to postmodern society is also indispensable.

Immigrants, like women and young people, were not actors and
thinkers in the first Quiet Revolution. With women and young people, they
too will have an important role to play in the success of the postmodern
Quiet Revolution. There are three reasons for this. First of all, their personal experience of changing societies has given them an intense experience
of remaking their own lives and thus the world. Secondly, they have a direct
knowledge of globalization and its migratory flows, since they have been
part of it. Finally, they have a special connection with the transnational networks that are of such great importance in this new context.

The First Nations also have a unique experience of adapting their culture to contemporary life in society. In addition, they have a head start in
terms of horizontal and transnational networks, since they have been
involved in them for a very long time. Indeed, most of them have ignored
our political borders and claimed transnational identities. Quebeckers have
the advantage of the presence in their society of native cultural and ethnic
communities of great richness and diversity, who will help them in this
postmodern period.

The groups in Quebec that are most advanced in the process of remaking their lives and thus remaking the world are therefore in a good position
to make the great leap towards postmodernism. One sign of things to come
is the fact that Quebeckers' contemporary heroes are undeniably "global"
figures: Céline Dion and Jacques Villeneuve. These two stars prove to Quebeckers that they can make a contribution on the world stage, that they have
their place in the sphere of influence, that "the others" are quite willing to
welcome them onto the front page of contemporary history, and that they
can even play important roles there. These are exceptions, some people say.
But they are not isolated cases. Thousands of Quebeckers are successfully
taking part in globalization and benefiting from it. From the Cirque du
Soleil, the Théâtre des Deux-Mondes, and director Robert Lepage, to Dr.
Jacques Genest in research and Laurent Beaudoin in industry, the examples
of organizations and individuals from Quebec who have distinguished
themselves throughout the world are too many to be counted.

For Tocqueville and Marx, although they came to contrary conclusions,
the social state took precedence over the political state. For both of them,
modern democracy is the egalitarian abstraction: in defining the human
being in terms of citizenship, it claims to provide a basis for the equality

that serves as a rule in the establishment of public sovereignty and, through the imagination, it extends this equality to all spheres of human activity. Marx concluded that the concrete individual was alienated, since democracy abstracts the citizen from the bourgeois as well as from the proletarian, and separates the communal aspect of the state from the conflictual individualism of the market. Globalization brings us back to this contradiction and, as I have said, we must not allow the fall of the Berlin Wall to lead to a "revenge of Marx." Quebec could become the first resolutely postmodern society. We therefore have to create the conditions that will encourage the development of civil society, of communities, and of individuals, because here as elsewhere, and perhaps more than elsewhere, they are in the throes of an identity crisis.

The Emergence of Regions in the World

Another characteristic of the new global system is the fact that it is economic regions and not necessarily nation-states that are determining world development. In this, a postmodern Quebec would have considerable advantages. Its unique character is an invaluable social and economic asset. There are many regions of the world that have distinguished themselves by their internal cohesion and their economic performance without having as many constitutional powers as Quebec does within the framework of Canadian federalism.

The *land* of Baden-Württemberg and the regions of Catalonia, Lombardy, and Rhône-Alpes, to mention only a few places, have established a cooperative vitality that makes them the "engines of Europe." These four regions in four different countries are partners in technological development, investment databases, and cooperation and exchange in culture, education, and higher learning. And the leaders of the *infranational* governments of these regions meet regularly. Under David Peterson, the Ontario government established cooperation with these four economic engines of Europe and the American Great Lakes states. Although this policy was very forward-looking, the New Democratic government that succeeded Peterson's government unfortunately maintained only some elements of it.

The Midwest, the old industrial heartland of the United States, battered by foreign competition in the early 1980s and left for dead in the early 1990s, is making a comeback. Its manufacturing economy in Ohio and Iowa has been transformed, its traditional base of car manufacturing replaced with new products that are in demand in the world. In this region, one manufacturing job out of six today depends on exports, particularly in the areas of semiconductors, financial services, and health care. Small high-tech, software, and biotechnology companies have sprouted around the various universities of the Midwest. And the private sector is not going through these profound changes alone. Every state in the region is fighting its hidebound bureaucracy and forming a government capable of responding. And yet these American states have much less sovereignty than Quebec. It all comes down to attitude.

Regions in unitary countries, such as Wales in Great Britain and the Osaka-Kobe industrial zone in Japan, are also joining transnational networks. Unlike Quebec, these regions do not have any legal sovereignty.

Why does Quebec, which already possesses a high degree of sovereignty, with substantial powers within the Canadian federal system, not follow a similar course? In the final analysis, beyond constitutional powers, what is required above all is a positive attitude to the economy, to postmodernity, and to tolerance, and a desire to take advantage of the current opportunities to prepare adequately for the future, rather than a mentality concerned with constitutional arrangements, legal "booty," and symbols of sovereignty.

Vertical Identity, or the Weakening of Sovereignty

The father of contemporary Europe, Jean Monnet,* wrote: "Sovereignty withers when it is frozen in the forms of the past. For it to live, it has to be transferred, as spheres of action open up, into a larger space where it merges with others destined for the same evolution. No sovereignty is lost in this transfer. On the contrary, all are strengthened."[8]

This has clearly been the experience of Quebeckers in the Canadian federation; they were simply ahead of their time in sharing their sovereignty with their neighbours in the nineteenth century. But today there is more to it. Whereas Monnet is talking about vertical sovereignty and the need to widen its sphere of action geographically, therefore territorially, our challenge now is to define sovereignty—that is, actual room to manoeuvre—horizontally. Sovereignty thus has to be redefined in a way that is less narrowly legalistic than what is proposed by the camp that calls itself sovereignist but that is really *indépendantiste*. Sovereignty, its capacity for action, would thus be espoused more responsibly, and Quebec would become a society that is even more distinct *in fact* than in the constitution. That, however, implies major changes in direction.

Opting for the independence of Quebec, on the other hand, would mean

---

* Jean-Pierre Derriennic says that in the school he attended as a child, Jean Monnet was beginning to replace Clemenceau as the exemplary citizen and there were more warnings against nationalism than exhortations to patriotism.[9]

using the methods of yesterday to solve the problems of tomorrow.* It would reduce Quebeckers' room to manoeuvre, their real sovereignty. By sanctioning the break-up of economic and political spaces, independence, far from strengthening Quebec's identity, would weaken it, and weaken it tragically, since it would, in fact, reduce it to a single dimension. Throughout the world, identities are becoming increasingly complex and allegiances are multiplying. The French, for example, are increasingly European, and each of their two identities reinforces the other. In the same way, the identity of Quebec is strengthened by the Canadian identity, especially because that Canadian identity is deeply rooted in the hearts and minds of Quebeckers, who have done so much to form it—to the great displeasure of the *indépendantiste* elites. More integrated into the North American context, the Canada-Quebec identity benefits many Quebec companies and groups and allows them to join transnational networks and world alliances. One has to lack any understanding of what is happening in the world today to imagine that the concentration of our identity in *québécitude* alone would strengthen it. On the contrary, that would exclude elements of richness and vitality, elements of the future. The strength of an identity, after all, comes more from its capacity to reflect the reality of a society than the constitutional status it establishes for itself. The facts are more important than their formal expression!

Horizontal Identity

Let us return for a moment to Céline Dion and Jacques Villeneuve. While refusing to take political positions, the two define themselves as both Quebeckers and Canadians, without the slightest problem. Céline Dion states, "I am a Quebecker and a Canadian." That is vertical identity. Then she quickly adds, "I am a singer." This is horizontal identity.**

The relationship between identity and otherness deserves some mention here. The definition of our identity often determines the nature of our relationships with others. If the other is perceived as a threat and arouses mistrust, then we naturally will prefer to be "among our own," where there is no risk of being questioned or challenged. But if, instead, the other becomes an

---

* This would amount to the same mistake as made by generals who prepare for the next war with their eyes fixed on the last one.

** However, Dion did not hesitate to say that the Order of Canada medal is more important to her than the necklace, with its famous 170-carat sapphire, that she wore at the Oscar ceremony to sing the song from the movie *Titanic*. With bad memories of the flood of criticism she received from very vocal *indépendantiste* circles after she expressed her disagreement with Quebec separation in Seville in 1992, she did not want to get into politics. Things have improved in spite of everything; this time she was able to express herself without incurring the wrath of the new clerics.[10]

opportunity for encounter and eventually "recognition," this allows us to deepen our own identity and enrich it with another perspective on the world and on life. Openness to others in trust and confidence thus becomes a condition of self-realization and fulfilment. Obviously, only this second attitude enables the individual to become a full person, a true subject. It is at the very heart of postmodernity and it has become fundamental in this era of migratory flows and porous borders. It is also the only attitude that enables the members of non-homogeneous societies—and what society is homogeneous today?—to live in respectful coexistence with others as one society.

It is therefore essential that Quebec show all the people throughout the world who are wondering about its future that, while it is geographically a border country, it does not intend to remain on the periphery. By becoming a resolutely postmodern society, Quebec should show that it intends to open the way for so many others who are seeking their path to the future.

Bertrand Badie maintains that we are currently witnessing in our societies a "regression from the idea of a contract towards the idea of bonds as natural and spontaneous, prescribed and innate. Politics is less and less the assertion of a desire to coexist with others, and more and more the organization of a community of the same."[11] As a political space of variable geometry, Canada, in my opinion, can help strengthen the political community in the midst of the crisis it is now facing, a crisis that has resulted from the economy and the market occupying such a huge place.

As essential as it is to reinvent politics and the political in order to prevent the dictatorship of the market and its laws in the economic and social spheres, it is equally necessary in order that the political function can begin again to do its work in the cultural sphere. If we accept that bonds be constructed in primal terms based on instinct rather than in political terms, the quest for accommodation, compromise, tolerance, and balance will be increasingly difficult. What will inevitably emerge will be ghettos, which Badie defines as "social spaces of homogeneity based on primal, monolithic, non-contractual, exclusive bonds."[12] It is no surprise, then, that Badie ends his article with the statement that this trend is leading to the "rebirth of intolerance and the refusal of otherness on the world stage."[13]

We Quebeckers, who have been politically astute in every way since the beginning of our history, will be capable of making a contribution to the strengthening and reinvention of politics. Quebec will not isolate itself on the periphery, on the northeastern borders of the North American continent. It will recreate itself as a postmodern society that is resolutely part of the dynamics of the world. It was Arnold Toynbee who wrote that at the end of history there would be two peoples left: the Chinese people, because of their enormous population, and the people of Quebec, because of their genius for survival.[14]

Chapter XVIII

The *Rouge* and the *Bleu*

THERE ARE TWO MAJOR POLITICAL CURRENTS IN QUEBEC, KNOWN as *bleu* and *rouge*, that have existed throughout our political history. In his book entitled *Regards sur le fédéralisme canadien*, Claude Ryan provides a very good description of these two opposing currents. The following passage is from his conclusion:

> For more than a century and a half—since the time of Louis-Joseph Papineau and Louis-Hippolyte LaFontaine—two profoundly different currents of thought have competed in Quebec society, one centred strongly on the protection and affirmation of Quebec values [the *bleu*], the other focusing more on openness to broader groups and values that we might share with different cultures [the *rouge*]. This opposition has been expressed in various ways through our history, but it has always been at the heart of our political struggles. Its most recent expression was certainly the fierce rivalry between René Lévesque and Pierre Elliott Trudeau. At one time or another, each camp hoped it might finally prevail over the other but, every time so far, the people of Quebec in their often baffling wisdom decided otherwise, preferring to be served by the two currents balancing and complementing each other than to draw on one of them only. Our federal system is certainly familiar with those sophisticated balancing games that the Quebec electorate is so good at in elections, and the conflicts they engender and sustain in terms of action often appear to go against the general interest. But it is not impossible that this very particular context is what gives political debates in Quebec their exceptional vitality.[1]

I know these two currents well, and they inspire equal respect in me, because some of my grandparents belonged to one and some to the other.

Along with my, so to speak, native understanding of these two sensibilities, I also inherited from my ancestors an enduring sense of the value of both of them. My own choice is unequivocal: I belong to the *rouge* current. But I recognize the value of the *bleu* current.

Pulled between the attraction of the unfettered global market and the temptation to turn inward, our society must obviously seek a moderate approach. It is a question of maintaining a balance while promoting vitality. The context of globalization represents such a major change that it may push these two sociopolitical currents to give the best of themselves to secure the future for Quebeckers, on condition that Quebeckers keep only the healthiest and most moderate elements of each. Such a combination would enable Quebec to become a postmodern society. It is clear, however, that the rouge current has to be dominant in the era of globalization and porous borders. The cost of withdrawal into the community would be exorbitant in a period of transnationality, when everything is moving more quickly.

Withdrawal into the Community

Turning inward has already cost us dearly. Our delayed entry into modernity, our delay in becoming interested in the economy— which is discussed in the next chapter—is largely due to the dominance of an extremely conservative elite that saw isolation as the source of salvation for French Canada. Certain quotations come to mind that are very revealing. Msgr. Ignace Bourget, the bishop of Montreal, went to France around 1840 and brought back large numbers of priests and nuns who had been unable to adjust to life after the Revolution. They were ultramontanes, determined to preserve here the values that had been lost there. It is during this time that people first began to talk of the conquest of Canada by the English rather than the ceding of Canada by France.[*] That was when the myth of the conquered people was born. It was this same Msgr. Bourget who stated that "the good Lord prefers smoke from censers to smoke from factories."[4]

Even today, there are people in my generation who say it is this attitude that enabled us to survive: the emphasis on the land and very large families. They do not seem to realize that in the years from 1870 to 1920 we

---

[*] Louis-Joseph Papineau himself protested against this reinterpretation of history.[2] Its promoters contributed to the development of the feeling of victimization that Lionel Groulx and then the Montreal School carried to the extreme. Before then, nobody in Quebec talked about conquest. On the contrary, there was a tradition that the famous quotation "Je me souviens," or "I remember," continued, "that, born under the lily, I grow under the rose"—our society, born French, developed under England. There is controversy about this; some claim that there are two separate slogans, both created by Eugène-Étienne Taché, the architect of the National Assembly in Quebec City, the first in 1883 and the second in 1908. This is the point of view expressed by Gaston Deschênes.[3]

lost a substantial part of our French-Canadian population to the factories of Massachusetts and New Hampshire, where they were quickly assimilated.

This suspicion of the economy, education, and progress was long sustained by the *bleu* current. For decades the *bleus* resisted the Liberals' calls and attempts to create a ministry of education in Quebec (Ontario has had one since the 1920s). During the 1939 electoral campaign, National Union candidate and solicitor general in Duplessis's first government Antoine Rivard argued: "We French Canadians have a long tradition of ignorance and poverty which we must preserve." Three years later, on January 20, 1942, Rivard went even further: "Education? Not too much! Our ancestors bequeathed us a heritage of poverty and ignorance, and it would be a betrayal to educate them."[5] Yet another accusation of betrayal levelled against the liberals! "Heaven is *bleu*, hell is *rouge*"—this is clearly an unfortunate constant in our history. Be that as it may, Rivard's comment shows a great deal of contempt for our people. The provincial premier at the time, Maurice Duplessis, "le cheuf," used to state triumphantly that "we have the best education system in the world." That accounts for the total inaction of his government in such a key sector all those years. This did not stop René Lévesque from rescuing Duplessis's statue from limbo in the basement of the Quebec National Assembly a year after the Parti Québécois took power in 1977. The things that are done to please supporters! But I am being facetious.)

I admit there is less obscurantism in the PQ, but to me, in the Union Nationale, "the union of the nation," and the Parti Québécois, "the party of Quebeckers," there is the same abuse, the same deception: the claim to speak in the name of all. Quebec is not a monolithic society either in its opinions or in its linguistic or ethnic make-up. I have always deplored the fact that Lévesque lost his battle against Gilles Grégoire of the Ralliement National, the co-founder of the PQ, over the name of the party; Lévesque favoured the name Sovereignty-Association Party. The very name Parti Québécois implies that people who do not share its policies or objectives are less fully Quebeckers.* This is blatant exclusion. In fact, the *indépendantiste* point of view is only one point of view in Quebec. It is not even the majority view. Why should anyone be allowed to monopolize the common name for all Quebeckers and the symbols that belong to all Quebeckers?

---

* I realized the extent of the harm this name can cause when a Montrealer whose linguistic background was not French told me in perfectly adequate French, "I am not Québécoise," meaning that she was going to vote for the Liberal Party, and thus for me, when I first ran for Parliament in March 1996. I had to explain to her that she was not a "Péquiste" but she *was* "Québécoise." She was not convinced. An expression that is monopolized and cheapened by a party tends to become partisan. This is sad for Quebeckers.

When the Bloc Québécois was founded in Ottawa, Lucien Bouchard demonstrated the same flagrant lack of respect for Quebeckers by using the same stratagem. The Péquistes and the Bloquistes would have shown a greater sense of democracy if they had called their organizations "indépendantiste" or "sovereignist." They could at least have called them "nationalist," which, although it does not indicate their prime objective of legal sovereignty for Quebec, would have had the virtue of describing the ideology they come closest to. But that would have weakened the insidious message intended to convince Quebeckers that they are being more faithful to their society if they support the sovereignists. This takes us back to the Union Nationale, "the union of the nation."

This deceptiveness gives rise to a public discourse that is distressing to democratic and liberal minds. The most recent example is the phrase "winning referendum," which came up in the last Quebec election campaign, in 1998. This expression, which is very typical of Bouchard's logic, implies that a referendum is a winning referendum only if the PQ wins. To the founder of the Bloc Québécois, now the leader of the Parti Québécois, Quebeckers win if the PQ wins. Pressured by questions regarding the necessity for a winning referendum, he added that Quebeckers could not say no to themselves a third time. But Quebeckers have never said no either to themselves or to Quebec. The majority of them have said no to the PQ option of independence or legal sovereignty. It shows a great deal of condescension towards Quebec democracy when the nationalist leaders accuse Quebeckers of saying no to themselves or to their society. Personally, as a Quebecker, I am offended by this rhetoric of exclusion. The preference for interdependence with other Canadians over independence is a perfectly respectable ideal, a legitimate choice and one, moreover, that is much more in step with contemporary history.

To me, a referendum is a winning referendum every time Quebeckers express themselves freely. The same is true for an election. For the parties, an election always means the victory of one and the defeat of the others. But at a higher level, democracy is always the winner in an election, whatever the outcome. Quebeckers, at least a majority of them, were by definition the winners of the last referendums. It is dishonest and contemptuous to say, as the PQ is all too quick to do, that Quebeckers have said no to themselves. As far as I am concerned, I have a passion for Quebec and I have too much consideration for Quebeckers to think they have ever said no to themselves. Quebeckers are simply capable of more than what the sovereignists are proposing.

Another example of this distressing public discourse is Bouchard's saying at the very beginning of the election campaign that Jean Charest did not love Quebec. Do you have to be a Péquiste to love Quebec? Did Maurice Duplessis love Quebec more than Jean Lesage? Coming from the premier, such a statement is extremely regrettable since it encourages the exclusion of a great many of our fellow citizens and fosters parochialism.

A party should define itself through policies, orientations, an ideology, an ethic, and not an ethnic group. Above all, when it forms a government, it must not limit itself to reflecting only the views and interests of those who make up the majority of the population.

Consensus in Quebec

In Quebec, we like to talk a lot about consensus. This predilection for consensus is part of this same tendency to want to merge into a whole. "But there is a consensus on this in Quebec" is the sledgehammer argument used to put an end to any discussion. While corporatism or intimidation may sometimes have led to a certain consensus, the true measure of a democracy is not its capacity to establish consensus, but the way those who participate in the consensus treat those who do not agree with them.

As Tocqueville wrote, any majority has a tendency towards tyranny.[6] That is why I tend systematically to take the side of the minority or the individual. This is my conception of democracy, a liberal conception, but it is not necessarily the form of democracy that is gaining ground in the world.[7] Where my country and my society are concerned, I aspire to a higher level of democracy, a political system that, in addition to free and fair elections, is based on the rule of law, the separation of powers, and the protection of freedom of expression, assembly, religion, and property. These freedoms, which are part of liberal constitutionalism, are conceptually and historically distinct from democracy.

Canada and Singular and Plural Majorities

Majority rule is fundamental in democracy. But political leaders can seek to build majorities very differently. Here again, the *rouge* and *bleu* currents are very distinct. Some political parties try to build a majority that, for lack of a better term, I will call singular: they are interested in an existing majority in a given territory, and encourage it, even incite it, to assert itself and take the place that rightly belongs to it. Their discourse flatters members of the majority group and pushes them to become even more "themselves"—that is, to impose their majority on others. This is the case for the Reform Party, which is as well established in Alberta as the PQ is in Quebec outside of Montreal. The discourse they use to mobilize their members is more emotional and appeals more to passion. It more readily arouses fervour, if not fever.

Other political parties seek to build majorities that I will call plural: they try to bring together minorities to form a majority. Their discourse is not one of self-affirmation but of respect for others and common values beyond the differences that may exist. This is certainly a more demanding political endeavour, a more complex exercise. Here, the mobilizing discourse is inevitably more rational and appeals more to the intellect. To me, whose political concern in this era of globalization is our ability to live "equal and different"—to borrow the subtitle of Alain Touraine's book—a plural majority will always be preferable to a singular majority.

These two currents have deep roots in our history, and both are essential in a society like ours. Moreover, I believe that one of the most successful things about Canada is that it allows them to coexist. This country made it possible for both of my grandfathers to be happy. As a child in the 1950s, I appreciated the value of being able to be *bleu* in Quebec and *rouge* in Ottawa. Each of my grandfathers had the satisfaction of being in power somewhere.*

In my view, the *rouge* current now has to take precedence, especially since the *bleu* current has been monopolized for thirty years by the promotion of sovereignty, which would lead to the elimination of the sphere of action that Canada represents for actors of the *rouge* current. Thus, the only possibility the *indépendantistes* offer for liberals is the alternation of the two currents in Quebec alone. And that is where the shoe pinches! The question of independence divides Quebeckers on a strategic issue, and not a minor one. This issue, in fact, has created a break in the historical debate with respect to Canada, the debate between the two currents Claude Ryan described as "one focusing on the preservation and enrichment of our values in Quebec itself, the other focusing on the honest acceptance of the wager of participation in a larger economic and political entity."[8] Indeed, since the dividing line between the two currents is now drawn essentially according to their respective attitudes to the nation-state, it is no longer possible to reach a reasonable balance between the two for the benefit of Quebec. The sovereignty question divides Quebeckers as never before, and this has consequences that go far beyond the government of the next four years; what is at stake is the country itself, and with it, the political meeting place of Quebeckers for generations.

A divergence on an issue as strategic as that of independence cannot be

---

* I must admit, however, that my *rouge* grandfather suffered more from the *bleu* side as a *rouge* Quebecker than my *bleu* grandfather was subjected to by the *rouges* in Ottawa. They both liked "Uncle Louis" (St. Laurent), who was a regular on the Grande-Allée in Quebec City. This may be the origin of my involvement with the Liberals.

without consequences, since, as I have already stated, the very originality of Canada lies largely in its rejection of the traditional nation-state dominated by *one* language, *one* religion, and *one* culture. In contrast to the sovereignist project, the Canadian mosaic resulting from this rejection brings a guarantee of respect for ethnic minorities. In light of this, it is hardly surprising that Canada is *the* choice of Quebec's ethnic communities. The spirit of accommodation in this conception of Canada and the exhilarating challenge of multi-ethnicity offer ethnic minorities a "security" that the conventional nation-state is quite simply incapable of providing. Behind this choice by the ethnic minorities lies a terrible condemnation of the sovereignists. What do they have to say on this point?

A Unique Balance between Similarities and Differences

Quebec, according to the Parti Québécois, can become "normal" only if it takes the road to sovereignty, implying that a normal people always creates a nation-state and that Quebec has to become normal like others. In fact, other countries, in most cases, are not as good as Canada at managing the dilemma posed by citizens who want to live both *together* and *different*, that is, who are as anxious to express their common traits as their distinctive ones. By this yardstick, Canada is a success story on the world scale and a model that the world of the next millennium very much needs, given the way societies and cultures are evolving.

Let me make myself clear. I am absolutely not asserting that Quebeckers are less tolerant than other Canadians. On the contrary, Montreal seems to me to be the living proof of our capacity to coexist with differences of all kinds embodied in our fellow citizens of extremely diverse backgrounds, whether they are recent or less recent arrivals. And immigrants in the regions, though far fewer in numbers, usually say they have been very well received. I also believe that the best majorities are those that have also experienced being minorities. Quebeckers are very familiar with the two realities of being a majority and a minority. Quite simply, I am of the opinion that the balance achieved in this respect by Canada is an exception, and an exception in the best sense of the word: a rare situation based on a practically unprecedented balance between common values and respect for differences within limits compatible with shared values. A nation-state concerned with "normality" would almost inevitably create institutions that would break this delicate balance. All things considered, the already old model of the sovereign nation-state cannot meet the very new challenge of the unprecedented sociocultural mixing we are now seeing in the world.[9]

It is clear that the balance achieved by Quebec within Canada has prepared it extremely well for the transition to postmodernity, in which Quebec could excel. Moreover, this political project could rally the support of three quarters of Quebeckers, or at least of a very large and very diverse majority of them. We are a long way, here, from the debate on the validity of a 50-percent-plus-one vote—but there's nothing wrong with being ambitious.

Sovereignty would not just be a victory of the *bleu* current for *one* mandate. It would be its institutionalization in a *single* central power, exercised exclusively in Quebec without any possibility of a counterbalance in Ottawa. For the regions, which want more powers and responsibilities, it would be a Pyrrhic victory, because this power, which is hardly inclined towards decentralization, would be very unlikely to take into account the specific characteristics of each region. And it must be admitted that the situation of Montreal, a jewel among North American cities, requires a great deal of finesse and flexibility.

Decentralization Is Not Provincialization

Regularly, all across Quebec, people of all political stripes in the regions tell me that they prefer dealing with the federal administration to dealing with that of the province. The example of the two ministries of revenue is notorious. But the phenomenon is more generalized; people greatly appreciate the fact that the federal administration leaves much more decision-making power with its civil servants in the regions than the very centralized provincial administration in Quebec City does.

The area of labour market training is revealing in this respect. The regional office in Chicoutimi, for example, could commit amounts of up to $350,000 before having to consult Human Resources Development Canada in Hull. Before the agreement on labour market training, the provincial offices in the regions could make decisions only involving up to $5,000. This means that federal decisions were made much more in the regions, by civil servants who knew the local actors, whereas provincial decisions were made by a remote bureaucracy in Quebec City that perhaps did not know the region at all. It also means that, with the transfer from the federal level to the provincial, important decisions in such a key sector as manpower were taken out of the hands of the people of the region. And finally, it means that, for the regions, a transfer to the province does not necessarily involve decentralization; on the contrary, it can involve centralization.[10] Fortunately, with the transfer of responsibilities, budgets, and a thousand civil servants, Quebec has adopted part of the federal culture and modified its standards to introduce more flexibility into decision-making.

Furthermore, it is a fact that the characteristic personality of Quebec has been much better treated within Canada than that of Montreal has been within Quebec. It is also a fact that Canadian federalism has made many more exceptions for the benefit of Quebec, whose development has shown and continues to show their effects, than Quebec itself has made for the benefit of Montreal, whose distinctive character calls for custom-tailored measures. Didn't the PQ get elected in 1976 with the endlessly repeated slogan "Montreal: a region like the others"? I think the same could be said of every region of Quebec, whose political system has not reflected or accommodated their specific characteristics and differences. What blindness!

The sovereignists of course have the right to propose their view of things. However, it is important to stress that Canadian federalism has been able to create a balance between the *bleu* and *rouge* currents that really takes both into account. It has been able to preserve the common values so dear to Canadians and *at the same time* to respect the characteristic traits of Quebec. It has been able to allow for the protection of the French language and *at the same time* the promotion of Quebec's culture, industry, and economy. Before elaborating on this last assertion, I would like to emphasize two crucial facts.

Postmodern Society and the Need for Protection

First of all, no matter what anyone says, the PQ's goal of sovereignty by definition entails destroying the balance between the *rouge* and *bleu* currents. Second, this would occur, in a most untimely way, at the very moment when globalization is creating a historic opportunity for reconciliation between these two approaches that are contradictory in so many ways, since one is primarily oriented towards protection and the other towards promotion. From a certain point of view, globalization is indeed favourable to the reconciliation of these two concerns, since it would allow Quebec simultaneously to affirm its personality and maintain its openness to progress in all forms—in other words, to become one of the first postmodern societies, a society capable of providing for both its protection and its promotion, because it knows that the former is not possible without the latter.

Quebeckers have been able to handle their need for protection in an extraordinary way in the context of Canada. Through Bill 101, for example, the government of Quebec explicitly protects the French language. And, contrary to prejudices that are too often accepted uncritically, the much-talked-about judgment of the Supreme Court of Canada does not weaken the impact of this law where it really counts; rather, it eliminates some of the difficulties, making it acceptable on the international level and thus clearing it at the UN, UNESCO, and many other world organizations concerned about human rights.

In addition to the legal protection of French, Quebeckers have benefited and continue to benefit from the geo-demographic protection afforded by buffer zones of French-speaking communities located along the Canadian borders of Quebec, both on the New Brunswick side in Acadia and on the Ontario side along the Ottawa Valley and in northern Ontario. The difference between the fate of the francophones who emigrated to the United States at the beginning of the century to work in the factories of New England and of those who remained in Canada speaks for itself. It took only one or two generations for those in the United States to lose their French language completely. In contrast, Canada has shown a real ability to protect French in the North American context. In spite of a certain amount of resistance, Quebeckers have been able to preserve their identity when they went elsewhere in Canada. Not to mention the wonderful, fertile blossoming of the French fact in Quebec—that is, within the boundaries of Canada, which, far from preventing Quebeckers from protecting themselves if they feel the need, has given them indispensable support in the promotion of Quebec.

Postmodern Society and the Need for Promotion

From the very outset, ever since it rejected the plans for assimilation that had been concocted by certain people, Canada has promoted Quebec. It is marvellous that French is protected. And the fact that Quebec culture as a whole receives ongoing support and is actively promoted is certainly important as well. Many federal institutions have effectively carried out this mission: the CBC, the National Film Board, Telefilm Canada, the Canada Council, and the Department of Foreign Affairs, whose grants have made it possible for so many Quebeckers to travel the world to study and further their knowledge or to perform and express themselves. As everyone acknowledges, many of these institutions that have been essential to the development of Quebec's francophone culture were established by Canadians, including many Quebeckers, at a time when the *bleu* current, dominated by Duplessis, was anti-intellectual and scorned culture; they provided essential oxygen when the air was thin. At that critical time, the effects of which are still felt today, federalism played an invaluable role in Quebec's cultural development.

The promotion of Quebeckers' interests by the Canadian government does not end with the cultural sphere. Canada has established various networks throughout the world, such as those that provide assistance to business. Canada also takes part in the activities of many organizations and associations, formal and informal, and these links benefit Quebeckers as they do all Canadians. The recent experiences of the Team Canada trade missions are irrefutable illustrations of this; one need only think of the economic benefits of these trips to appreciate their value.

Having always recognized the double need for protection and for promotion of Quebeckers' interests, I am continually surprised that the public discourse in Quebec, which is well reflected in the questions asked in polls, is very much more interested in the need for protection than the need for promotion of our interests. "Who can best defend Quebeckers' interests?" politicians and pollsters constantly ask. The question itself suggests that we are under attack; defence implies aggression. Why should we be surprised, then, when the strength of the *bleu* current is systematically overestimated in polls? Of course, when a question about defence is asked, it appeals to the mythology of victimization, or at least the fearful sensibility of a society that has been encouraged to turn inward and isolate itself by Msgr. Bourget's ultramontanes, Lionel Groulx, and the new clerics of narrow nationalism. The often fearful answer thus reflects this mistrustful sensibility. I am willing to bet that if prominent federalists and pollsters asked instead "Who can best promote Quebeckers' interests?" the *rouge* current would gain several points, because when we speak of promotion, we are appealing to confidence in our own capacities.

The Canadian Model

In the final analysis, the double need for protection and for promotion of Quebec has been magnificently served in Canada, which is increasingly being used as a model by other countries. Canadian federalism obviously needs to be modernized. It must, for example, grant and even encourage greater regional autonomy where it benefits everyone; this will legitimately preserve Quebec's ability to protect itself. But it must also strengthen cooperation from sea to sea, especially economic cooperation, which is indispensable for competitiveness.

If the two broad currents—the *rouge* and the *bleu*—are essential in a society like that of Quebec, Canadian federalism, with its two levels of government, is an exceptionally advantageous formula for their coexistence. These two tendencies both exist in Canada, and in Quebec they are extremely strong. Each can make a decisive contribution to community and individual development, and our country must be able to reflect them both. Better yet, these two tendencies should be harmonized in order that we may finally achieve all we know we are capable of. One way or another, everyone will benefit from this new situation. And above all, in this era of globalization, we will be making a contribution to the whole world, one that is our moral duty, given our comparative advantages.

Chapter XIX

Trust and Mistrust
in Quebec[1]

JUST AS QUEBEC ENTERED POLITICAL MODERNITY LATE, THE MODERN economy of Quebec was on the whole late in developing, even though British Montreal, which was mostly English and Scottish and therefore mainly Protestant, was Canada's first industrial base. However, since 1960, the francophones of Quebec have to a large extent been able to catch up with other groups in many regions of North America, including Ontario. We have already seen how much the Quiet Revolution contributed to this development, both by changing attitudes to the economy and by creating the tools of a modern state, such as the Caisse de dépôt et placement and Hydro-Québec.

The traditional factors of labour and capital do not explain Quebec's lag; it is explained, rather, by the absence, until then, of a collective attitude favourable to the economy. For generations, industry, business, and trade were treated with open contempt by Quebec's French-speaking elite, as they were in most Catholic societies, especially the ultramontane ones. As has often been pointed out, this elite encouraged the vast majority of our ancestors to live on the land and allowed just a few of them to enter the liberal professions or religious orders. Finance, industry, and trade were left to others, the British, and soon the Jews who were arriving from central Europe and who, denied access to French (Catholic) schools, joined the ranks of the English-speaking community. Steinberg in Montreal and Pollack in Quebec City are examples of the latter.

To go back to the relationship between trust and development, Quebec's historical record is clear: the collective attitude to the economy was for a long time imbued with mistrust. Its future, however, is less obvious: the two attitudes, trust and mistrust, are in real competition, although trust has definitely gained ground in the past forty years. Let us reconsider the past, however, before looking forward to the future.

For a long time, to return briefly to Fukuyama's analysis, Quebec was on the whole a low-trust society, that is, a society in which spontaneous groups outside the family were rare. With little aid from the state, family businesses were barely able to make a go of it. Under these conditions, how many of them survived to the second generation? Obviously, the founding entrepreneur, not wanting to extend the ownership outside the family, had only his own offspring to carry on his work. And since they did not always share his talent, energy, or interest, the business would often go under.

Let us also take a closer look at Peyrefitte's thesis. Rejecting Weber's theological arguments, Peyrefitte focuses on the Church's influence on attitudes and temporal matters. Economic development and the corresponding human advances, which remain the exception in the world, appeared initially in southern Europe, thus in that part of Europe that was to remain Catholic. From this we see that there is no fundamental incompatibility between Catholicism and economic development. But the fact remains that the rise of capitalism took place primarily in the societies of northern Europe, and then in the United States—that is, in Protestant societies. Why? Essentially because of the role allowed to individual initiative. With the Council of Trent, the Catholic Church responded to the attacks of the Lutheran and Calvinist Reformation by becoming rigid. It went on the defensive before launching its counter-attack.[2]

The Council of Trent Condemns Confidence

The Council of Trent, the first council following the great schism of Western Christianity in the fourteenth century, led to a hardening of many aspects of Catholic economic and social teaching, dogma, organization, and culture. Taboos against profit and usury, a rejection of innovation and modernity, the claim to a monopoly on truth, and a mistrust of personal freedom would be essential to the doctrine of Rome until Pope John XXIII and the Vatican II Council. Trying to dissociate itself from the Reformation, the Church at the time of the Council of Trent harshly condemned confidence, which was a central element of the doctrine of the new churches as well as a fundamental ingredient of economic development; the Church saw it as nothing but pride and presumption. Peyrefitte amuses himself by turning into positives such formulas of the council as its admonition against people who thought for themselves and acted with self-confidence rather than submitting to an external authority.[3]

The French Revolution in 1789 led to a further hardening on the part of the Church. Since the Revolution was carried out in the name of freedom,

Rome found renewed vigour in fighting this freedom. Since the Revolution pushed to the limit the demand of sovereignty for political power, Rome in response demanded the right for the Church to direct society spiritually. The Pope exercised his authority in a Church that became increasingly ultramontane, closing ranks around its leader. The nineteenth century was a time in which the Church experienced more defeats than victories. In its teaching it tried as much as possible to resist the conditions of the modern world.[4]

In 1888, a century after the French Revolution, Pope Leo XIII started to make some adjustments. He presented the Catholic Church as an enemy of liberalism but not of freedom, and, recalling the liberating mission of Jesus Christ, even as the guardian of freedom. Because the freedom of the modern liberals implied no necessity to obey a supreme and eternal law, it was seen as usurping the name of freedom for pure licence, and liberals were likened to Lucifer in their refusal to serve.[5]

Rerum novarum, in 1891, again denounced the evil of liberalism while rejecting the socialist remedy of collective ownership. In it, Leo XIII sought to firmly establish private, personal property as a "natural right,"[6] and deplored the demise of the old trade guilds, condemned usury,[*] and denounced the inhumanity of competition. These ills were regarded as arising from liberalism, that thirst for feverish and dangerous agitation. While extending the concept of natural right to immovable and movable property, Leo XIII professed a nostalgia for the rural economy, for the worker toiling on his land:

> The land, surely, that has been worked by the hand and the art of the tiller greatly changes in aspect. The wilderness is made fruitful; the barren field, fertile. But those things through which the soil has been improved so inhere in the soil and are so thoroughly intermingled with it, that they are for the most part quite inseparable from it.[**][7]

Historically, the clergy of Quebec, although it had no ideological competition from the merchant and administrative class, saw its mission as protecting its flocks from its enemies: beginning in 1763, from the Protestant

---

[*] The miser Séraphin Poudrier, the main character in Claude-Henri Grignon's novel *The Woman and the Miser*, which was broadcast on radio and then on Radio-Canada television, would have grown up at that time.

[**] This sounds just like Father Labelle, the deputy minister for colonization in Grignon's novel.

threat, which led it also to denounce confidence; then, following the French Revolution, from the liberal threat.[8] As we saw above, the clergy active in Quebec from 1840 on followed Msgr. Bourget, who belonged to the most severe element of the clergy with respect to values. They were particularly vigilant about applying the full doctrine of the Church and they were extremely rigid, Jansenist with respect to morals and ultramontane with respect to institutions. Bourget's campaign against the Institut Canadien and the liberals was part of that universal crusade.

Msgr. Bourget's Campaign against the *Rouges*

"In the nineteenth century, French-Canadian society, like that of Catholic Europe, experienced a revolt by liberal intellectuals against the rigorous orthodoxy of ultramontanism."[9] The liberals' goal was the separation of church and state. Ultramontanism—which literally means "what is beyond the mountains (the Alps)"—sought to impose doctrines and positions favourable to the Church of Rome, and, in Quebec as elsewhere, was marked by a reactionary spirit hostile to the modern world. The ultramontanes rejected the separation of church and state.

The *rouges* congregated around the Institut Canadien, encouraged by the liberal tide in Europe and especially the revolutions of 1848. They assembled a library, published several newspapers, and gained the support of a minority of French Canadians. Their main adversary, Msgr. Bourget, dreamed of making his episcopal city a little Rome, and his Church a well-organized and prestigious Canadian Church. The Church was often willing to use excommunication, as in the Guibord affair, when it refused to allow the burial of Joseph Guibord in the Catholic Côte-des-Neiges Cemetery because of his membership in the Institut Canadien. Msgr. Bourget was supported by the majority of French-Canadian political leaders and by Rome, at least until his excesses became so extreme that the Privy Council and even Rome called the ultramontanes to order.

However, the ultramontanes in 1875 won the abolition of the ministry of education, which had existed since the LaFontaine-Baldwin administration and in the first government of Quebec after Confederation in 1867. An education expert, and already superintendent of education, Premier Pierre-Joseph-Olivier Chauveau had at the beginning of his government created a ministry of education, with himself as minister.[10] It would take nearly a century before Quebec renounced its system of traditional values and set up another ministry of education.[11]

As we have seen, Quebec had a deep mistrust of industry, the economy, progress, and education. We can understand now why this mistrust was so

visceral; the liberals' confidence, which was so essential to social development, was perceived as misplaced pride, while freedom was perceived as
absurd licence. *Rerum novarum*, however, began to define the role of the
state, the owner, and the worker in human terms. There was a rapproche-
ment with the state, although the Church resisted a great deal at first, having seen the field of political decision-making considerably extended at its
expense. The encyclical made a great many concrete proposals on charitable institutions, associations for mutual aid, and Christian trade unions. We
see here the beginning of social thought on the organization of *this* world,
though there is still an invitation to give up worldly goods. Work is seen as
expiation, and wealth and poverty are both seen as trials, or as being unim-
portant, since it is how wealth is used that is considered to determine a person's merits for the next life, the only true one.[12] The first principle is that
man must accept his condition with patience. Historically, Quebec has
essentially been dominated by this current of thought, fostering mistrust
and condemning liberalism. As elsewhere, however, there was always some
room for confidence and liberal ideas.

In practice, the ethos of a given society—like the ethos of individuals—
is never pure. Confidence and mistrust fight for the head and heart, the
reflexes and reason of every one of us, and of every society. But confidence
and mistrust have in them a dynamic principle; in action, one wins out over
the other.[13] The question is which one is dominant.

A long-time Gaullist who can hardly be suspected of antipathy towards
francophone nationalisms, including Quebec nationalism, Peyrefitte
describes what he calls "the ethos of competitive confidence" as an engine
of prosperity; this is an ethos in which, according to his analysis, France is
relatively lacking. Let us remember that Fukuyama also classifies France
among low-trust countries. I believe that Peyrefitte is right in showing that
the factor of Protestantism, without the religious determinism Max Weber
attributed to it, is a simple intervening variable in the relationship between
attitudes and economic progress.[14]

Vatican II Reinstates Confidence

Catholic thought has come a long way in this regard, especially with Pope
Pius XI on the fortieth anniversary of *Rerum novarum*. Always seeking a
third way between what it saw as the errors of socialism and the false the-
ories of human freedom,[15] this thought continued its evolution with Pope
John XXIII, who with Vatican II began the internal reform of the Catholic
Church that the Council of Trent had not dared to undertake.

Vatican II led, among other things, to a tremendous rise in confidence.

In his encyclical *Mater et magistra* in 1961, John XXIII called for personal initiative and autonomy in economic matters.[16] Quebec went through a remarkably parallel development with the Quiet Revolution, which officially began with the election of Jean Lesage's Liberals in 1960. This encyclical marks, if not a break, at the very least a major evolution in the opening up of the Church to modernity and individual autonomy, especially in the economic sphere. John XXIII acknowledged the end of the Church's monopoly and recognized that the economy and society were now characterized by pluralism. Since Catholics could not by themselves shape a reality in keeping with their ideas, their goal was to put a human and Christian emphasis on modern civilization.[17]

The truly innovative formulation of the principle of subsidiarity, which was traditional in the Church, emphasized the autonomy of private initiative: "In accordance with the principle of subsidiary function, public authority must encourage and assist private enterprise, entrusting to it, wherever possible, the continuation of economic development."[18] The principle has shifted; it is no longer a matter of relegating minor affairs to a lower level, but of leaving at the lower level everything that is not indispensable at the higher level.[19]

The following is Peyrefitte's concluding paragraph on John XXIII's encyclical *Mater et magistra*:

> Autonomy, initiative, adaptation, and participation are the key concepts of an encyclical that also emphasizes "trust" and, even more, "mutual understanding" among economic partners in different sectors. This marks the end of doctrines calling for the inexorable restoration of an old social order. With John XXIII, the achievement of the human person in this world becomes the striving of the Catholic Church, which thus makes up its lag of more than four centuries behind the economic and social teaching of Calvin.[20]

Mater et magistra opened the way for Pope Paul VI, who stated that development was the new name for peace.[21] What a long way the Church had come to make such a statement!

The change made by John XXIII and confirmed by Paul VI came to its logical culmination in 1991 with Pope John Paul II's encyclical *Centesimus annus*, which marked the centenary of *Rerum novarum*.[22] The pope from the Eastern bloc of course repeats the condemnation of socialism—which should be understood here as meaning Marxism—whose error is seen as anthropological in nature in that it regards the individual as a mere element, a molecule in the social organism. And on the question of confidence, while John Paul II condemns liberal philosophy, he lays all the foundations for it. Peyrefitte attributes his condemnation to his respect for his predecessors. But, in fact, he rejects only the extreme version of liberalism, the "unbridled affirmation of self-interest."[23]

Private property is still defended, and the market and profit are now seen as having a positive role. More interesting still—fundamentally more interesting—John Paul II elaborates further on the theme of human labour:

> In our time, in particular, there exists another form of ownership which is becoming no less important than land: *the possession of know-how, technology and skill.* The wealth of the industrialized nations is based much more on this kind of ownership than on natural resources.[24]

With this, the mental factor is finally recognized. Not only is human labour more important than capital but, in that labour, the stress is on the capacity for knowledge, foresight, initiative, and entrepreneurship.

While he denounces the idolatry of the market, John Paul II limits himself to criticizing its excesses. More generally, he states that economic freedom is only one element of human freedom.[25] But he sees it as an essential element. Without free initiative, there is no economic development. And without economic development, there is no freedom. From the economic sphere to the spiritual sphere, there is a continuity of freedom, and the same dignity and the same necessity are recognized in economic freedom and spiritual freedom. The deep humanism of the Church has again come to the fore. Life takes precedence over dogma. The pope returns to its place of honour a remodelled principle of subsidiary function, which is another name for confidence and trust in personal, interpersonal, and contractual initiative, something the state limits itself to guaranteeing within legal and institutional frameworks, because this initiative alone gives meaning and value to human activity.

Even though Quebeckers have turned away from the Church since 1960, it would be illuminating to look more closely at the development of the Church's social and economic thought, which has marked us for so long. Whether or not it is coincidental, it is striking that the evolution of Quebec since the Quiet Revolution has gone in the same direction. However, what is important from the point of view of development is that the attitude of confidence and trust has become emphatically dominant.

The Quebec Question and the *Rouge* and *Bleu* Currents

Since Quebec and the rest of Canada are today among the most developed societies in the world, it is understandable that in recent years economic arguments have played a large role in the political debate we are engaged in. Much has been said about the public finances of an independent Quebec, the division of the federal debt, jobs related to trade with the rest of Canada, and the capacity of a sovereign Quebec to maintain the same social programs as Canada even though its gross domestic product is proportionally smaller than that of Canada. Perhaps because the sovereignist arguments on these points are rather precarious, Lucien Bouchard refused to engage in a debate on the results of the Le Hir studies. And perhaps because of the weakness of the sovereignist arguments on the anticipated deficit of a sovereign Quebec, *indépendantiste* political leaders have diverted attention from the remarkable work of one of the most eminent researchers at the Institut national de la recherche scientifique, Georges Mathews, whose sovereignist sympathies are no secret to anyone.[26]

In any event, during the last referendum, the debate veered over into another area, that of—surprisingly, after the fall of the Berlin Wall—class struggle as it was seen in Quebec in the 1960s. Not that it mattered much, because behind the war of numbers, it was not so much classes confronting each other as two extremely different attitudes to the economy: the traditional attitude, well rooted in our history, which is imbued with mistrust, and the more modern, more recent attitude that is full of confidence, which nonetheless has deep roots and is making considerable progress in Quebec. These two antagonistic attitudes to the economy are more and more clearly associated with the two sides of the referendum debate. At the very least, it is encouraging to see such consistency between people's political and economic orientations.

On the federalist side there is the *rouge* current, made up of those who want Quebec's solidarity to be directed towards the creation of wealth and the economic promotion of Quebec internationally. Merely by making this choice, proponents of this orientation are expressing an attitude to the economy that is marked by confidence and trust. This of course is the same attitude the *rouge* current showed in forthrightly accepting the wager that Canada represented for them. In the sovereignist camp, which represents the *bleu* current, we find mainly those who are concerned with the redistribution of wealth, without, however, being concerned with creating it. Here, mistrust of the economy prevails. Merely by making this choice, the sovereignist leaders are orienting Quebec's solidarity towards demands and protection, which indeed makes them true representatives of the *bleu* current.

All things considered, the federalist camp aims for prosperity, the creation of wealth, and openness to competition, whereas the sovereignist camp promotes the redistribution and protection of assets within a single state. In other words, the former wants to make the biggest possible pie, whereas the latter is concerned with having its rightful share of the pie. These are some of the new expressions of the traditional opposition between the *rouge* current and the *bleu* current. Whom should we believe in these circumstances? Laurent Beaudoin or Gérald Larose—Bombardier or the Confederation of National Trade Unions?

A Quebec of Trust or of Mistrust?

Quebec faces a crucial choice. It must resolutely choose the party of confidence and trust, the party of development and forthright acceptance of the wager of participation in the larger economic and political unit that is Canada. Social and economic growth go hand in hand, which implies that the economic and political spheres are connected. It is therefore impossible to consider a political choice of paramount importance as if it were devoid of economic consequences. In choosing Canada, Quebeckers are making two choices at the same time. They are choosing both a country and a particular attitude towards the economy.

The obvious relationship of confidence and trust to development offers an important lesson to Quebeckers, especially at the dawn of the twenty-first century, when they want to lay the foundations for their future growth. The question is not whether the state should be denied any role, but rather what form of state—federal or unitary—will best be able to stimulate, maintain, and orient the confidence and the economic initiatives that are most conducive to collective prosperity.

In a speech to the Montreal Chamber of Commerce in 1995, Laurent Beaudoin clearly showed, for anyone willing to take the trouble to understand, how much Bombardier, the company he heads, benefits from the Canadian economic unit. If we consider the size of the Canadian state and the size of the Quebec state—that is, the arena in which they exercise their respective sovereignties—we see that they are at the low end of the scale of states capable of supporting high-tech companies in the heavy transportation equipment industry, and even more so in the aeronautics sector. This is an undeniable reality for Bombardier and many other Quebec companies that are now competitive abroad, although the state is obviously not the only variable in the equation.

As we saw in chapter IV, Peyrefitte identifies an elective affinity between individual economic initiative and certain religious choices (which themselves determine the kind of state that develops). This observation is extremely pertinent to the current debate, especially when we consider that the Quebec state has replaced the Church in Quebec's collective attitude. As Professor Robert Melançon of the French department of the Université de Montréal said some time ago in *Le Devoir*, "The nationalists have taken over from the priests of the past." And he added, "Nationalist dogma has replaced religious dogma, with the same sterilizing effects on thought."*[27]

And that is not all. The religious affiliation that marked Quebec from its beginnings until well after Confederation continues to make itself felt in the fact that many Quebeckers are still more comfortable with public money than with private money. However, public money, like private money, comes essentially from individual productivity, which even the Catholic Church has recognized since John XXIII and John Paul II. No government today, with the possible exception of those of Brunei and a few Persian Gulf countries, makes enough "profit" to be able to replace taxation. With a public debt proportionally higher than that of any other Canadian province, higher taxes than anywhere else in Canada, and a gross domestic product 10 percent below the Canadian average, the Quebec state by itself does not have the means to exercise the solidarity desired by Quebeckers. It is all very nice to "have a heart," but Quebec must either organize itself so that private prosperity supports it through taxes, or else compromise the assets of future generations, which are already heavily mortgaged, by increasing debt. In the light of this information, is it not significant that the vast majority of PQ supporters are in the public, parapublic, trade union, and community sectors—that is, in activities involving the redistribution of wealth more than its creation?

During the referendum debate in 1995, opinions expressed by spokespersons for several large Quebec companies were attacked as the views of "arrogant privileged people . . . with the superiority complex of the jet set." Jacques Parizeau, the premier, spoke of those who "bite the hand that feeds them," of "billionaires who spit on us."[29] These outbursts are annoying reminders of the ideological rantings of the 1960s, if not of

---

* Anyone who doubts that there is still a close kinship between the two institutions, especially when the government is led by the Parti Québécois, should read about the state funeral of MNA Yves Blais. The whole PQ government and caucus as well as some six hundred other people came to pay their last respects, not to a work colleague but to a genuine friend, who is described as "a voice for Quebec." The account continues: "'I hope that in heaven, sovereignty has already been achieved,' cried the officiating priest, who was dressed for the occasion in a Quebec-blue shawl decorated with fleurs de lys. 'If not, you'll spend a good part of your eternity working for it.' A burst of energetic applause. The gathering delighted in this appeal to their nationalist feelings. 'You've gone to join those of your kind—like Doris Lussier, Gérald Godin, Pauline Julien, and Félix Leclerc. And we're sure that, together, you'll ask God to push this little people to achieve its ideal.'"[28]

the Council of Trent's condemnation of confidence, which it saw as nothing but pride and presumption. Once again, heavy rhetoric was used to avoid the basic arguments. However, many valid comments by our decision-makers provided food for thought. When people like Laurent Beaudoin, Marcel Dutil, and Guy Saint-Pierre say they need Canada to ensure the survival and growth of their companies, they are speaking, among other things, of the conditions that will foster a competitive attitude. This is far from inconsequential. Because the opposite attitude—that of disengagement, turning inward, constitutional haggling, and legalistic claims for debts the state no longer has the means to honour—has been overtaken by current economic realities and—to say the least—hardly belongs in the world of global markets.

Money and the "Ethnics"

Jacques Parizeau's deplorable remark on the night of the 1995 referendum also shows the consistency of the attitudes of the two currents. In attributing his party's failure to money and the "ethnics," and even blaming them for it, he showed the *bleu* current's traditional contempt for money, an old, very Jansenist and ultramontane reflex, as well as his mistrust of his fellow citizens of various backgrounds and his attitude of exclusion. Parizeau did not blame the very many French Canadians who did not support his cause, nor the English Canadians: "For them, it's 'normal.' They want to be part of the majority." He pointed a finger only at the "ethnics." Yet for them, as I have said, the choice of Canada and the Canadian mosaic may be eminently rational and more attractive than the "normal" choice of the nation-state promised by the *indépendantistes*. Indeed, they show good instincts by ardently defending Canada. They know from experience that a federal society like ours—because of the sheer diversity of the interests it must accommodate within it—is more conducive to the free development of their own values and simply to the growth of freedom.

One fact that is absolutely crucial is that among Quebeckers who have a positive attitude to the economy and want to orient Quebec's solidarity towards the creation of wealth, international promotion, and collective well-being, there is a very strong majority in favour of Canadian federalism. And over the last ten years, on a worldwide scale, everything has contributed to making precisely this attitude the source of prosperity, a prosperity without which—and this is another crucial fact—no worthwhile redistribution is possible.

Chapter XX

The Disadvantages of Legal Sovereignty[1]

SINCE WE FIND OURSELVES IN AN INTERNATIONAL ORDER—SOME would call it a global disorder—that is forced to deal with the juxtaposition of the new global perspective and the old international perspective, we ought to consider the pertinence of sovereignty in both cases, because these two worlds will coexist for a long time yet. We have seen that sovereignty would have no effect on Quebec's capacity to adapt to globalization and the transnational forces it releases, since the action occurs largely outside the state. Now I would like to assess the effect of sovereignty on Quebec's real room to manoeuvre in the international order, that order in which the state continues, and will continue for a long time, to play a paramount role.

The United Nations

Quebec society would be well advised to turn its energy and channel its nationalism towards the emerging world, with its transnational networks and its complex configuration of allegiances. As this world is becoming increasingly autonomous in relation to the state, since it puts the priority on direct relationships between individuals and groups, Quebec has no need for sovereignty in order to be part of it. Not only does Canada not prevent Quebec society from fully taking part in the emerging transnational world, but it enables it to play a role in traditional international affairs that would otherwise be inaccessible to it. Canada's international personality and its influence, so much greater than its population would justify, owe a great deal to Quebeckers, of course, and serve their interests very well too.

Obviously, independence would enable Quebec in the short or medium term to take part directly, rather than through the Canadian federal state, in the deliberations of the General Assembly of the United Nations. However, equality of nation-states is the rule at the UN, and Quebec would exercise only a very symbolic role. The resolutions of the General Assembly have no real impact unless they are adopted by the Security Council. Not counting the five permanent members, Canada will be the only Western country to sit on the Security Council for six terms; it will serve its sixth term in 1999–2000. Sweden and Finland have sat on the council only twice, Norway three times, Greece and Portugal only once. It is inconceivable that Quebec could do better than these countries, which have already been far outdone by Canada.

The G-7, the P-8, and Other Major Organizations

As Canadians, Quebeckers take part in the G-7, which today exercises considerable influence over the evolution of the world. Bringing together the leaders of the seven richest industrialized countries, the G-7 is a place of cooperation and coordination that has enormous influence on both the transnational world that is gaining strength and the international order it is gradually supplanting. As a group, the G-7 plays a true leadership role in the world, although—or perhaps even because—unlike the Security Council, it has no legal status.

An independent Quebec would never have the preferential access to the Great Powers that Quebec has through Canada. And it is worth mentioning that for twenty of the twenty-two years the G-7 has existed, Quebeckers have led the Canadian delegation to it. At the Halifax Summit in June 1995, Jean Chrétien was host to the heads of government, while André Ouellet was host to the foreign ministers and Paul Martin to the ministers of finance. Thus, three Quebeckers were the privileged partners and interlocutors of the representatives of Washington, Tokyo, Bonn, London, Paris, and Rome.

Independence would also mean Quebec's exclusion from the P-8, the G-7 plus Russia, which makes very serious political and strategic decisions. Similarly, Quebec would no longer belong to the Quadrilateral Commission, the forum for economic and trade consultation in which the United States, Japan, the European Union, and Canada discuss the most delicate and most important subjects *before* negotiating with some one hundred and ten member countries of the World Trade Organization (WTO).

Quebec also takes part in APEC, the Asia-Pacific Economic Cooperation Council, an organization that is crucial for our relations with many of the economies that today are experiencing the most remarkable growth; only as part of the Canadian federation does Quebec satisfy the geographical condition for membership in APEC. Among the growing industrial sectors in the Asia-Pacific region are many in which Quebec has major competitive advantages, such as telecommunications, transportation, energy, and development infrastructure. Independence would also mean Quebec's exclusion from the Team Canada trade missions and the loss of the resulting economic and trade advantages for Quebec companies. Canada's reputation and the strength that comes from bringing together the economic and political leaders of a major country—which is also an influential actor in many of the most exclusive centres of power—have contributed greatly to opening the doors to many markets and the successful negotiation of many business agreements.

Quebec therefore has no need for independence in order to participate in all these forums. Nor does it need it to belong to La Francophonie, since it already enjoys the status of a participating government, and thus was able to keep its opinion to itself regarding French nuclear tests so as not to displease its Gaullist allies—an indication of the real autonomy it has within Canadian federalism.

Canadian Diplomacy: Unique and Irreplaceable

For Quebec to choose independence would mean excluding itself from a great many decision-making forums and influential and prestigious strategic organizations. It would also mean giving up a first-class, highly competent, well regarded diplomatic corps, and losing embassies in almost every country in the world and consulates in many strategic regions. Quebeckers, with seven million citizens, will never have the means to maintain diplomatic representation on this scale. And this does not even take into account the additional costs required to establish a defence policy for a sovereign Quebec, nor the costs that would be involved in its eventual membership in NATO.

Quebec independence would force us to join the majority of countries, which at best are able to express their political, economic, and social interests and wishes to the world's leaders and decision-makers, including Canada. Austria, Australia, Norway, Sweden, and Switzerland have to go through Canada or another member of the G-7 or the other exclusive organizations to put forward their views. And their diplomats solicit meetings with ours in order to help their sovereign governments better understand future directions. Canada's exceptional reputation is certainly due to its contribution in two world wars and its role in United Nations peacekeeping forces, but it is maintained above all because dozens of countries in the world value Canada's role as an intermediary in international bodies.

As Quebeckers and as Canadians, we have a responsibility to maintain this role and continue this mission in the world, and it is also to our advantage; it represents a huge asset for all of us. Having access to privileged information and being able to rely on the good will of friendly countries has strategic value for our businesses and our cultural, political, and social institutions—in short, for our society as a whole. This is an advantage that Quebeckers should never give up if they really want to develop their society.

NAFTA: Washington Would Destroy "Québec Inc."

It is on our own North American continent that sovereignty would mean the greatest change for Quebec. Let us be frank; membership of a sovereign Quebec in the North American Free Trade Agreement (NAFTA) would be neither automatic nor easy. People who claim the opposite do not know what they are talking about or, worse—but this is a possibility that cannot be excluded—they are concealing what they know very well. In any event, statements on this subject by the undersecretary of state for trade in Washington, Bill Merkin, by the former U.S. ambassador in Ottawa, James Blanchard, and by Laura Tyson, an economic adviser to President Clinton, are very clear.

Quebec would be subject to the will of the United States Congress, where it would likely find itself at the mercy of bargaining and issues that had very little to do with what it was asking. Membership for Quebec would be extremely complex in the absence of a "supranational partnership" with Canada. And the negotiations—the political time—would be very long. We have already paid a high price to obtain the agreement with the United States. It would be necessary for Quebec to pay a second time to join again. Membership for Quebec would require, at the very least, a renegotiation of the original rules and conditions for the regulated trade in automobiles, textiles, and agricultural produce. Thousands of jobs would be at stake.

But there is much more. It is clear that the independence of Quebec would greatly reduce its room to manoeuvre within NAFTA, if and when it gained membership. Thus, paradoxically, sovereignty would be a direct threat to the Quebec model of economic development. But the Canadian economic union accommodates "Québec Inc." very well, and Quebeckers defend it in the federal context, where Quebec has a political weight that is often greater than its proportion of the population. Above all, this economic model, which is based on a special and sometimes very close relationship between the state, the business world, financial institutions, and the Caisse de dépôt et placement, is part of Canadian tradition. "Québec Inc." was built within the framework of the Canadian federation and is readily supported by political and economic leaders in the rest of Canada. One would hope that those who most value "Québec Inc." would not want to be responsible for hastening its demise!

But what would happen if Quebec had to renegotiate its membership in the North American Free Trade Agreement? It would find itself alone facing the United States, which has a strong aversion to this economic approach. The Americans would certainly not accept in the closeness of a free trade area what they denounce and fight against, in the case of Japan, on the multilateral level. What, then, would be the demands of the Americans?

The Provincial Status of Quebec: Protection within NAFTA

In the best-case scenario, Quebec would be asked to sign the current NAFTA agreement, but we would be deluding ourselves to think that this would preserve the status quo. In fact, since Quebec would go from the status of a provincial zone to that of a national state, and since certain provisions of the agreement apply to national institutions but not provincial institutions, these provisions would then apply to Quebec. For example, NAFTA prohibits preferential government procurement policies in twenty-two departments and ten agencies of the *federal* government, but does not at all limit those of American states or Canadian *provinces*. Quebec independence would make Quebec public procurement, including purchasing by Hydro-Québec, *national* purchasing, which would then be subject to the restrictions of NAFTA. In the logic of negotiations, this could only be avoided by making costly concessions elsewhere.

As a worthy successor to the Free Trade Agreement with the United States (FTA), NAFTA is primarily an exercise in the economic disarmament of the *federal* governments. This explains why the provinces kept most of their powers of economic intervention. For example, chapter 14 of NAFTA exempts American residents from restrictions on foreign ownership of financial institutions under *federal* jurisdiction but does not give them the same privileges for institutions under *provincial* jurisdiction. If Quebec became a country, it could no longer protect its financial institutions against possible takeover by Americans.

There is another strategic element the Americans would have their eye on: the special relationship between financial institutions and business. Strictly applied in a Quebec that had become a national state, chapter 14 would have serious consequences in many sectors. This would especially be the case regarding the close links between the financial sector—including the Mouvement Desjardins and the Caisse de dépôt et placement, which are regulated by *provincial* and not *federal* laws—and the commercial and industrial sectors, which are the core of Quebec's industrial strategy. Quebec's provincial status has thus protected its "distinct" model.

Its provincial status also protects Quebec in the World Trade

Organization, which allows regional development grants throughout Quebec because its average GDP is lower than that of Canada. If Quebec became independent and joined the WTO, only the regions of Quebec whose GDP was below the average Quebec GDP would be entitled to these grants. This would exclude large areas of Quebec.

Sovereignty versus Room to Manoeuvre

If Quebec became a sovereign country with a national state, the restrictions of NAFTA would destroy "Québec Inc.," which was built within Canadian federalism. Those who are nostalgic for the 1960s and the days of "Maîtres chez nous" (Masters in our own house) would do well to realize quickly that globalization of the economy has made the concept of sovereignty extremely relative, not to say anachronistic. By doing without a few of the symbols and attributes of the nation-state, which these days serve mostly to flatter the elites, Quebec can keep more room to manoeuvre for the benefit of all its citizens, including workers and the less affluent. Globalization of the economy leads to the creation of blocs, that is, to a high degree of continentalization. As neighbours of the United States, we have to define our sovereignty, or better, our room to manoeuvre, in the North American context.

Canadian federalism, far from curtailing Quebec's development, has proven to be an excellent framework for integration that is helping Quebec to better face the future. Let us be realistic. In the long run, whether in Canada, with the United States, or in the WTO, the Quebec model is threatened by the universal trend towards liberalization. Independence would dangerously hasten the demise of this model at a time when it can still contribute substantially to improving the structure of Quebec's economy.

Of all the provinces, it is Quebec that depends the most on the Canadian domestic market. The share of Quebec's exports that goes to the Canadian market is almost equal to the share that goes to the whole of the United States. In 1989, 27 percent of Quebec's manufacturing production found buyers in the other provinces. In comparison, Ontario exported only 17 percent of its production to the other provinces, and the Canadian average is 19 percent. If negotiations with the other Canadian provinces failed, Quebec would thus suffer more than they would. In the event of a break-up of the monetary union, a key element of any economic union, Quebec would find itself isolated, and it is essential for small- and medium-sized economies to have access to a large economic unit. Except for the formula of the unitary state, no form of political and economic union provides such strong guarantees as federalism.

Sovereignists have to be clear-minded enough to recognize that the partnership they are proposing, whatever its form, will still be light-years away from a true economic union that is capable of guaranteeing the free circulation of goods, services, people, and capital. During the last referendum campaign, Jacques Parizeau refused to make his partnership offer public, because the only way to move towards his stated objectives was precisely a kind of supranationality very much oriented towards federalism. And that is not what he wanted. Instead, he emphasized certain ambiguities that would provide him with circumstantial allies and allow him to sneak through in disguised form a legal sovereignty that Quebeckers do not want.

Sovereignty in Disguise

To achieve this sovereignty—which among other things would wipe out the promise Quebec holds in the context of Canada—the sovereignist camp plans negotiations with its Canadian "partner," which in the meantime it belligerently accuses of misleading Quebeckers and treating them with disrespect. At the same time, it tries to get Quebeckers to swallow the pill by promising they can keep the Canadian citizenship they cherish, the Canadian passport, which is one of the most highly regarded in the world, and Canadian currency. In short, having lost everything but its *symbolic meaning* and thus its power to motivate, the sovereignty that is being proposed would only reduce Quebeckers' possibilities and could make them the laughingstock of the world.

Disorder in North America

Legal sovereignty would inevitably reduce Quebec's room to manoeuvre in North America. Destabilized at its very core, Canada could eventually break up into three or four new countries, leading to disorder in North America, which would favour the diktats of the market at the expense of politics, which would be reduced to a servant of the economy. The new nation-state of Quebec would have to compete with these three or four new countries to get the political attention of Washington and the economic attention of investors in New York and elsewhere in the world. This would lead to strong downward pressure on Quebec's environmental standards, social legislation, and perhaps even linguistic arrangements. The new state, which would have exploited society's energy to conquer an illusory sovereignty, would have considerably increased the insecurity of the business world and it would be forced to accept some of the lowliest tasks in the new technological hierarchy.

Sovereignty would lead to the isolation of Quebec and deprive it of the intra-Canadian alliances it might make, depending on its interests, with Ontario, the West, or the Atlantic provinces. It would separate the political and economic spheres. But Quebeckers' strength has always been their proverbial ability to exploit their assets on the political and economic fronts at the same time. The very concept of "Québec Inc.," of which sovereignists are so proud, is the fruit of a skilful and original combination of politics and economics, the state and the market. And "Québec Inc."—this can never be repeated enough—has benefited enormously from the context, the market, and the possibilities for alliances that Canada offers. If many important aspects of "Québec Inc." survived the negotiations for the Free Trade Agreement with the United States, it is because the FTA imposed restrictions on the federal governments and not on the governments of the states or the provinces; this is equally true of NAFTA. If it became sovereign, these restrictions would be mercilessly applied to Quebec.

Long, Uncertain Negotiations

In choosing legal sovereignty, Quebeckers would be making a useless, difficult, and deceptive detour at a time when legal sovereignty is hardly more than a decoy, because the state is no longer a major player in development and the effectiveness of its traditional means is decreasing every day. Why invest so many years and so much energy and thought in long and difficult negotiations whose outcome would be very uncertain, negotiations that would be infinitely more complex than the current federal-provincial negotiations because of the scope of the issues and the question of legitimacy that would arise for the Canadian negotiators? Why go to such lengths to try to get from Ottawa the means that are already available to Quebeckers, our businesses, our interest groups, and our artists, since they belong to us too? Economic time is accelerating in this period when transnational networks are quickly being established. The time of political negotiations, on the contrary, is constantly getting longer, since more and more individuals and interest groups want to have a say. Independence would only accentuate the gap between these two time frames that are already so different.

It is true that the solution of the 1960s, that of a strong central state, allowed Quebec to make up the lag of two or three generations behind Ontario and the rest of North America that its political and religious elites had inflicted on it. It should not be forgotten, however, that it did so within the Canadian federation, but during the golden age of internationalization and decolonization following Bandung, thus at the height of the welfare state and the state in the United Nations. But that was forty years ago! Today, the sense of security sovereignty would bring would be illusory and would even constitute a serious danger. The sovereignty of the Quebec state—because that is what this is really about, since Quebec society and Quebeckers themselves are already sovereign—is the standard solution to the problems of a bygone day, a solution that is completely unsuited to the present era of globalization.

A "Normal" People

Modern, democratic peoples are searching for new models better suited to their reality and their needs. Conscious of the limitations of the nation-state, Europeans were the first, soon after the war of 1939–45, to take the supranational path. They first of all opted for integration on a functional basis: for coal and steel, they created the ECSC (European Coal and Steel Community); for atomic energy, they set up Euratom; and, to develop a real common market, they conceived and established the European Economic Community (EEC). Since then, the European Union of the Maastricht Treaty has boldly adopted federalist methods, objectives, and aims in order to further European integration and, especially, to eliminate the persistent democratic deficit in European Community institutions, those institutions that sovereignists persist in seeing as a model.

As a political model, the nation-state has had its day. Without excluding the territorial impulse, Quebec nationalism in the twenty-first century will have to show it is modern and assert itself economically, technologically, culturally, and financially. Quebec does not need the obsolete attribute of sovereignty, that creates so much disorder because of the fragmentation and exclusion it leads to.

Quebeckers have, here and now, the extraordinary opportunity to prove that a "normal" people chooses to express its originality, its determination, and its intelligence by redefining its priorities and its sovereignty in the light of the future rather than the past. Quebeckers must take advantage of that opportunity.

The concerns of Quebeckers today are not related to sovereignty, which in any case is poorly defined, stripped of its symbols, and devoid of any vision of society. What Quebeckers want is the greatest possible room to manoeuvre in order to reinvigorate Montreal, strengthen the regions, provide people with well-paying and meaningful employment, energize their language and their culture, and ensure a healthy environment for tomorrow. Let us not weaken Quebec again by trying to make it stronger.

Conclusion

W E ARE LUCKY TO BE LIVING IN A FASCINATING TIME WHEN humanity is on the verge of a major evolution that will change the world and change life: a genuine change of civilization. Young people are even more fortunate than their elders because, since this change will take place over several generations, they will have a greater influence on the world of tomorrow; at the very least, they will know more of the answers to all the questions we are asking today. And God knows we have a lot of questions! There are so many questions that I find it hard to understand people who speak and act with so much certainty. Doubt, which leads to insecurity for so many people, seems to me to be much wiser and basically much less threatening to the freedom of others.

I have a strong impression that we are living at a turning point where postmodernity could take a concrete form and usher in a new era. The time is ripe for it. Other border countries, such as Scotland, are also experimenting. But I believe Quebeckers have crucial choices and important decisions to make that will enable them to be the first to enter postmodernity with confidence. I would find it deeply regrettable if, instead, they chose to stop the parade and take the obsolete path of legal sovereignty.

Many are watching what is happening in Quebec. Every one of our individual and collective actions therefore has an impact on the world that is taking shape. To the historical grievances that have been endlessly rehashed to the point that they have become myths, the young people of Quebec are capable of countering a new, deeper, broader, more personal consciousness. They, along with women and members of minority groups and ethnic communities, will be capable of involving Quebec in large transnational networks while furthering their own experience. They will be able to reconcile the economy and culture, private life and public life, as never before.

Not only is this path compatible with the country of Canada, but it provides an incentive for this original country, this space of variable geometry in constant evolution, to continue to offer the world a model. Indeed, as a country that is first "political," Canada must more than ever affirm that submission only to the laws of the market and economic flows does not serve the interests of human beings. And that the pluralism that is integral to the personality, the very identity of the country, is better than turning inward. Canada is the site of an experiment that has been able to resist the fashions and truisms of the times. A pioneer in every way, it can show the rest of the world that interdependence is a higher moral value than independence. Even the strongest, most robust person knows that in the snows of the North cooperation is essential to survival. The Canadian contribution to globalization could be precisely to help put it at the service of humanity. This will demonstrate the proper place of political activity in providing the arbitration that is necessary for all life in society.

Globalization is a challenge to the established order. Many institutions, such as the state and then the market that arose in a suitable territory, have contributed to producing a level of economic development that is without parallel in the history of humanity. These institutions also made possible a remarkable growth in human freedom. But this modernity had its limits, particularly the fact that it was based too exclusively on reason.

The postmodernity that globalization is opening up for us should be an opportunity to recognize the person more completely. Its institutions should give rise to new progress for humanity, and not regression in terms of economic development, quality of life, and freedom. It should therefore maintain certain aspects of the order that arose with modernity, but give free rein to human beings' full creativity. Living in a time of great change always gives rise to insecurity. Yesterday's order fulfilled some of our aspirations, but disorder fulfils other aspirations, and it can spur us to new heights.

I would like to express my own enthusiasm for the future by sharing these beautiful words by Christian Bobin: "Holiness has little to do with perfection; it is its absolute opposite. Perfection is the spoiled little sister of death. Holiness is a powerful taste of this life as it is, a childlike capacity to find delight in what is without asking for anything else."[1] Besides, nowhere is it written that order must be the main feature of life. There is such a thing as the joy of life, which often gives rise to an abundance that disorients us and impels us to recreate an ordered world. In this sense, disorder is a source of irreplaceable energy, and this should be seen as an indisputably positive aspect of it. The same applies to doubt, which often generates discomfort, but which is an unequalled stimulus to curiosity, the desire to understand, and the will to act.

Disorder and doubt spur creativity.

Endnotes

Chapter I
History, Politics, and Freedom

[1] Adam Smith, *An Inquiry into the Nature and Causes of the Wealth of Nations*. This book is still a classic and I cannot recommend it too highly. Complete references for all publications cited as well as other works drawn on in this book may be found in the bibliography.

[2] Alain Peyrefitte, *La Société de confiance*; Francis Fukuyama, *Trust: The Social Virtues and the Creation of Prosperity*.

Chapter II
Upheavals and Global Disorder:
The Internal Contradictions of Triumphant Capitalism

[1] In this chapter and in chapters III and IV, I expand on the first two articles in my newspaper series "Le Québec dans un monde global" [Quebec in a global world], *La Presse*, September 26 and 27, 1995, p. B3.

[2] On these questions, which are essential to an understanding of my thesis, the curious reader may consult the following books: Alain Peyrefitte, *Du "miracle" en économie. Leçons au Collège de France* [On "Miracles" in the Economy: Lectures at the Collège de France]; the remarkable survey by Douglas C. North and Robert P. Thomas, *The Rise of the Western World*; and the monumental work by Immanuel Wallerstein, *Modern World System II: Mercantilism and the Consolidation of the European World Economy, 1600–1750*.

[3] Alain Peyrefitte, *Du "miracle" en économie. Leçons au Collège de France*, p. 44.

[4] The General Agreement on Tariffs and Trade, which recently became the World Trade Organization (WTO), was established in January 1948. It has organized many negotiations to reduce the barriers to trade among countries.

[5] World Trade Organization, *International Trade 1995: Trends and Statistics*, 1995, pp. 1–4.

[6] Immanuel Kant, *Perpetual Peace, a Philosophical Essay*, 1795.

Chapter III
The Divorce of State and Market

[1] Paul Hazard, *La Crise de la conscience européenne, 1680–1715*, p. vii. (Translators' note: Our translation.) Hazard provides an excellent account of this evolution that was in fact a revolution.

[2] Étienne Bonnot de Condillac, "Puissance," *Dictionnaire des synonymes*, p. 467. (Translators' note: Our translation.) See also Paul Foulquié, *Dictionnaire de la langue philosophique*, p. 595.

[3] Thomas J. Peters and Robert H. Waterman, Jr., *In Search of Excellence: Lessons from America's Best-Run Companies*.

[4] "The Fortune directory of the 500 largest U.S. industrial corporations," *Fortune*, vol. 111, no. 9, April 29, 1985, pp. 252–319.

[5] Compare "The Fortune directory of the 500 largest U.S. industrial corporations," *Fortune*, vol. 99, no. 9 (May 7, 1979), pp. 268–89, with "Fortune's service 500: The largest U.S. service corporations," *Fortune*, vol. 127, no. 11 (May 31, 1993), pp. 200–279.

[6] Ghislain Fortin, "La mondialisation de l'économie," *Relations*, no. 587, January-February 1993, pp. 9–12.

[7] Jessica T. Mathews, "Power shift," *Foreign Affairs*, vol. 76, no. 1, January-February 1997, p. 53. This article provides an extremely lucid analysis.

[8] Jacques Julliard, "Lionel Jospin ou l'exception française," *Le Débat*, no. 100, May-August 1998.

[9] James Rosenau, "Patterned chaos in global life: structure and process in the two worlds of world politics," *International Political Science Review*, vol. 9, no. 4 (October 1988), pp. 357–94. See also his *Turbulence in World Politics*.

[10] Bertrand Badie, *La Fin des territoires. Essai sur le désordre international et sur l'utilité sociale du respect*.

[11] Bertrand Badie and Marie-Claude Smouts, *Le Retournement du monde. Sociologie de la scène internationale*.

Chapter IV
Confidence and Development

[1] Bertrand Badie and Marie-Claude Smouts, pp. 199 and 201. (Translators' note: Our translation.)

[2] Jean-François Bayart, *The State in Africa: The Politics of the Belly* (London and New York: Longman, 1993).

[3] "Many estimates have been made of the total revenue accruing to the illicit drug industry—most range from US$300bn to US$500bn. However, a growing body of evidence suggests that the true figure lies somewhere around the US$400bn level. A US$400bn turnover would be equivalent to approximately 8 per cent of total international trade. In 1994 this figure would have been larger

than the international trade in iron and steel and motor vehicles and about the same size as the total international trade in textiles." United Nations, *World Drug Report*, p. 124. See also "Observatoire géopolitique des drogues" (Geopolitical Drug Watch), *The World Geopolitics of Drugs 1995–1996*. Annual report.

4 Alain Peyrefitte, *La Societé de confiance*.

5 *Ibid.*, p. 49 ff. Note that this is the subject of his previous book, *Du "miracle" en économie*.

6 Max Weber's classic, *The Protestant Ethic and the Spirit of Capitalism*, remains indisputably one of the most illuminating works on this subject.

7 Peyrefitte even speaks of a correlation with Olympic medals (*La Societé de confiance*, p. 52).

Chapter V

The State and the Conquest of State Allegiance

1 Readers who wish to know more about the place given to the individual by and in the state, historically, may consult the remarkable overview by Moses I. Finley, *Politics in the Ancient World*.

2 Much has been written on this question. However, there are some classic texts that have not been surpassed. *Leviathan* by Thomas Hobbes and *The Social Contract* by Jean-Jacques Rousseau are two of them.

3 Jean-Louis Levet and Jean-Claude Tourret, *La Révolution des pouvoirs. Les patriotismes économiques à l'épreuve de la mondialisation*, p. 125 ff.

4 Bertrand Badie and Marie-Claude Smouts, *Le Retournement du monde. Sociologie de la scène internationale*, p. 39. (Translators' note: Our translation.)

5 *Ibid.*, pp. 39–40. (Translators' note: Our translation.) See also Karl Deutsch, *Nationalism and Social Communication* and *Nationalism and Its Alternatives*, and Ernest Gellner, *Nation and Nationalism*.

6 Francis Fukuyama, *Trust: The Social Virtues and the Creation of Prosperity*.

7 Levet and Tourret, *La Révolution des pouvoirs*, p. 129. See also Alain Peyrefitte, *La Société de confiance; passim*.

8 Levet and Tourret, *La Révolution des pouvoirs*, p. 131.

9 This expression is from *Le Grand Espoir du XXe siècle*, by Jean Fourastié. (Translators' note: Our translation.)

10 And the awakening was brutal. See Philippe Bénéton, *Le Fléau du bien. Essai sur les politiques sociales occidentales (1960–1980)*.

11 Levet and Tourret, *La Révolution des pouvoirs*, p. 107.

12 *Ibid.*, p. 108.

Chapter VI
Identity Crisis and the Pain of Loss

[1] There is a great deal of information available on this issue. To my knowledge, the most recent analysis is that of Bruce Benson, "Crime control through private enterprise," *The Independent Review*, vol. 2 (Winter 1998), pp. 341–71, which maintains that already in 1983 the work force of private security services in the United States was more than double that of the public services, and that the ratio reached 2.5:1 in 1991, a year when a total of $52 billion (US) is estimated to have been spent on private security services, including the cost of the 1.3 million full-time employees in the industry.

[2] This social contract was first described by the philosopher Thomas Hobbes.

[3] Touraine, *Pourrons-nous vivre ensemble? Égaux et différents*, p. 19. (Translators' note: Our translation.) I am deeply indebted, particularly in this chapter and the next, to this book.

[4] Alain Touraine, *Pourrons-nous vivre ensemble?*, pp. 43–44. (Translators' note: Our translation.) In *The Gutenberg Galaxy*, Marshall McLuhan had already examined the influence of media technology on human life. His contribution to the subject remains unsurpassed to this day.

Chapter VII
The Subject — at the Centre of a New Aesthetic Experience

[1] Philip Resnick, *Twenty-First Century Democracy* (Montreal: McGill-Queen's University Press, 1997), p. 142.

[2] Of the many editions of Descartes's *Discourse on Method*, the one [in French] with an introduction and notes by Étienne Gilson is filled with useful information for the modern reader. Descartes's intellectual system is not immune to criticism. See, for example, Jean-François Revel's preface to the *Discours de la méthode* in his *Descartes inutile et incertain*.

[3] To write this section, I went back to the notes from my course on epistemology in the Department of Philosophy at the Université du Québec à Trois-Rivières with Professor Naud, of whom I have fond memories. These were largely inspired by Bernard Lonergan, *Insight: A Study of Human Understanding* (New York: Philosophical Library, 1957), pp. 181–89.

[4] Touraine, op. cit., p. 224.

[5] He even uses this expression as the subtitle of his book, *Voltaire's Bastards: The Dictatorship of Reason in the West*.

[6] Kant's *Critique of Judgment* contains analyses of the beautiful and the sublime that have never been surpassed.

[7] Here again I am referring to the course notes of Julien Naud, S.J.

[8] On this subject, Luigi Pirandello's play *Six Characters in Search of an Author* is worth reading.

⁹ This book was as much the inspiration for this chapter as *Pourrons-nous vivre ensemble? Égaux et différents*, by Alain Touraine, and Professor Julien Naud's course notes.

¹⁰ Francisco Alberoni, pp. 17, 71, 72.

¹¹ Touraine, p. 175.

¹² Rainer Maria Rilke, *Letters to a Young Poet*, translated by Stephen Mitchell (New York: Random House, 1984), letter three, pp. 25–26.

¹³ Alberoni, pp. 13–14.

¹⁴ *Ibid.*, p. 60.

¹⁵ Touraine, p. 175. (Translators' note: Our translation.)

¹⁶ Touraine, pp. 246–47. (Translators' note: Our translation.)

¹⁷ *Ibid.*

¹⁸ Raymond Boudon, "Critique de la bienveillance universelle ou De la nature de la rationalité axiologique," in Guy Laforest and Philippe de Lara (editors), *Charles Taylor et l'interprétation de l'identité moderne*, p. 285 ff.

Chapter VIII
Remaking the World: Politics, Ethics, and the Common Good

¹ See the section in chapter III entitled "The Emergence of a Global Civil Society."

² Bertrand Badie, "L'État-nation: un modèle en épuisement?" Serge Cordelier and Béatrice Didio (editors), *L'État du monde 1996. Annuaire économique et géopolitique mondial*, p. 74.

³ Alain Touraine, pp. 359–60.

4 Élisabeth and Robert Badinter point out in their Condorcet (1743–1794). Un intellectuel en politique that Condorcet was practically the only thinker of the time to support women's right to vote (see p. 333).

5 I have borrowed the essence of this argument from Alain Touraine, pp. 228–31.

6 *McGill Law Journal / Revue de droit de McGill*, no. 42, 1997, p. 91. See also Diana T. Meyers and Eva Feder Kittay (editors), *Women and Moral Theory*, and in particular the article by Mary Fainsod Katzenstein and David D. Laitin, "Politics, feminism, and the ethics of care," pp. 261–81.

7 The Church and the Modern World, Pastoral Constitution. [De Ecclesia in mundo huius temporis (Gaudium et Spes)].

8 Michael Novak, *Free Persons and the Common Good*.

⁹ I am indebted for these observations to Bertrand Badie and Marie-Claude Smouts, *Le Retournement du monde. Sociologie de la scène internationale*, especially pp. 215–16, 229, and 232.

[10] Known as absolute advantage, this principle and the associated trade benefits were well explained by Ricardo in his classic work, *The Principles of Political Economy and Taxation* (1817).

Chapter IX
The Country That Refused to Become a Nation-State

[1] Michel Tournier, *The Ogre*, translated by Barbara Bray (Baltimore: Johns Hopkins University Press, 1997).

[2] Yisrael Gutman and Michael Berenbaum, *Anatomy of the Auschwitz Death Camps*, pp. 250–51.

[3] François Bayrou, *Henri IV, le roi libre*, p. 380. (Translators' note: Our translation.)

[4] *Ibid.*, p. 432. (Translators' note: Our translation.)

[5] *Lord Durham's Report on the Affairs of British North America* (1839), edited by C. P. Lucas, 3 vols. (London: Oxford UP, 1912), v. 2, pp. 16, 292.

[6] John Ralston Saul, *Reflections of a Siamese Twin*, p. 65.

7 Claude Ryan used to like to tell this very Liberal and very Canadian anecdote when I was his executive assistant.

8 Lawrence Martin, *The Presidents and the Prime Ministers. Washington and Ottawa Face to Face: The Myth of Bilateral Bliss, 1867–1982*, pp. 139–40.

9 *In the Eye of the Eagle* (Toronto: HarperCollins, 1990), pp. 5, 278–79.

Chapter X
The Country of the Third Way, or the Passion for Balance

[1] This chapter is based largely on my speech to the National Women's Liberal Commission at the biennial convention of the Liberal Party of Canada in March 1998, and on a speech I made to senior officials in my department in Cornwall.

[2] René Lévesque, *An Option for Quebec*, Toronto/Montréal: McClelland and Stewart, 1968.

[3] Bernard Landry, "Quelle politique tue l'économie?" *La Presse*, July 4, 1998, p. B3. Landry attributes Quebec's economic lag to eight causes, eight "federal" decisions taken over the last hundred and twenty-five years. No decision taken in Quebec or Quebec City is mentioned.

[4] Saul, *Reflections of a Siamese Twin*, chapter 12.

[5] Saul, pp. 185–96.

[6] KPMG, "The Competitive Alternative: A Comparison of Business Costs in Canada and the United States."

[7] Alain Touraine, pp. 182–83.

[8] Will Hutton, *The State to Come* (London: Vintage, 1997), p. 62. This book is a

companion volume to another book by the same author, *The State We're In.*

[9] Hutton, p. 4.

[10] John Kenneth Galbraith, *The Culture of Contentment* (Boston: Houghton Mifflin, 1992).

[11] Lester Charles Thurow, *The Future of Capitalism: How Today's Economic Forces Shape Tomorrow's World*, chapter 13, pp. 242–78.

[12] Hutton, p. 107.

[13] Charles Taylor, *The Malaise of Modernity.*

[14] *Voltaire's Bastards*, by John Ralston Saul, is full of thought-provoking observations. I recommend it highly.

[15] *Rethinking Social Policy: Race, Poverty and the Underclass*, pp. 202–203.

Chapter XI
A Status Quo in Constant Evolution

[1] Stéphane Dion, *The Ethic of Federalism*, section 1, "The Necessary Cohabitation of Cultures," on the Internet: <http://www.pco-bcp.gc.ca/aia/ro/doc/spchst3096.htm>

[2] I am thinking, for example, of some of the arguments put forward by Maurice Séguin, the former holder of the Lionel Groulx Chair; see his *Histoire de deux nationalismes au Canada.*

[3] I have borrowed this idea from Jean-François Gaudreault-DesBiens, who quoted it in a brief presented on June 4, 1998, to the Commission des institutions de l'Assemblée nationale du Québec, *De la Déclaration de Calgary, de sa réception au Québec et de quelques pathologies du discours constitutionnel majoritaire dans notre société au caractère "unique."*

Chapter XII
One Constitution, Two Cultures, Four Myths

[1] Claude Ryan, *Regards sur le fédéralisme canadien*, p. 8. (Translators' note: Our translation.)

[2] See the section entitled "Is Canadian federalism really a gridlocked system that cannot be reformed?" in Stéphane Dion's speech, Federalism: A System in Evolution, on the Internet: <http://www.pco-bcp.gc.ca/aia/ro/doc/apex4_e.htm>

[3] Much could be said on this, but I do not want to pile up quotations from the two or three dozen works that illustrate my argument. Therefore I will just mention a few of the more recent ones. Serious authors in English Canada have for a long time been examining what was particular about French Canadians' membership in Confederation. A. I. Silver's *The French-Canadian Idea of Confederation, 1864–1900* expresses this extremely well, and an epilogue to the second edition emphasizes the topicality of the question. In the same vein, I would like to cite Jeremy Webber's *Reimagining Canada: Language, Culture, Community, and the Canadian Constitution*, Samuel V. LaSelva's *The Moral Foundation of Canadian Federalism*, and Kenneth McRoberts's *Misconceiving Canada: The Struggle for National Unity.*

Chapter XIII
Renewing the Canadian Social Union
and Canadian Federalism: A Twofold Project

[1] This text was first presented as a speech at a luncheon hosted by the Laval Chamber of Commerce in November 1997.

[2] Negotiations with Ontario are still taking place.

[3] Jean-Guy Genest, *Godbout*.

[4] *La Presse,*"Les normes nationales: une menace ou une opportutnité?" Claude Castonguay, September 3, 1997, p. B3.

[5] Interview with Pierre Maisonneuve, *Maisonneuve à l'écoute*, RDI network, May 26, 1998. (Translators' note: Our translation.)

Chapter XIV
Canada's International Personality

[1] Henry Kissinger makes this observation in his memoir *White House Years* (Boston: Little Brown, 1979).

[2] Frédéric Moulène, "L'essence du néolibéralisme," *Le Monde diplomatique*, June 1998, p. 2. (Translators' note: Our translation.)

[3] The following sections are based partly on *Canada 2005, Global Challenges and Opportunities 1997*, a publication of the government of Canada.

Chapter XV
A New Quiet Revolution:
From the "Obelix State" to the "Asterix State"

[1] This chapter is based on a talk I gave to the Montreal Chamber of Commerce at a lunch on November 10, 1992. Obélix and Astérix are two characters of a popular French comic book. "Astérix" tells the adventures of a Gaulish village resisting Caesar's Rome. The village's Druid prepares a magic potion giving villagers extraordinary physical strength to fight Roman invasion attempts. Obélix, as a child, fell in the potion and has therefore grown much taller and bigger than his fellow villagers. He retains his exeptional strength, which becomes available to others only in case of emergencies. Astérix is small, even smaller than most, but much smarter, and he plans and charts both attack and resistance strategies. Therefore the analogy.

[2] Yves Frenette, *Brève Histoire des Canadiens français*, p. 160. (Translators' note: Our translation.)

[3] Yves Frenette states that the number of vocations dropped dramatically in a relatively short period of time: from some two thousand priests ordained in Quebec in 1947, the number fell to eighty in 1970. In addition, priests, monks, and nuns by the hundreds returned to secular life. *Ibid.*, p. 165.

[4] *Ibid.*, p. 163.

[5] I first used this expression in my talk to the Montreal Chamber of Commerce

on November 10, 1992. I was very happy that the French management expert Hervé Sérieyx, a skilled communicator, found it sufficiently convincing to use it in a book he published the following year.

⁶ Some provinces had developed a great deal of expertise in certain sectors, such as Saskatchewan in the field of health, for example, but they were exceptions.

⁷ See Alain Lapointe and Stéphane Fortin, *L'économie du savoir marquerait-elle la fin du déclin pour Montréal?*, a report presented to a conference of ASDEQ [Quebec association of economists], March 25, 1998.

⁸ This section owes a great deal to Gérard De Sélys, *Tableau noir. Appel à la résistance contre la privatisation de l'enseignement*, which was discussed in *Le Monde diplomatique* in June 1998.

⁹ OECD, *Adult Learning on Technology in OECD Countries*.

¹⁰ I wrote this section in Rabat, Morocco, in early July 1998, where I headed a delegation of representatives of colleges and universities. Laval University's centre for distance education aroused a great deal of interest.

¹¹ "ESAS, the European skill accreditation system," undated information memo.

¹² Minutes of the Council of Education Ministers, May 6, 1996.

¹³ OECD, International Conference on Learning Beyond Schooling 1994, *The Future of Post-Secondary Education and the Role of Information and Communication Technology: A Clarifying Report* (conference proceedings), Paris: OECD.

¹⁴ European Round Table, *Investing in Knowledge: The Integration of Technology in European Education*.

¹⁵ Jean Paré, "Constitution d'accord, éducation d'abord," *Je persiste et signe* (Montreal: Boréal, 1996), pp. 229–30. The article was originally written in March 1995. (Translators' note: Our translation.)

Chapter XVI
Decentralization, not Provincialization

¹ Pierre-Paul Proulx, "L'avenir économique de Montréal," *Forces*, no. 99 (fall 1992), p. 56, citing SRI International, *The Emergence of New City-Regions and the Issues of Economic Growth and Governance for Canada*, 1992.

Chapter XVII
A Postmodern Quiet Revolution: The Strength of Quebec

¹ This chapter elaborates on topics I discussed in "Opter pour la souveraineté, ce serait entrer dans l'avenir à reculons" [To choose sovereignty would be to enter the future backwards], the third article in my series "Le Québec dans un monde global" [Quebec in a global world], *La Presse*, September 28, 1995, p. B3.

² Interview with the Montreal weekly *Voir* in November 1995, quoted in Jacques Godbout and Richard Martineau, *Le Buffet. Dialogue sur le Québec à l'an 2000*, p. 112. (Translators' note: Our translation.)

³ Chantal Bouchard, *La Langue et le Nombril. Histoire d'une obsession québécoise*, pp. 34–35. (Translators' note: Our translation.)

⁴ Bertrand Badie, *Culture et Politique*, p. 130, quoted in Chantal Bouchard, p. 35. (Translators' note: Our translation.)

⁵ Lise Bissonnette, "Nouvel équilibre, nouveau partage. Un progrès qui est au surplus une lumière," *Forces*, no. 119, p. 5. Bissonnette was at the time the editor of the newspaper *Le Devoir*. On the twenty-fifth anniversary of the Quebec Council on the Status of Women, *Forces* devoted an issue to Quebec women.

⁶ *Ibid.*, p. 7.

⁷ *Ibid.*, p. 4.

⁸ Quoted in André Burelle, Le Mal canadien. Essai de diagnostic et esquisse d'une thérapie, p. 121. (Translators' note: Our translation.)

⁹ *Nationalisme et Démocratie. Réflexions sur les illusions des indépendantistes québécois*, p. 27.

¹⁰ *La Presse*, May 2, 1998.

¹¹ Bertrand Badie, "L'essor des politiques de ghetto devient une source d'instabilité internationale," *L'État du monde 1998*, p. 40. (Translators' note: Our translation.)

¹² *Ibid.* (Translators' note: Our translation.)

¹³ *Ibid.*, p. 42. (Translators' note: Our translation.)

¹⁴ Marc Renaud quoted this comment by the great historian at the first Quebec forum on social development at the Quebec City convention centre during a discussion on globalization and its consequences for Quebec. On this subject, see Alain Bouchard, "1er forum sur le développement social. Consensus sur le bonheur égalitaire," *Le Soleil*, vol. 102, no. 103, May 2, 1998, p. A19.

Chapter XVIII
The *Rouge* and the *Bleu*

1 Claude Ryan, *Regardes sur le fédéralisme canadien*, pp. 191–92 and 239–40. (Translator's note: Our translation.)

2 Saul, p. 20.

3 "Un mythe tenace," *Le Devoir*, August 30, 1994.

4 Translators' note: Our translation.

5 Paul Gérin-Lajoie quotes Antoine Rivard in his book *Combats d'un révolutionnaire tranquille*, p. 29. These were originally quoted by Jean-Louis Gagnon in *Les Apostasies*, vol II, p. 33. (Translators' note: Our translation.)

6 I would have to cite the complete works of Alexis de Tocqueville, since this is a recurring theme in his thought. I can, however, refer specifically to the section on the tyranny of the majority in chapter 7 of the second part of his *Democracy in America*.

[7] Fareed Zakaria, "The rise of illiberal democracy," *Foreign Affairs*, vol. 76, no. 6 (November-December, 1997), pp. 22–43.

[8] Claude Ryan, p. 191. (Translators' note: Our translation.)

[9] *The Clash of Civilizations and the Remaking of World Order*, by Samuel P. Huntington, is undeniably one of the most lucid analyses of this whole question, which is certainly being played out on the world stage but whose ramifications have a profound effect on the domestic situation of every country. It is interesting to note here that former prime minister Lester B. Pearson, a universally admired statesman, foresaw this whole situation. See his ground-breaking work, *Democracy in World Politics*.

[10] Henry Mintzberg, a professor at McGill University and the European Institute of Business Administration in France, is known the world over for his books on management and organization. He has done considerable work on the thesis that *decentralize* should not be synonymous with *provincialize*. See chapter 3 of his book, *The Canadian Condition: Reflections of a "Pure Cotton"* (Toronto: Stoddart, 1995).

Chapter XIX
Trust and Mistrust in Quebec

[1] This chapter is based on an article I published with Professor Yves-Marie Morissette, entitled "Deux conceptions antagonistes de l'économie s'affrontent dans le débat référendaire" [Two opposing conceptions of the economy confront each other in the referendum debate], *La Presse*, October 25, 1995, p. B3. The first pages, on the social and economic teaching of the Catholic Church, are based on part six, entitled "Église catholique et modernité économique," of Alain Peyrefitte's *La Société de confiance*.

[2] Peyrefitte, p. 321.

[3] *Ibid.*, p. 403.

[4] *Ibid.*, p. 323.

[5] *Ibid.*, p. 325. See also Arthur Utz, *La Doctrine de l'Église à travers les siècles*, Volume I, *Libertas praestantissimum* (June 20, 1988), p. 177.

[6] *Ibid.*, p. 330. See also *Rerum novarum* (May 15, 1871).

[7] Peyrefitte, p. 330. *Rerum novarum* (May 15, 1871), paragraph 16.

[8] For readers interested in the situation of Catholicism in Quebec before Msgr. Bourget took charge, see Raymond Brodeur, *Catéchisme et Identité culturelle dans le diocèse de Québec de 1815*, in particular chapter 2, "Constituer la félicité d'un people," on the efforts of Msgr. Plessis and the development of our catechism.

[9] Jacques Lacoursière, Jean Provencher, and Denis Vaugeois, *Canada-Québec. Synthèse historique*, p. 382. (Translators' note: Our translation.)

[10] Philippe Sylvain and Nive Voisine, *L'Histoire du catholicisme québécois*, vol. II: *Réveil et Consolidation*, 1840–1898, p. 397.

[11] For readers interested in learning more about the influence of the Church in nineteenth-century Quebec, see Philippe Sylvain and Nive Voisine, op. cit.; Roberto Perin, *Rome and Canada*, and Leon Pouliot, *Mgr Bourget et son temps*.

[12] Peyrefitte, p. 331.

[13] Peyrefitte, p. 414.

[14] Alain Peyrefitte, *Du "miracle" en économie. Leçons au Collège de France*, p. 52. (Translators' note: Our translation.)

[15] Peyrefitte, *La Société de confiance*, p. 334.

[16] *Mater et magistra* (July 15, 1961).

[17] Peyrefitte, *La Société de confiance*, pp. 340–41.

[18] *Mater et magistra: Encyclical of Pope John XXIII on May 15, 1961.*

[19] Peyrefitte, *La Société de confiance.*

[20] Peyrefitte, *La Société de confiance*, p. 342. (Translators' note: Our translation.)

[21] Quoted in Peyrefitte, *La Société de confiance*, p. 321.

[22] *Ibid.*, pp. 343–48.

[23] *Centesimus annus*, paragraph 17, quoted in Alain Peyrefitte, *La Société de confiance*, p. 345.

[24] *Ibid.*, paragraph 32 (italics in original).

[25] Quoted in Peyrefitte, *La Société de confiance*, p. 347.

[26] Georges Mathews, *La Pièce manquante du casse-tête: le déficit budgétaire d'un Québec souverain*. On Mathews's sovereignist views, see his *L'Accord. Comment Robert Bourassa fera l'indépendance*.

[27] Robert Melançon, "Les nationalistes, ces nouveaux curés. Peut-on penser à autre chose qu'à la souveraineté?" *Le Devoir*, August 12, 1995, p. A7. (Translators' note: Our translation.)

28   Hélène Buzetti, *Le Devoir*, November 28, 1998.

29   (Translators' note: Our translation.) Many will remember hearing Parizeau make remarks such as these. For readers who wish to verify the quotations and the ensuing climate, see Michel Venne, "Bilan de campagne. L'incroyable remontée du OUI," Le Devoir, October 28, 1996, p. A6.

Chapter XX

The Disadvantages of Legal Sovereignty

[1] This chapter consists essentially of the fourth and fifth articles of my series "Le Québec dans un monde global" [Quebec in a global world], "Le G-7 est plus important que l'assemblée de l'ONU" [The G-7 is more important than the UN General Assembly] and "Aléna: Washington affaiblirait Québec Inc." [NAFTA: Washington would weaken Québec Inc.], in *La Presse*, September 29 and 30, 1995, p. B3.

Conclusion

1 Christian Bobin, *L'Éloignement du monde*, p. 56. (Translators' note: Our translation.)

Bibliography

Adler, Nancy J., and Dafna N. Izraeli. *Competitive Frontiers: Women Managers in the Global Economy.* Cambridge, Mass.: Blackwell, 1994.

Alberoni, Francesco. *Falling in Love.* Translated by Lawrence Venuti. New York: Random House, 1984.

Alberoni, Francesco. *La Morale.* Paris: Plon, 1993.

Amin, Samir, Jorge Semprun, et al. *Penser la fin du communisme, l'Europe, l'état, la politique, l'histoire.* Paris: Monde-Éditions, 1994.

Aron, Raymond. *Memoirs: Fifty Years of Political Reflection.* Translated by George Holoch. With a foreword by Henry A. Kissinger. New York: Holmes and Meier, 1990.

Attali, Jacques. *Dictionnaire du xxie siècle.* Paris: Fayard, 1998.

Badie, Bertrand. *Culture et Politique.* Paris: Economica, 1983.

Badie, Bertrand. "L'État-nation, un modèle en épuisement?" *L'État du monde 1996. Annuaire économique et géopolitique mondial.* Edited by Serge Cordelier and Béatrice Didiot, 70–74. Montreal: Boréal, 1995.

Badie, Bertrand. *La Fin des territoires. Essai sur le désordre international et sur l'utilité sociale du respect.* Paris: Fayard, 1995.

Badie, Bertrand. "L'essor des politiques de ghetto devient une source d'instabilité internationale." *L'État du monde 1998,* 40–42. Paris/Montreal: La Découverte/Boréal, 1997.

Badie, Bertrand, and Marie-Claude Smouts. *Le Retournement du monde. Sociologie de la scène internationale.* Paris: Presse de la Fondation nationale des sciences politiques and Dalloz, 1992.

Badinter, Élisabeth, and Robert Badinter. *Condorcet (1743–1794). Un intellectuel en politique.* Paris: Fayard, 1988.

Bayart, Jean-François. *The State in Africa: The Politics of the Belly.* Translated by Christopher Harrison. London and New York: Longman, 1993.

Bayart, Jean-François. *L'Illusion identitaire.* Paris: Fayard, 1996.

Bayart, Jean-François, editor. *La Réinvention du capitalisme.* Paris: Karthala, 1993.

Bayrou, François. *Henri IV, le roi libre*. Paris: Flammarion, 1994.

Bénéton, Philippe. *Le Fléau du bien. Essai sur les politiques sociales occidentales (1960–1980)*. Paris: Robert Laffont, 1983.

Benson, Bruce. "Crime control through private enterprise." *The Independent Review*, vol. 2 (winter 1998), pp. 341–71.

Bernard, Michel. *L'Utopie néolibérale*. With a preface by Michel Chartrand. Montreal: Éditions du Renouveau québécois and Chaire d'études socio-économiques de l'UQAM, 1997.

Bissonnette, Lise. "Nouvel équilibre, nouveau partage. Un progrès qui est au surplus une lumière." *Forces*, no. 119 (1998): 4–8.

Bobin, Christian. *L'Éloignement du monde*. Paris: Lettres Vives, 1993.

Boublil, Alain. *Keynes, reviens! Ils sont devenus fous . . . .* Monaco: Éditions du Rocher, 1996.

Bouchard, Alain. "1er forum sur le développement social. Consensus sur le bonheur égalitaire. Stéphan Tremblay n'est pas le seul à s'inquiéter des écarts grandissants entre les riches et les pauvres." *Le Soleil*, May 2, 1998, p. 2.

Bouchard, Chantal. *La Langue et le Nombril. Histoire d'une obsession québécoise*. Montreal: Fides, 1998.

Bouveresse, Jacques. *La Demande philosophique. Que veut la philosophie et que peut-on vouloir d'elle?, leçon inaugurale du Collège de France, 6 octobre 1995*. Paris: Éditions de l'Éclat, 1996.

Brodeur, Raymond. *Catéchisme et Identité culturelle dans le diocèse de Québec en 1815*. Québec: Presses de l'Université Laval, 1998.

Bruckner, Pascal. *La Mélancolie démocratique*. Paris: Seuil, 1990.

Bucaille, Alain, and Bérold Costa de Beauregard. *Les États, acteurs de la concurrence industrielle. Rapport de la Direction Générale de l'Industrie sur les aides des États à leurs industries*. Paris: Economica, 1988.

Bull, Hedley. *The Anarchical Society: A Study of Order in World Politics*. London: Macmillan, 1977.

Burelle, André. *Le Mal canadien: Essai de diagnostic et esquisse d'une thérapie*. Montreal: Fides, 1995.

Buzetti, Hélène. "Le dernier soupir d'un 'bâtisseur de pays.'" *Le Devoir*, Nov. 28, 1998.

Carfantan, Jean-Yves. *Le Grand Désordre du monde. Les chemins de l'intégration*. Paris: Seuil, 1993.

CEE/ESAS. "The European skill accreditation system." Undated information memo.

Clark, Michael T., and Simon Serfaty, editors. *New Thinking and Old Realities: America, Europe, and Russia*. Washington: Seven Locks Press in association with the Johns Hopkins Foreign Policy Institute, 1991.

Condillac, Étienne Bonnot de. *Dictionnaire des synonymes*. Edited by Raymond Bayer. *Corpus général des philosophes français*. Vol. XXXIII: *Auteurs modernes:*

Oeuvres philosophiques de Condillac. Vol. III. Paris: Presses Universitaires de France, 1951.

Derriennic, Jean-Pierre. *Nationalismes et Démocratie. Réflexions sur les illusions des indépendantistes québécois.* Montreal: Boréal, 1995.

Descartes, René. *Discours de la méthode.* With an introduction and commentary by Étienne Gilson. Paris: Vrin, 1964.

Descartes, René. *Discourse on Method.*

Deschênes, Gaston. "Un mythe tenace." *Le Devoir,* Aug. 30, 1994.

De Sélys, Gérard. *Tableau noir. Appel à la résistance contre la privatisation de l'enseignement.* Brussels: EPO, 1998.

Deutsch, Karl W. *Nationalism and Social Communication: An Inquiry into the Foundations of Nationality.* 2nd edition. Cambridge, Mass.: M.I.T. Press, 1962.

Deutsch, Karl W. *Nationalism and Its Alternatives.* New York: Knopf, 1969.

Dicken, Peter. *Transforming the World Economy.* 2nd edition. London: Paul Chapman, 1992.

Dion, Stéphane. Federalism: A System in Evolution. Speech given to APEX, April 25, 1996. Internet:http://www.pcobcp.gc.ca/aia/ro/doc/apex4_e.htm.

Dion, Stéphane. The Ethic of Federalism. Speech given at the conference "Identities—Involvement—Living Together in Federal States: International Aspects of Federalism," Sainte-Foy, Quebec, September 30, 1996. Internet: http://www.pco-bcp.gc.ca/aia/ro/doc/spchst3096.htm.

Drucker, Peter F. *Managing in Turbulent Times.* New York: Harper and Row, 1980.

Drucker, Peter F. *The New Realities.* New York: Harper and Row, 1989.

Dumont, Fernand. *Le Lieu de l'homme. La culture comme distance et mémoire.* Montreal: Éditions HMH, 1968.

Durham, John George. *Lord Durham's Report on the Affairs of British North America* (1839). Edited and with an introduction by C. P. Lucas. 3 vols. London: Oxford University Press, 1912.

Elbaz, Mikhaël, Andrée Fortin, and Guy Laforest, editors. *Les Frontières de l'identité. Modernité et postmodernisme au Québec.* Québec/Paris: Presses de l'Université Laval/L'Harmattan, 1996.

European Round Table. *Investing in Knowledge: The Integration of Technology in European Education.* Brussels: ERT, 1997.

Fainsod Katzenstein, Mary, and David D. Laitin, "Politics, feminism, and the ethics of care." In *Women and Moral Theory.* Edited by Eva Feder Kittay and Diana T. Meyers, 261–81. New York: Rowman and Littlefield, 1987.

Finkielkraut, Alain. *The Defeat of the Mind.* Translated and with an introduction by Judith Friedlander. New York: Columbia University Press, 1995.

Finley, Moses I. *Politics in the Ancient World.* Cambridge: Cambridge University Press, 1983.

Fortin, Ghislain. "La mondialisation de l'économie." *Relations*, no. 587 (Jan.-Feb. 1993): 9–12.

Fortune. "The Fortune directory of the 500 largest U.S. industrial corporations." *Fortune*, vol. 99, no. 9 (May 7,1979): 268–89.

Fortune. "The Fortune directory of the 500 largest U.S. industrial corporations." *Fortune*, vol. 111, no. 9 (Apr. 29,1985): 252–319.

Fortune. "Fortune's service 500: The largest U.S. service corporations." *Fortune*, vol. 127, no. 11 (May 31, 1993): 200–279.

Foucauld, Jean-Baptiste de, and Denis Piveteau. *Une société en quête de sens*. Paris: Odile Jacob, 1995.

Foulquié, Paul, with Raymond St-Jean. *Dictionnaire de la langue philosophique*. Paris: Presses Universitaires de France, 1962.

Fourastié, Jean. *Le Grand Espoir du XXe siècle*. Definitive edition. Paris: Gallimard, 1963.

Frenette, Yves. *Brève Histoire des Canadiens français*. Montreal: Boréal, 1998.

Frost, Robert. *The Poetry of Robert Frost*. Edited by Edward Connery Lathem. New York: Holt Rinehart, 1969.

Fukuyama, Francis. *The End of History and the Last Man*. New York: The Free Press/Macmillan, 1992.

Fukuyama, Francis. *Trust: The Social Virtues and the Creation of Prosperity*. New York: The Free Press, 1995.

Gagnon, Jean-Louis. *Les Apostasies*. Montreal: Les Editions La Presse, 1988.

Galbraith, John Kenneth. *The Culture of Contentment*. Boston: Houghton Mifflin, 1992.

Gaudin, Thierry. *Les Métamorphoses du futur. Essai de prospective technologique*. Paris: Economica, 1988.

Gaudin, Thierry. *2100. Récit du prochain siècle*. Paris: Payot, 1990.

Gaudreault-DesBiens, Jean-François. *De la Déclaration de Calgary, de sa réception au Québec et de quelques pathologies du discours constitutionnel majoritaire dans notre société au caractère "unique."* Brief presented to the Commission des institutions de l'Assemblée nationale du Québec, June 4,1998.

Gellner, Ernest. *Nations and Nationalism*. Ithaca, N.Y., and London: Cornell University Press, 1983.

Généreux, Jacques. *Une raison d'espérer*. Paris: Plon, 1997.

Genest, Jean-Guy. *Godbout*. Sillery: Éditions du Septentrion, 1996.

Gérin-Lajoie, Paul. *Combats d'un révolutionnaire tranquille*. Centre éducatif et culturel, Anjou, 1989.

Godbout, Jacques, and Richard Martineau. *Le Buffet. Dialogue sur le Québec à l'an 2000*. Montreal: Boréal, 1998.

GRECO CNRS EFIQ. *Conflits et Négociations dans le commerce international: l'Uruguay Round*. Fourth conference of GRECO CNRS EFIQ. Paris: Economica, 1989.

Greenspon, Edward, and Anthony Wilson-Smith. *Double Vision: The Inside Story of the Liberals in Power*. Toronto: Doubleday, 1996.

Group of Lisbon. *Limits to Competition: For a New World Contract*. Cambridge, Mass.: M.I.T. Press, 1995.

Gutman, Yisrael, and Michael Berenbaum, editors. *Anatomy of the Auschwitz Death Camps*. Bloomington: Indiana University Press, 1994.

Gutmann, Amy. *Liberal Equality*. Cambridge: Cambridge University Press, 1980.

Hart, Michael. *What's Next: Canada, the Global Economy and the New Trade Policy*. Ottawa: Centre for Trade Policy and Law, 1994.

Haus, Leah A. *Globalizing the GATT: The Soviet Union's Successor States, Eastern Europe, and the International Trading System*. Washington: The Brookings Institution, 1992.

Hazard, Paul. *La Crise de la conscience européenne, 1680–1715*. Paris: Fayard, 1967.

Hesse, Hermann. *Narcissus and Goldmund*. Translated by Ursule Molinaro. New York: Farrar, Straus and Giroux, 1968.

Hobbes, Thomas. *Leviathan*.

Huntington, Samuel P. *The Clash of Civilizations and the Remaking of World Order*. New York: Simon and Schuster, 1996.

Hutton, Will. *The State We're In*. London: Jonathan Cape/Random House, 1995.

Hutton, Will. *The State to Come*. London: Vintage Books, 1997.

Jacobs, Jane. *By Way of Advice: Growth Strategies for the Market-Driven World*. Oakville: Mosaic Press, 1991.

Jacquard, Albert. *J'accuse l'économie triomphante*. Paris: Calmann-Lévy, 1995.

Jacquard, Albert. *Petite Philosophie à l'usage des non-philosophes*. Paris: Calmann-Lévy, 1997.

Jencks, Christopher. *Rethinking Social Policy: Race, Poverty, and the Underclass*. Cambridge, Mass.: Harvard University Press, 1992.

John XXIII, Pope. *Mater et magistra*. Encyclical letter given in Rome May 15, 1961. Internet: http://listserv.american.edu/catholic/church/papal/john.xxiii/j23mater.txt.

John Paul II, Pope. *Centesimus annus*. Encyclical letter given in Rome May 1, 1991. Internet: http://www.vatican.va/holy_father/john_paul_ii/encyclicals/john-paul-ii_encyclical_1-may-1991_centesimus-annus_english.shtml.

Julliard, Jacques, "Lionel Jospin ou l'expression française." *Le Débat*, no. 100 (May-Aug. 1998).

Kant, Immanuel. *Critique of Judgment*.

Kant, Immanuel. *Perpetual Peace, a Philosophical Essay*.

Kattan, Naïm. *Culture: alibi ou liberté?* Montreal: Hurtubise/HMH, 1996.

Kissinger, Henry. *White House Years*. Boston: Little Brown, 1979.

KPMG Management Consulting. *The Competitive Alternative: A Comparison of*

Business Costs in Canada and the United States. Ottawa: Prospectus Inc., 1997.

Lacoste, Yves, et al. *Nation et Nationalisme.* Paris: La Découverte, 1995.

Lacoursière, Jacques, Jean Provencher, and Denis Vaugeois. *Canada-Québec. Synthèse historique.* Montreal: Éditions du Renouveau Pédagogique, 1970.

Lafay, Gérard, et al. *Commerce international: la fin des avantages acquis.* Paris: Economica, 1989.

Laforest, Guy, and Douglas Brown. *Integration and Fragmentation: The Paradox of the Late Twentieth Century.* Kingston: Institute of Intergovernmental Relations, Queen's University, 1994.

Laforest, Guy, and Philippe de Lara, editors. *Charles Taylor et l'interprétation de l'identité moderne,* Québec/Paris: Presses de l'Université Laval/Éditions du Cerf, 1998.

Laidi, Zaki. *A World without Meaning: The Crisis of Meaning in International Politics.* Translated by June Burnham and Jenny Coulon. London and New York: Routledge, 1998.

Landry, Bernard. "Quelle politique tue l'économie?" *La Presse,* July 4, 1998.

Lapointe, Alain, and Stéphane Fortin. *L'économie du savoir marquerait-elle la fin du déclin pour Montréal?* Report presented at the conference of ASDEQ, Mar. 25,1998.

LaSelva, Samuel V. *The Moral Foundation of Canadian Federalism.* Kingston: McGill-Queen's University Press, 1996.

Latouche, Daniel. *Plaidoyer pour le Québec.* Montreal: Boréal, 1995.

Laulan, Yves-Marie. *La Planète balkanisée.* Paris: Economica, 1991.

Leo XIII, Pope. *Rerum novarum.* Encyclical letter given in Rome May 15, 1891. Internet: gopher://wiretap.Spies.COM:70/00/Library/Religion/Catholic/Leo_XIII/Rerum_novarum.

Lévêque, Raphaël. *Unité et Diversité.* Paris: Presses Universitaires de France, 1963.

Lévesque, René. *An Option for Quebec.* Toronto and Montreal: McClelland and Stewart, 1968.

Levet, Jean-Louis, and Jean-Claude Tourret. *La Révolution des pouvoirs. Les patriotismes économiques à l'épreuve de la mondialisation.* Paris: Economica, 1992.

Lion, Robert. *L'État passion.* Paris: Plon, 1992.

Lisée, Jean-François. *In the Eye of the Eagle.* Toronto: HarperCollins, 1990.

Lonergan, Bernard. *Insight: A Study of Human Understanding.* New York: Philosophical Library, 1957.

Martin, Lawrence. *The Presidents and the Prime Ministers. Washington and Ottawa Face to Face: The Myth of Bilateral Bliss, 1867–1982.* Toronto and Garden City, N.J.: Doubleday, 1982.

Mathews, Georges. *L'Accord. Comment Robert Bourassa fera l'indépendance.* Montreal: Le Jour, 1990.

Mathews, Georges. *La Pièce manquante du casse-tête: le déficit budgétaire d'un Québec souverain.* Montreal: Institut national de la recherche scientifique, 1995.

Mathews, Jessica T. "Power shift." *Foreign Affairs*, vol. 76, no. 1 (Jan.-Feb. 1997): 50–66.

McLuhan, Marshall. *The Gutenberg Galaxy.* Toronto: University of Toronto Press, 1962.

McRoberts, Kenneth, *Misconceiving Canada: The Struggle for National Unity.* Toronto: Oxford University Press, 1997.

Melançon, Robert. "Les nationalistes, ces nouveaux curés. Peut-on penser à autre chose qu'à la souveraineté?" *Le Devoir*, Aug. 12, 1995, p. A7.

Merle, Marcel. *Les Acteurs dans les relations internationales.* Paris: Economica, 1986.

Minc, Alain. *L'Argent fou.* Paris: Bernard Grasset, 1990.

Minc, Alain. *La Vengeance des nations.* Paris: Bernard Grasset, 1990.

Mintzberg, Henry. *The Canadian Condition: Reflections of a "Pure Cotton."* Toronto: Stoddart, 1995.

Monnet, Jean. *Memoirs.* Translated by Richard Mayne, with a foreword by Roy Jenkins. London: Collins, 1978.

Morissette, Yves-Marie. "La conciliation des différences. Les valeurs que partagent les Canadiens." *Cahiers du fédéralisme*, no. 1 (1998): 1–7.

Morissette, Yves-Marie, and Pierre S. Pettigrew. "Deux conceptions antagonistes de l'économie s'affrontent dans le débat référendaire." *La Presse*, Oct. 25, 1995, p. B3.

Moulène, Frédéric. "L'essence du néolibéralisme." *Le Monde diplomatique*, June 1998: 2.

Mowers, Cleo. *Towards a New Liberalism: Re-Creating Canada and the Liberal Party.* Victoria: Orca, 1991.

Nedelsky, Jennifer. "Embodied diversity and the challenges to law." *McGill Law Journal/Revue de droit de McGill*, no. 42 (1997): 91.

North, Douglas C., and Robert P. Thomas. *The Rise of the Western World.* Cambridge: Cambridge University Press, 1973.

Novak, Michael. *Free Persons and the Common Good.* Lanham: Madison Books, 1989.

Observatoire géopolitique des drogues [Geopolitical Drug Watch]. *The World Geopolitics of Drugs 1995–1996.* Annual report. Paris: La Découverte, 1997. Internet: http://www.ogd.org/rapport/RP01_RAP.html.

OECD. *The Future of Post-Secondary Education and the Role of Information and Communication Technology: A Clarifying Report.* Proceedings of the International Conference on Learning Beyond Schooling,1994. Paris: OECD.

OECD. *Adult Learning on Technology in OECD Countries.* Paris: OECD, 1996.

Paré, Jean. *Je persiste et signe.* Montreal: Boréal, 1996.

Paul VI, Pope. *Pastoral Constitution on the Church in the Modern World: Gaudium et Spes.* Promulgated on December 7, 1965. Internet: http://www.vatican.va/archive/ii_vatican_council/constitutions/vatican-ii_constitution_7-dec-1965_gaudium-et-spes_english.shtml.

Pearson, Lester Bowles. *Democracy in World Politics.* Princeton: Princeton University Press, 1955.

Perin, Roberto. *Rome in Canada: The Vatican and Canadian Affairs in the Late Victorian Age.* Toronto: University of Toronto Press, 1990.

Peters, Thomas J., and Robert H. Waterman, Jr. *In Search of Excellence: Lessons from America's Best-Run Companies.* New York: Harper and Row, 1982.

Pettigrew, Pierre S. "Le Québec dans un monde global." *La Presse,* Sept. 26–30, 1995, p. B3.

Peyrefitte, Alain. *Du "miracle" en économie. Leçons au Collège de France.* Paris: Odile Jacob, 1995.

Peyrefitte, Alain. *La Société de confiance.* Paris: Odile Jacob, 1995.

Pinard, Maurice, Robert Bernier, and Vincent Lemieux. *Un combat inachevé.* Sainte-Foy: Presses de l'Université du Québec, 1997.

Pirandello, Luigi. *Six Characters in Search of an Author.* Translated by Frederick May. London: Heinemann, 1954.

Pouliot, Léon. *Monseigneur Bourget et son temps.* Vol. I: *Les Années de préparation (1799–1840).* Montreal: Beauchemin, 1955. Vol. II: *L'Évêque de Montréal;* part one: *L'Organisation du diocèse de Montréal (1840–1846).* Montreal: Beauchemin, 1956. Vol. III: *L'Évêque de Montréal;* part two: *La Marche en avant du diocèse (1846–1876).* Montreal: Bellarmin, 1972. Vol. IV: *L'Affrontement avec l'Institut canadien (1858–1870).* Montreal: Bellarmin, 1974. Vol. V: *Les Derniers Combats. Le démembrement de la paroisse Notre-Dame (1865). Vingt-cinq années de luttes universitaires (1851–1876).* Montreal: Bellarmin, 1977.

Proulx, Pierre-Paul. "L'avenir économique de Montréal." *Forces,* no. 99 (fall 1992): 56.

Putnam, Robert D., with Robert Leonardi and Raffaella Y. Nanetti. *Making Democracy Work: Civic Traditions in Modern Italy.* Princeton: Princeton University Press, 1993.

Reich, Robert. *The Work of Nations: Preparing Ourselves for 21st-Century Capitalism.* New York: Knopf, 1991.

Resnick, Philip. *Twenty-First Century Democracy.* Montreal: McGill-Queen's University Press, 1997.

Revel, Jean-François. *Descartes inutile et incertain.* Paris: Stock, 1976.

Rey, Jean-Jacques. *Institutions économiques internationales.* Brussels: Bruylant, 1988.

Ricardo, David. *The Principles of Political Economy and Taxation.* With an introduction by Michael P. Fogarty. London: Dent, 1955.

Rilke, Rainer-Maria. *Letters to a Young Poet.* Translated by Stephen Mitchell. New York: Random House, 1984.

Rosanvallon, Pierre. *La Nouvelle Question sociale*. Paris: Seuil, 1976.

Rosenau, James. "Patterned chaos in global life: Structure and process in the two worlds of world politics." *International Political Science Review*, vol. 9, no. 4 (Oct. 1988): 327–64.

Rosenau, James. *Turbulence in World Politics*. Princeton: Princeton University Press, 1990.

Rousseau, Jean-Jacques. *The Social Contract*.

Ryan, Claude. *Regards sur le fédéralisme canadien*. Montreal: Boréal, 1995.

Sandel, Michael J. *Democracy's Discontent: America in Search of a Public Philosophy*. Cambridge, Mass., and London: Belknap Press of Harvard University Press, 1996.

Saul, John Ralston. *Voltaire's Bastards: The Dictatorship of Reason in the West*. New York: The Free Press, 1992.

Saul, John Ralston. *Reflections of a Siamese Twin: Canada at the End of the Twentieth Century*. Toronto: Viking, 1996.

Schiller, Herbert I. *Culture Inc.: The Corporate Takeover of Public Expression*. New York: Oxford University Press, 1989.

Séguin, Maurice. *Histoire de deux nationalismes au Canada*. Edited and with an introduction by Bruno Deshaies. Montreal: Guérin, 1997.

Seligman, A. B. *The Problem of Trust*. Princeton: Princeton University Press, 1997.

Silver, A. I. *The French-Canadian Idea of Confederation, 1864–1900*. 2nd edition. Toronto: University of Toronto Press, 1997.

Slama, Alain-Gérard. *La Régression démocratique*. Paris: Fayard, 1995.

Smith, Adam. *An Inquiry into the Nature and Causes of the Wealth of Nations*. With an introduction by M. Blaug. 2 vol. Homewood, Ill.: R. D. Irwin, 1963.

Stopford, John, Susan Strange, and John S. Henley. *Rival States, Rival Firms: Competition for World Market Shares*. Toronto: Cambridge University Press, 1991.

Sylvain, Philippe, and Nive Voisine. *L'Histoire du catholicisme québécois*. Vol. II: *Réveil et Consolidation, 1840–1898*. Montreal: Boréal, 1991.

Taylor, Charles. *The Malaise of Modernity*. Toronto: Anansi Press, 1991.

Taylor, Charles. *Multiculturalism and "The Politics of Recognition": An Essay*. With commentary by Amy Gutmann. Princeton: Princeton University Press, 1992.

Taylor, Charles. *Reconciling the Solitudes: Essays on Canadian Federalism and Nationalism*. Montreal and Kingston: McGill-Queen's University Press, 1993.

Thomson, Dale C. *Jean Lesage and the Quiet Revolution*. Toronto: Macmillan of Canada, 1984.

Thureau-Dangin, Philippe. *La Concurrence et la Mort*. Paris: Syros, 1995.

Thurow, Lester C. *The Future of Capitalism: How Today's Economic Forces Shape Tomorrow's World*. New York: William Morrow, 1996.

Tocqueville, Alexis de. *Democracy in America*.

Touraine, Alain. *Pourrons-nous vivre ensemble? Égaux et différents*. Paris: Fayard, 1997.

Touraine, Marisol. *Le Bouleversement du monde. Géopolitique du XXIe siècle*. Paris: Seuil, 1995.

Tournier, Michel. *The Ogre*. Translated by Barbara Bray. Baltimore: Johns Hopkins University Press, 1997.

Tsurumi, Yoshi. *Multinational Management: Business Strategy and Government Policy*. 2nd edition. Cambridge, Mass.: Ballinger, 1984.

United Nations. *World Drug Report*. New York: International Drug Control Programme, 1997. Internet: http://www.un.org/ga/20special/wdr/wdr.htm.

Utz, Arthur. *La Doctrine de l'Église à travers les siècles*. Vol. I: *Libertas praestantissimum*. Fribourg, Switzerland: Éditions Valores, 1970.

Valance, Georges. *Les Maîtres du monde: Allemagne, États-Unis, Japon*. Paris: Flammarion, 1992.

Venne, Michel. "Bilan de campagne. L'incroyable remontée du OUI." *Le Devoir*, Oct. 28, 1996, p. A6.

Wallerstein, Immanuel. *The Modern World-System*. Vol. I: *Capitalist Agriculture and the Origins of the European World-Economy in the Sixteenth Century*. New York: Academic Press, 1976. Vol. II: *Mercantilism and the Consolidation of the European World-Economy, 1600–1750*. New York: Academic Press, 1980.

Webber, Jeremy. *Reimagining Canada: Language, Culture, Community, and the Canadian Constitution*. Kingston: McGill-Queen's University Press, 1994.

Weber, Max. *The Protestant Ethic and the Spirit of Capitalism*. Translated by Talcott Parsons.

World Trade Organization. *International Trade 1995: Trends and Statistics*. Geneva: World Trade Organization, 1995.

Young-Bruehl, Elizabeth. *Hannah Arendt for the Love of the World*. New Haven, Conn.: Yale University Press, 1982.

Zakaria, Fareed. "The rise of illiberal democracy." *Foreign Affairs*, vol. 76, no. 6 (Nov.-Dec. 1997), pp. 22–43.

Index

in Quebec, 122
international law, 23
International Monetary
    Fund, 14*n*, 20, 25, 108
international trade
    agreements, 112
Internet, 20, 126
Italy
    as a low-trust society, 26
    as a nation-state, 66
    public spending in, 96
    and unity, 66

Jacquard, Albert, 70*n*
Jacques, Jocelyn, 131*n*
Japan
    and distance education,
        126
    as a high-trust society, 26
    and the internal
        consistency of societies,
        52
    and trade unionism, 26
    and the tradition of
        interventionism, 121
Jencks, Christopher, 81
Julliard, Jacques, 22

Kant, Immanuel, 14
King, Mackenzie, 71*n*
Kittay, Eva Feder, 60*n*
knowledge-based economy,
    75–76, 112–13

labour, 100–101, 121
    and capital, 156
    international division of,
        28
labour market agreement, 102
labour market training, 152
LaFontaine, Louis-
    Hippolyte, 69, 70, 145
La Francophonie, 107, 109,
    169
Landry, Bernard, 73
Larose, Gérald, 164
Latin America
    and free trade, 109
    and the logic of
        integration, 28
    NGOs in, 21
Lavallée, Calixa, 89*n*
leadership, 80–82
Leonardo da Vinci
    program, 126
Lepage, Robert, 140
Lesage, Jean, 85, 88–89,
    103–4, 119, 120, 161

Lévesque, René, 73, 145,
    147
Lévy, Bernard-Henri, 136
liberal capitalism, 6, 76
liberalism, 6, 9, 10, 25, 35
liberalization, 9, 10
    of trade, 13
liberals, 3
life cycle of products, 14
lifelong learning, 125–27
Lisée, Jean-François, 71*n*
logic of exclusion, 5, 28–29
logic of integration, 27–28
low-trust societies, 26–27,
    157
Lower Canada, 69, 91
Lyon, Sterling, 92

Maastricht Treaty, 175
Mackenzie, William Lyon,
    69
"Maîtres chez nous," 89,
    172
majority rule, 149
management science, 36
Mandela, Nelson, 60*n*
Manitoba, 90, 92
    regional identity in, 82
Manitoba school laws, 70
Manning, Preston, 70*n*
marginalized world, 28–29,
    114
market, the
    globalization and, 30–31,
        32, 105, 130
    idolatry of, 162
    law of, *xvii*
    nation-state and, 34–35
    "too-exclusively-
        economic," *xviii*
    tribulations of, 24–25
Martin, Paul, 168
Martineau, Richard, 136,
    137
Marx, Karl, 6, 24, 43, 140,
    141
Mathews, Georges, 163
media, dissociating effect
    on society, 42–43
Meech Lake Accord, 86,
    93, 96
Melançon, Robert, 165
melting-pot, 67, 71, 88, 133
Merkin, Bill, 170
Meyers, Diana L., 60*n*
microelectronics, 20
military power, 112, 114
Minc, Alain, 106
Ministerial Council on
    Social Policy, 100, 101

mistrust, 6. *See also*
    confidence, trust
Monnet, Jean, 142
Montreal, 69, 90, 115, 122,
    128, 129, 132–34, 152,
    153, 156
mosaic, 67, 68, 71
Moulène, Frédéric, 108
multicentric world, 23, 24,
    55, 137
multilateralism, 108
multimedia educational
    software, 126
multinationals, 18–19

NAFTA. *See* North
    American Free Trade
    Agreement
narcissism of small
    differences, 90
national allegiance, 24
national child benefit, 80,
    101–2
National Film Board, 154
national markets, *xvii*, 32,
    34, 35
nation-state, 33, 65–72, 99,
    151
    Canada's refusal to
        become, 66
    and the market, 34–35
    and sociocultural
        uniformity, 66–67
    and the United Nations,
        167
NATO. *See* North Atlantic
    Treaty Organization
natural resources, 110
    Quebec, 122
natural right, 158
Naud, Julien, S.J., 46
Nedelsky, Jennifer, 60*n*
New Brunswick, 109, 154
New Deal, 5
Newfoundland, 94
New France, 86
new international order, 56
new world order, 8
    globalization, 9
Nietzsche, Friedrich, 52
non-governmental
    organizations (NGOs),
    20, 21–23
nordicity, 83
North American Free
    Trade Agreement
    (NAFTA), 109, 134,
    170–71
    and provincial status of
        Quebec, 171